The DevOps 2.2 Toolkit

Self-Sufficient Docker Clusters

Viktor Farcic

BIRMINGHAM MUMBAI

The DevOps 2.2 Toolkit

Acquisition Editor: Dominic Shakeshaft
Technical Editor: Nidhisha Shetty
Indexer: Aishwarya Gangawane
Production Coordinator: Arvindkumar Gupta

First published: March 2018
Production reference: 1090318

Published by Packt Publishing Ltd.
Livery Place
35 Livery Street
Birmingham
B3 2PB, UK.

ISBN 978-1-78899-127-8

www.packtpub.com

I noticed that authors sometimes thank famous people for the help they never received. At other times, they publish introduction written by well-established authors who probably didn't even read their book. There must be a reason behind that. Maybe it helps to have well-known names. Perhaps listing famous people invokes some unknown powers. There might be a kind of a Vudu magic that binds a reader to the book. Even though I doubt that thanking people helps, I'll do it anyways. It's better not to risk it. I wish to thank the following people: Larry David for being weirder than me; Uncle Bob whose books are always in front of mines in Amazon; Donald Trump for writing entertaining tweets; Josip Broz Tito for not living over 100 years; Netflix for entertaining my daughter while I work; David Heinemeier Hansson for explaining that Ruby On Rails is untestable; Douglas Adams for letting me use his quote at the end of this book. There are many others I could thank, but my humility compels me to stop and list a few others who are not (yet) famous. This book is dedicated to my daughter Sara that gives me the strength to wake up every morning and do an insane number of working hours. Her smile after coming back from school is all the encouragement I need. To my wife Eva, without whose never-failing support this book would never have been finished. I love you girls, more than anything in the world. This book is dedicated to you. To caffeine and sugar, essential ingredients for long nights of writing. To pizza delivery boy without whom I'd starve to death.

– Viktor Farcic

Contributor

About the author

Viktor Farcic is a senior consultant at CloudBees(`https://www.cloudbees.com/`), a member of the Docker Captains(`https://www.docker.com/docker-captains`) group, and books' author.

Viktor coded using a plethora of languages starting with Pascal (yes, he is old), Basic (before it got the Visual prefix), ASP (before it got the .Net suffix), C, C++, Perl, Python, ASP.Net, Visual Basic, C#, JavaScript, Java, Scala, and so on. He never worked with Fortran. His current favorite is Go. His big passions are Microservices, Continuous Deployment, and **Test-Driven Development** (**TDD**).

Viktor often speaks at community gatherings and conferences.

Viktor wrote *The DevOps 2.0 Toolkit: Automating the Continuous Deployment Pipeline with Containerized Microservices, The DevOps 2.1 Toolkit: Docker Swarm: Building, testing, deploying, and monitoring services inside Docker Swarm clusters*, and *Test-Driven Java Development* all by *Packt Publishing*. His random thoughts and tutorials can be found at his blog TechnologyConversations.com (`https://technologyconversations.com/`).

Packt is searching for authors like you

If you're interested in becoming an author for Packt, please visit `authors.packtpub.com` and apply today. We have worked with thousands of developers and tech professionals, just like you, to help them share their insight with the global tech community. You can make a general application, apply for a specific hot topic that we are recruiting an author for, or submit your own idea.

`mapt.io`

Mapt is an online digital library that gives you full access to over 5,000 books and videos, as well as industry leading tools to help you plan your personal development and advance your career. For more information, please visit our website.

Why subscribe?

- Spend less time learning and more time coding with practical eBooks and Videos from over 4,000 industry professionals

- Improve your learning with Skill Plans built especially for you

- Get a free eBook or video every month

- Mapt is fully searchable

- Copy and paste, print, and bookmark content

PacktPub.com

Did you know that Packt offers eBook versions of every book published, with PDF and ePub files available? You can upgrade to the eBook version at `www.PacktPub.com` and as a print book customer, you are entitled to a discount on the eBook copy. Get in touch with us at `service@packtpub.com` for more details.

At `www.PacktPub.com`, you can also read a collection of free technical articles, sign up for a range of free newsletters, and receive exclusive discounts and offers on Packt books and eBooks.

Table of Contents

Preface

It seems that with each new book the scope gets fuzzier and less precise. When I started writing Test-Driven Java Development the scope of the whole book was done in advance. I had a team working with me. We defined the index and a short description of each chapter. From there on we worked on a schedule as most technical authors do. Then I started writing the second book. The scope was more obscure. I wanted to write about DevOps practices and processes and had only a very broad idea what will be the outcome. I knew that Docker had to be there. I knew that configuration management is a must. Microservices, centralized logging, and a few other practices and tools that I used in my projects were part of the initial scope. For that book I had no one behind me. There was no team but me, a lot of pizzas, an unknown number of cans of Red Bull, and many sleepless nights. The result is *The DevOps 2.0 Toolkit: Automating the Continuous Deployment Pipeline with Containerized Microservices*. With the third book, the initial scope became even more obscure. I started writing without a plan. It was supposed to be about cluster management. After a couple of months of work, I attended DockerCon in Seattle where we were presented with the new Docker Swarm Mode. My immediate reaction was to throw everything I wrote to trash and start over. I did not know what will the book be about except that it must be something about Docker Swarm. I was impressed with the new design. Something about Swarm ended up being *The DevOps 2.1 Toolkit: Docker Swarm: Building, testing, deploying, and monitoring services inside Docker Swarm clusters*. While working on it, I decided to make **DevOps Toolkit Series**. I thought that it would be great to record my experiences from different experiments, and from working with various companies and open source projects. So, naturally, I started thinking and planning the third installment in the series; **The DevOps Toolkit 2.2**. The only problem is that, this time, I truly don't have a clue what will it be about. One idea was to do a deep comparison of different schedulers (for example, Docker Swarm, Kubernetes, and Mesos/Maraton). The another was to explore serverless. Even though it is a terrible name (there are servers, we just don't manage them), it is a great subject. The ideas kept coming but there was no clear winner. So, I decided not to define the scope. Instead, I defined some general objectives.

The goals I set in front of me is to build a **self-adaptive** and **self-healing** system based on Docker. The only problem is that I do not yet know how I will do that. There are different bits of practices and tools I've been using, but there is no clearly visible light at the end of the tunnel. Instead of defining what the book will be, I defined what I want to accomplish. You can think of this book as my recording of the journey. I will need to explore a lot. I will probably need to adopt some new tools and write some code myself. I don't know, yet. Maybe it will turn out to be something completely different, and there will not be a self-adaptive and self-healing system. We'll see. Think of this book as "Viktor's diary while trying to do stuff."

So, for now, the objectives are to go beyond a simple setup of a cluster, services, continuous deployment, and all the other things you probably already know. If you don't, read my older books. I do not yet know the scope, nor I know what will be the result. Typically, when you write a book, you start with an outline and an index, write your chapters one by one and, at the end of the process, write a preface. It makes us (authors) look intelligent and in control. That is not the case. I did not write the preface at the end of the process (as an editor would advise me). I'm trying to be honest with you. I don't have a plan.

You've been warned! I don't know where this book is going nor whether I will manage to fulfill my self-defined objectives. I'll do my best to outline the steps towards a self-adapting and self-healing system in the same way as I am exploring them myself.

Overview

This book will not teach you DevOps practices. It will not show you how Docker works. It will not explore how to build images, deploy services, operate Swarm clusters, nor how to do continuous deployment. We will not develop microservices nor will we go through practices and tools that allow us to create and manage our infrastructure. This book assumes that you already know all that. If you do not, please read *The DevOps 2.0 Toolkit: Automating the Continuous Deployment Pipeline with Containerized Microservices* for a general overview of DevOps tools and practices and *The DevOps 2.1 Toolkit: Docker Swarm: Building, testing, deploying, and monitoring services inside Docker Swarm clusters* for an in depth examination of how Docker Swarm clusters work.

Now that you know what this book is NOT about, you are probably wondering what it is. Well... I don't know yet. I decided to skip the planning and just start coding and writing about solutions that go beyond a simple cluster management and deployment of services. The objective is to create a self-adapting and self-healing system. That's all I know for now. I'm not sure how I will do it nor whether I will succeed. What I do know is that I will write down every step of the journey.

While there will be a lot of theory, this is a hands-on book. You won't be able to complete it by reading it in a metro on the way to work. You'll have to read this book while in front of a computer getting your hands dirty. Eventually, you might get stuck and in need of help. Or you might want to write a review or comment on the book's content. Please join the DevOps20 (`http://slack.devops20toolkit.com/`) Slack channel and post your thoughts, ask questions, or simply participate in a discussion. If you prefer a more one-on-one communication, you can use Slack to send me a private message or send an email to `viktor@farcic.com`. All the books I wrote are very dear to me, and I want you to have a good experience reading them. Part of that experience is the option to reach out to me. Don't be shy.

Please note that this, just as the previous book, is self-published. I believe that having no intermediaries between the writer and the reader is the best way to go. It allows me to write faster, update the book more frequently, and have a more direct communication with you. Your feedback is part of the process. No matter whether you purchased the book while only a few or all chapters were written, the idea is that it will never be truly finished. As time passes, it will require updates so that it is aligned with the change in technology or processes. When possible, I will try to keep it up to date and release updates whenever that makes sense. Eventually, things might change so much that updates are not a good option anymore, and that will be a sign that a whole new book is required. **I will keep writing as long as I continue getting your support**.

Download the example code files

You can download the example code files for this book from your account at `www.packtpub.com`. If you purchased this book elsewhere, you can visit `www.packtpub.com/support` and register to have the files emailed directly to you.

You can download the code files by following these steps:

1. Log in or register at `www.packtpub.com`.
2. Select the **SUPPORT** tab.
3. Click on **Code Downloads & Errata**.
4. Enter the name of the book in the **Search** box and follow the onscreen instructions.

Once the file is downloaded, please make sure that you unzip or extract the folder using the latest version of:

- WinRAR/7-Zip for Windows
- Zipeg/iZip/UnRarX for Mac
- 7-Zip/PeaZip for Linux

The code bundle for the book is also hosted on GitHub at `https://github.com/PacktPublishing/The-DevOps-2.2-Toolkit`. We also have other code bundles from our rich catalog of books and videos available at `https://github.com/PacktPublishing/`. Check them out!

Download the color images

We also provide a PDF file that has color images of the screenshots/diagrams used in this book. You can download it here: `http://www.packtpub.com/sites/default/files/downloads/TheDevOps2.2Toolkit_ColorImages.pdf`.

Conventions used

There are a number of text conventions used throughout this book.

`CodeInText`: Indicates code words in text, database table names, folder names, filenames, file extensions, pathnames, dummy URLs, user input, and Twitter handles. Here is an example: "Mount the downloaded `WebStorm-10*.dmg` disk image file as another disk in your system."

A block of code is set as follows:

```
docker service create \
    --name util \
    --network monitor \
    --mode global \
    alpine sleep 100000000
```

When we wish to draw your attention to a particular part of a code block, the relevant lines or items are set in bold:

```
docker service create \
    --name util \
    --network monitor \
    --mode global \
    alpine sleep 100000000
```

Any command-line input or output is written as follows:

```
docker container exec -it $ID \
    curl node-exporter:9100/metrics
```

Bold: Indicates a new term, an important word, or words that you see onscreen. For example, words in menus or dialog boxes appear in the text like this. Here is an example: " Depending on the view, you should see three values in **Console** or three lines in the **Graph** tab"

Warnings or important notes appear like this.

Tips and tricks appear like this.

Get in touch

Feedback from our readers is always welcome.

General feedback: Email feedback@packtpub.com and mention the book title in the subject of your message. If you have questions about any aspect of this book, please email us at questions@packtpub.com.

Errata: Although we have taken every care to ensure the accuracy of our content, mistakes do happen. If you have found a mistake in this book, we would be grateful if you would report this to us. Please visit www.packtpub.com/submit-errata, selecting your book, clicking on the Errata Submission Form link, and entering the details.

Piracy: If you come across any illegal copies of our works in any form on the Internet, we would be grateful if you would provide us with the location address or website name. Please contact us at copyright@packtpub.com with a link to the material.

If you are interested in becoming an author: If there is a topic that you have expertise in and you are interested in either writing or contributing to a book, please visit authors.packtpub.com.

1
Introduction to Self-Adapting and Self-Healing Systems

Microservices, microservices, microservices. We are all in the process of rewriting or planning to rewrite our monoliths into microservices. Some of us already did it. We are putting them into containers and deploying them through one of the schedulers. We are marching into a glorious future. There's nothing that can stop us now. Except... We, as an industry, are not yet ready for microservices. One thing is to design our services in a way that they are stateless, fault tolerant, scalable, and so on. The other is to incorporate those services into a system as a whole.

Unless you just started a new project, the chances are that you still did not reach "microservices nirvana" and that quite a few legacy services are floating around. However, for the sake of brevity and the urge to get to the point, I will assume that all the services you're in control of are truly microservices. Does that mean that the whole system reached that nirvana state? Is deployment of a service (no matter who wrote it) entirely independent from the rest of the system? Most likely it isn't.

You are practicing continuous deployment, aren't you? I will assume you are. Now, let's say that you just finished the first release of your new service. That first version is the first commit to your code repository. Your CD tool of choice detected the change in your code repository and started the CD pipeline. At the end of it, the service will be deployed to production. I can see a smile on your face. It's that expression of happiness that can be seen only after a child is born, or a service is deployed to production for the first time. That smile should not be long lasting since deploying a service is only the beginning. It needs to be integrated with the rest of the system. The proxy needs to be reconfigured. Logs parser needs to be updated with the format produced by the new service. Monitoring system needs to become aware of the new service. Alerts need to be created with the goal of sending warning and error notifications when the state of the service reaches certain thresholds. The whole system has to adapt to the new service and incorporate the new variables introduced with the commit we made a few moments ago.

How do we adapt the system so that it takes the new service into account? How do we make that service be an integral part of the system?

Unless you are writing everything yourself (in which case you must be Google), your system consists of a mixture of services developed by you and services written and maintained by others. You probably use a third-party proxy (hopefully that's Docker Flow Proxy - `https://proxy.dockerflow.com/`). You might have chosen the ELK stack or Splunk for centralized logging. How about monitoring? Maybe it's Nagios, or it might be Prometheus. No matter the choices you made, you are not in control of the architecture of the whole system. Heck, you're probably not even in control of all the services you wrote.

Most of the third-party services are not designed to work in a highly dynamic cluster. When you deployed that first release of the service, you might have had to configure the proxy manually. You might have had to add a few parsing rules to your LogStash config. Your Prometheus targets had to be updated. New alerting rules had to be added. And so on, and so forth. Even if all those tasks are automated, the CD pipeline would have to become too big, and the process would be too flaky.

I will try to be an optimist and assume that you survived the hurdle of configuring all your third-party tools to work seamlessly with the new service. There will be no time to rest since that same service (or some other) will soon be updated. Someone will make a change that will result in a higher memory threshold. That means that, for example, monitoring tool needs to be reconfigured. You might say that's OK since it happens occasionally but that would not be true either. If we adopted microservices and continuous deployment, "occasionally" might mean "on any of the frequent commits." Remember, teams are small, and they are independent. A change that affects the rest of the system might come at any moment, and we need to be ready for it.

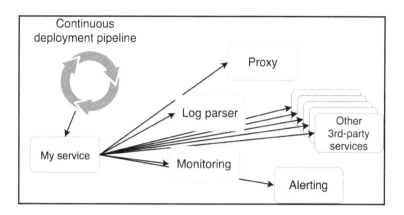

Figure 1-1: Traditional deployment where the source of truth about a service is scattered across many different places

Most third-party services were designed in an era when clusters were a collection of static servers. Only a handful of those were designed to work well with containers and even fewer were truly adapted to work with schedulers (for example, Swarm, Kubernetes, or Mesos/Marathon).

One of the major limitations of third-party services is their reliance on static configuration. Take Prometheus as an example. It is, potentially, in charge of monitoring all of your services as well as hardware, networking, and what so not. Each of the targets it observes might have a different set of metrics and a different set of conditions that will fire alerts. Every time we want to add a new target, we need to modify Prometheus configuration and reload it. That means that, for fault tolerance, we have to store that configuration file on a network drive, have some templating mechanism which updates it with every new service and, potentially, with every update of an existing service. So, we would deploy our fancy new service, update the template that generates Prometheus config, create a new config, overwrite the one stored on the network drive, and reload Prometheus. Even that is not enough because data that fuels those templates needs to be stored somewhere meaning that we need to register every service in a service registry (or use the one baked in Docker) and make sure that templating solution reads from it.

Part of the mess could be avoided if Prometheus would be configurable through its API. Still, configuration API more would remove the need for templates but would not eliminate the need for a network drive. Its configuration is its state, and it has to be preserved.

This line of thinking is historical. We are used to monolithic based systems where information is scattered all over the place. We are slowly moving towards a different model. The system is broken into many smaller services, and each of them is a complete source of truth for a problem domain it solves. If you need information about a service, ask for it, or have a mechanism that will push that information to you. A service does not know nor it should care who uses it and how.

The service itself should contain all the data that describes it. If it should reconfigure a proxy, that info should be part of the service. It should contain a pattern it uses to output logs. It should have the addresses of targets that a monitoring tool should scrape from. It should have the info that will be used to launch alerts. In other words, everything that a service needs should be defined in that service. Not somewhere else. The origin of the data we need to adapt a system to the new service should not be distributed across multiple locations, but inside the service we're deploying. Since we are all using containers (aren't we?), the best place to define all that info are service labels.

If your service should be accessible on a path `/v1/my-fancy-service`, define a label by using argument `--label servicePath=/v1/my-fancy-service`. If Prometheus should scrape metrics on port `8080`, define a label `--label scrapePort=8080`. And so on and so forth.

Why is all that significant? Among other reasons, when we define all the data a service needs inside that service, we have a single place that contains the complete truth about a service. That makes configuration easier, it makes the team in charge of a service self-sufficient, it makes deployments more manageable and less error prone, and so on and so forth.

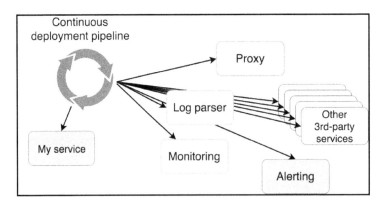

Figure 1-2: A service is the single source of truth that, often through an intermediary, announces to the rest of the system its existence

Defining all the info of a service we're developing inside that same service is not a problem. The problem is that most of the third-party services we're using are not designed to leverage that info. Remember, the data about a service needs to be distributed across the cluster. It needs to reach all other services that work in conjunction with the services we're developing and deploying. We do not want to define that info in multiple locations since that increases maintenance costs and introduces potential problems caused by human errors. Instead, we want to define everything inside a service we're deploying and propagate that information throughout the cluster.

We do not want to define and maintain the same info in multiple locations, and we do want to keep that info at the source, but the third-party services are incapable of obtaining that data from the source. If we discard the option of modifying third-party services, the only choice left is to extend them so that they can pull or receive the data they need.

What we truly need are third-party services capable of discovering information from services we are deploying. That discovery can be pull (a service pulls info from another service) or push based (a service acts as a middle-men and pushes data from one service to another). No matter whether discovery relies on push or pull, a service that receives data needs to be able to reconfigure itself. All that needs to be combined with a system that will be able to detect that a service was deployed or updated and notify all interested parties.

The ultimate goal is to design a system that is capable of adapting to any service we throw at it, as well as to changed conditions of a cluster. The final objective is to have a **self-adapting** and **self-healing** system that will continue operating efficiently even when we are on vacations.

What is a self-adaptive system?

A self-adaptive system is a system that adapts to changing conditions. That was evident, wasn't it? In practical terms, when operating a cluster and deploying services, that means that a system should adapt when a new service is deployed, or an existing one is updated. When conditions in a cluster change, the whole system should change by adapting to those conditions. If a new service is deployed, the monitoring solution should get the information about that service and change its configuration. A logging system should start processing the logs of that service and parse it correctly. The number of nodes in the cluster should adjust. And so on and so forth. The most important requirement for a system to self-adapt is to create it in such a way that human intervention is not needed. Otherwise, we can just as well change the name from self-adaptive to John-adapts-it system.

What is a self-healing system?

A self-healing system needs to be adaptive. Without the capability to adapt to the changes in the environment, we cannot self-heal. While adaptation is more permanent or longer lasting, healing is a temporary action. Take a number of requests as an example. Let's imagine that it increased permanently because now we have more users or because the new design of the UI is so good that users are spending more using our frontend. As a result of such an increase, our system needs to adapt and permanently (or, at least, longer lastingly) increase the number of replicas of our services. That increase should match the minimum expected load. Maybe we run five replicas of our shopping cart, and that was enough in most circumstances but, since our number of users increased, the number of instances of the shopping cart needs to increase to, let's say, ten replicas. It does not need to be a fixed number. It can, for example, vary from seven (lowest expected load) to twelve (highest expected load).

Self-healing is a reaction to unexpected and has a temporary nature. Take us (humans) as an example. When a virus attacks us, our body reacts and fights it back. Once the virus is annihilated, the state of the emergency ceases and we go back to the normal state. It started with a virus entering and ended once it's removed. A side effect is that we might adapt during the process and permanently create a better immune system. We can apply the same logic to our clusters. We can create processes that will react to external threats and execute reactive measures. Some of those measures will be removed as soon as the threat is gone while others might result in permanent changes to our system.

Self-healing does not always work. Both us (humans) and software systems sometimes need external help. If all else fails, and we cannot self-heal ourselves and eliminate the problem internally, we might go to a doctor. Similarly, if a cluster cannot fix itself it should send a notification to an operator who will, hopefully, be able to fix the problem, write a post-mortem, and improve the system so that the next time the same problem occurs it can self-heal itself.

This need for an external help outlines an effective way to build a self-healing system. We cannot predict all the combinations that might occur in a system. However, what we can do is make sure that when unexpected happens, it is not unexpected for long. A good engineer will try to make himself obsolete. He will try to do the same action only once, and the only way to accomplish that is through an ever-increasing level of automated processes. Everything that is expected should be scripted and fall into self-adapting and self-healing processes executed by the system. We should react only when unexpected happens.

What now?

Let us start building a self-adaptive and self-healing system. The first thing we'll need is metrics. Without metrics, neither the system nor we can make decisions. We'll start by choosing the right tool for the job.

2
Choosing a Solution for Metrics Storage and Query

Every cluster needs to collect metrics. They are the basis of any alerting system we might want to employ. Without the information about the current and the past state of a cluster, we would not be able to react to problems when they occur nor would we be able to prevent them from happening in the first place. Actually, that is not entirely accurate. We could do all those things, but not in a way that is efficient and scalable.

A good analogy is blindness. Being blind does not mean that we cannot feel our way through an environment. Similarly, we are not helpless without a way to collect and query metrics. We can SSH into each of the nodes and check the system manually. We can start by fiddling with `top`, `mem`, `df`, and other commands. We can check the status of the containers with the `docker stats` command. We can go from one container to another and check their logs. We can do all those things, but such an approach does not scale. We cannot increase the number of operators with the same rhythm as the number of servers. We cannot convert ourselves into human machines. Even if we could, we would be terrible at it. That's why we have tools to help us. And, if they do not fulfill our needs, we can build our own solutions on top of them.

There are many tools we can choose. It would be impossible to compare them all, so we'll limit the scope to only a handful.

We'll focus on open source projects only. Some of the tools we'll discuss have a paid enterprise offering in the form of additional features. We'll exclude them from the comparison. The reason behind the exclusion lies in my belief that we should always start with open source software, get comfortable with it, and only once it proves its worth, evaluate whether it is worthwhile switching to the enterprise version.

Moreover, we'll introduce one more limitation. We will explore only the solutions that we can host ourselves. That excludes hosted services like, for example, Scout (`https://scoutapp.com/`) or DataDog (`https://www.datadoghq.com/`). The reason behind such a decision is two-fold. Many organizations are not willing to "give" their data to a third-party hosted service. Even if there is no such restriction, a hosted service would need to be able to send alerts back to our system and that would be a huge security breach. If neither of those matters to you, they are not flexible enough. None of the services I know will give us enough flexibility to build a *self-adapting* and *self-healing* system. Besides, the purpose of this book is to give you free solutions, hence the insistence on open source solutions that you can host yourself.

That does not mean that paid software is not worth the price nor that we should not use, and pay for, hosted service. Quite the contrary. However, I felt it would be better to start with things we can build ourselves and explore the limits. From there on, you will have a better understanding what you need and whether paying money for that is worthwhile.

A note to The DevOps 2.1 Toolkit readers
You might be able to guess which tool will be chosen. Nevertheless, this chapter provides a more detailed explanation behind the choice. I think that the overview that follows is important since it provides a short description of the types of the solutions for storing and querying metrics as well as some of the pros and cons of some of the tools on the market.

Non-dimensional versus dimensional metrics

Before we explore the tools we'll choose from, we should discuss different approaches to storing and collecting metrics.

We can divide the tools by dimensions. Some can store data with dimensions while others cannot. Representatives of those that are dimensionless would be Graphite and Nagios. Truth be told, there is a semblance of dimensions in Graphite, but they are so limited in their nature that we'll treat it as dimensionless. Some of the solutions that do support dimensions are, for example, InfluxDB and Prometheus. The former supports them in the form of key/value pairs while the latter uses labels.

Non-dimensional (or dimensionless) metric storage belongs to the *old world* when servers were relatively static, and the number of targets that were monitored was relatively small. That can be seen from the time those tools were created. Both Nagios and Graphite are older tools than InfluxDB and Prometheus.

Why are dimensions relevant? Query language needs them to be effective. Without dimensions, the language is bound to be limited in its capabilities. That does not mean that we always need dimensions. For a simple monitoring, they might be an overhead. However, running a scalable cluster where services are continuously deployed, scaled, updated, and moved around is far from simple. We need metrics that can represent all the dimensions of our cluster and the services running on top of it. A dynamic system requires dynamic analytics, and that is accomplished with metrics that include dimensions.

An example of a dimensionless metric would be `container_memory_usage`. Compare that with `container_memory_usage{service_name="my-service", task_name="my-service.2.###", memory_limit="20000000", ...}"`. The latter example provides much more freedom. We can calculate average memory usage as we'd do with dimensionless but we can also deduce what the memory limit is, what is the name of the service, which replica (task) it is, and so on, and so forth.

Dimensions, when added to metrics, can be combined into innumerable combinations, and paint an accurate picture of the system and answer complex questions.

Are dimensions (or lack of them) the only thing that distinguishes tools for storing and analyzing metrics? Among others, the way those metrics end up in a database makes a difference that might be significant. Some of the tools expect data to be pushed while others will pull (or scrape) them.

If we stick with the tools we mentioned previously, representatives of a push method would be Graphite and InfluxDB, while Nagios and Prometheus would belong to the pull group.

Those that fall into the push category are expecting data to come to them. They are passive (at least when metrics gathering is concerned). Each of the services that collect data is supposed to push them into one central location. Popular examples would be `collectD` and `statsD`. Pull system, on the other hand, is active. It will scrape data from all specified targets. Data collectors do not know about the existence of the database. Their only purpose is to gather data and expose them through a protocol acceptable to the system that will pull them.

A discussion about pros and cons of each system is raging for quite some time. There are many arguments in favor of one over the other system, and we could spend a lot of time going through all of them. Instead, we'll discuss discovery, the argument that is, in my opinion, the most relevant.

With the push system, discovery is easy. All that data collectors need to know is the address of the metrics storage and push data. As long as that address keeps being operational, the configuration is very straight forward. With the pull system, the system needs to know the location of all the data collectors (or exporters). When there are only a few, that is easy to configure. If that number jumps to tens, hundreds, or even thousands of targets, the configuration can become very tedious. That situation clearly favors the push model. But, technology changed. We have reliable systems that provide service discovery. Docker Swarm, for example, has it baked in as part of Docker Engine. Finding targets is easy and, assuming that we trust service discovery, we always have up to date information about all the data collectors.

With a proper service discovery in place, pull versus push debate becomes, more or less, irrelevant. That brings us to an argument that makes pull more appealing. It is much easier to discover a failed instance or a missing service when pulling data. When a system expects data collectors to push data, it is oblivious whether something is missing. We can summarize the problem with "I don't know what I don't know." Pull systems, on the other hand, know what to expect. They know what their targets are and it is very easy to deduce that when a scraping target does not respond, the likely cause is that it stopped working.

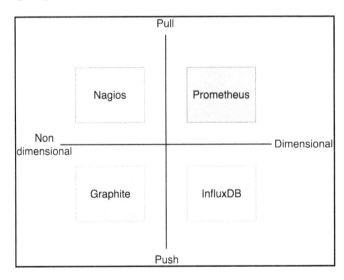

Figure 2-1: Monitoring tools placement based on dimensions and data collection methods

Neither of the arguments for push or pull are definitive, and we should not make a choice only based on that criteria. Instead, we'll explore the tools we discussed a bit more.

The first one on the list is Graphite.

Graphite

Graphite is a passive metrics storage tool. The reason we call it passive lies in its inability to collect metrics. They need to be collected and pushed in a separate process.

It is a time series database with its own query language and capabilities to produce graphs. Querying API is powerful. Or, to be more precise, was considered powerful when it appeared. Today, when compared with some other tools, its query language is limiting, mainly due to its dimensionless format for storing metrics.

Graphite stores numeric data in time series format. Its metric names consist of dot-separated elements.

Data is stored on a local disk.

InfluxDB

Just like Graphite, InfluxDB is a time series database. Unlike Graphite, Influx DB data model is based on key/value pairs in the form of labels.

InfluxDB (open source version, to be more precise) relies on local storage for storing data, and its scraping, rule processing, and alerting.

Nagios and Sensu

Nagios is a monitoring system that originated in the 90s as NetSaint. It is primarily about alerting based on the exit codes of scripts.

Unlike other solutions, the amount and types of data it stores is limited to check state making it suitable only for a very basic monitoring.

Sensu can be considered a more modern version of Nagios. The primary difference is that Sensu clients register themselves, and can determine the checks to run either from a central or local configuration. There is also a client socket permitting arbitrary check results to be pushed into Sensu.

Sensu uses (almost) the same data model as Nagios and shares its limitation of the format it uses to store metrics.

Prometheus

Prometheus is a full monitoring and trending system that includes built-in and active scraping, storing, querying, graphing, and alerting based on time series data. It has knowledge about what the world should look like (which endpoints should exist, what time series patterns mean trouble, and so on.), and actively tries to find faults.

Prometheus has a rich data model and probably the most powerful query language among time series databases. It encodes dimensions explicitly as key-value pairs (labels) attached to a metric name. That allows easy filtering, grouping, and matching by these labels via in the query language.

Which tool should we choose?

All the tools we listed are (or were) good in their merit. They are different in many aspects while similar in others.

Nagios and Sensu served us well in the past. They were designed in a different era and based on principles that are today considered obsolete. They work well with static clusters and monolithic applications and services running on predefined locations. The metrics they store (or lack of them) are not suitable for more complex decision making. We would have a hard time using them as means to accomplish our goals of operating a scheduler like Docker Swarm running in an auto-scalable cluster. Among the solutions we explored, they are the first ones we should discard. One is out; three are left to choose from.

Dot-separated metrics format used by Graphite is limiting. Excluding elements of a metric with asterisks (*) is often inadequate for proper filtering, grouping, and other operations. Its query language, when compared with InfluxDB and Prometheus, is the main reason we'll discard it.

We're left with InfluxDB and Prometheus as finalists and are facing only minor differences.

InfluxDB and Prometheus are similar in many ways, so the choice is not going to be an easy one. Truth be told, we cannot make a wrong decision. Whichever we choose of the two, the choice will be based on slight differences.

If we would not limit ourselves to open source solutions as the only candidates, InfluxDB enterprise version could be the winner due to its scalability. However, we will discard it in favor of Prometheus. It provides a more complete solution. More importantly, Prometheus is slowly becoming the de-facto standard, at least when working with schedulers. It is a preferred solution in Kubernetes. Docker (and therefore Swarm) is soon going to expose its metrics in Prometheus format. That, in itself, is the tipping point that should make us lean slightly more towards Prometheus.

The decision is made. We'll use Prometheus to store metrics, to query them, and to trigger alerts.

What now?

Now that we decided which tool will be the basis for storing metrics, we should proceed with the setup. Since we will be using Docker Swarm services, deploying Prometheus in its most basic form will be a breeze.

3

Deploying and Configuring Prometheus

On the first look, deploying Prometheus is simple. Create a compose file and execute `docker stack deploy` command. Complications emerge once we start integrating services with Prometheus. Soon, you will have a first-hand chance to experience the integration problems.

Like any good story, this chapter will start on a happy note. Among engineers, happy means that it's simple and it works. Let's see how simple looks in practice.

Deploying Prometheus stack

We'll start by cloning `vfarcic/docker-flow-monitor` repository from `https://github.com/vfarcic/docker-flow-monitor`. It contains all the scripts and Docker stacks we'll use throughout this chapter.

 All the commands from this chapter are available in the `03-deploying-prometheus.sh` Gist at `https://gist.github.com/vfarcic/e597004e626fbffc47de72bdc75a3498`.

```
git clone \
    https://github.com/vfarcic/docker-flow-monitor.git

cd docker-flow-monitor
```

The rest of the chapter will require Docker machine. Please set it up using the installation instructions at (`https://docs.docker.com/machine/install-machine/`). If you are a Windows user, please run all the commands from *Git Bash* (installed through *Git*) or any other bash you might have.

Before we create a Prometheus service, we need to have a cluster. It will consist of three nodes created with Docker machine.

Feel free to skip the commands that follow if you already have a working Swarm cluster.

```
chmod +x scripts/dm-swarm.sh

./scripts/dm-swarm.sh

eval $(docker-machine env swarm-1)
```

The `dm-swarm.sh` script created the nodes and joined them into a Swarm cluster.

I will assume that you are already familiar with Docker Swarm and do not need an explanation of the script. If that's not the case, please consider reading *The DevOps 2.1 Toolkit: Docker Swarm* for an in-depth examination of how Docker Swarm clusters work.

Now we can create the first Prometheus service. We'll start small and slowly move toward a more robust solution.

We'll deploy the stack defined in `stacks/prometheus.yml`. It is as follows:

```
version: "3"

services:

  prometheus:
    image: prom/prometheus
    ports:
      - 9090:9090
```

As you can see, it is as simple as it can get. It specifies the image and the port that should be opened.

Let's deploy the stack.

```
docker stack deploy \
    -c stacks/prometheus.yml \
    monitor
```

Please wait a few moments until the image is pulled and deployed. You can monitor the status by executing the `docker stack ps monitor` command.

Let's confirm that Prometheus service is indeed up-and-running.

```
open "http://$(docker-machine ip swarm-1):9090"
```

 If you're a Windows user, Git Bash might not be able to use the `open` command. If that's the case, replace the `open` command with `echo`. As a result, you'll get the full address that should be opened directly in your browser of choice.

You should see the Prometheus graph screen.

Let's take a look at the configuration.

```
open "http://$(docker-machine ip swarm-1):9090/config"
```

You should see the default config that does not define much more than intervals and internal scraping. In its current state, Prometheus is not very useful, so we'll have to spice it up a bit.

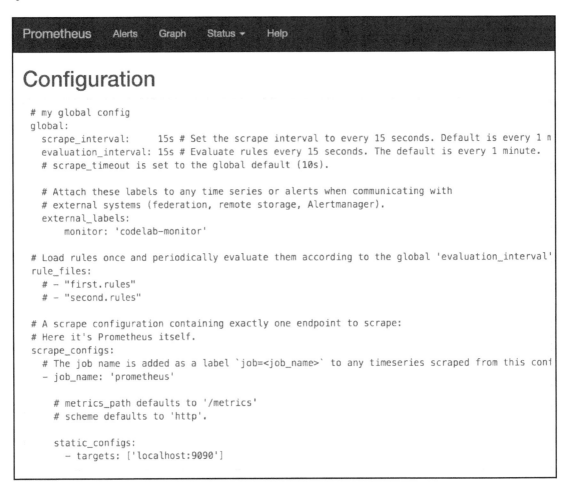

Figure 3-1: Prometheus with the default configuration

We should start fine tuning Prometheus. There are quite a few ways we can do that.

We can create a new Docker image that would extend the one we used and add our own configuration file. That solution has a distinct advantage of being immutable and, hence, very reliable. Since Docker image cannot be changed, we can guarantee that the configuration is exactly as we want it to be no matter where we deploy it. If the service fails, Swarm will reschedule it and, since the configuration is baked into the image, it'll be preserved. The problem with that approach is that it is not suitable for microservices architecture. If Prometheus has to be reconfigured with every new service (or at least those that expose metrics), we would need to build it quite often and tie that build to CD processes executed for the services we're developing. This approach is suitable only for a relatively static cluster and monolithic applications. Discarded!

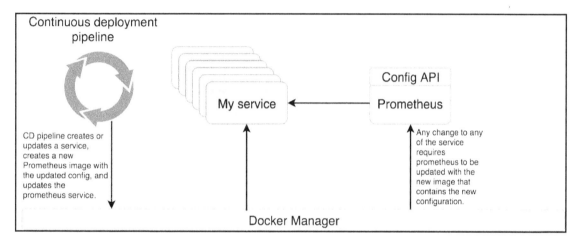

Figure 3-2: Creating a new image every time Prometheus config change

What would be the alternative approach?

We can enter a running Prometheus container, modify its configuration, and reload it. While this allows a higher level of dynamism, it is not fault-tolerant. If Prometheus fails, Swarm will reschedule it, and all the changes we made will be lost. Besides fault tolerance, modifying a config in a running container poses additional problems when running it as a service inside a cluster. We need to find out the node it is running in, SSH into it, figure out the ID of the container, and, only then, we can `exec` into it, modify the config, and send a reload request. While those steps are not overly complicated and can be scripted, they will pose an unnecessary operational complexity. Discarded!

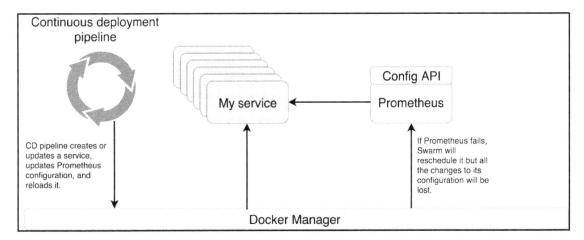

Figure 3-3: Updating Prometheus configuration inside a container

Among other reasons, we discarded the previous solution because it is not fault-tolerant.

We could mount a network volume to the service. That would solve persistence, but would still leave the problem created by a dynamic nature of a cluster. We still, potentially, need to change the configuration and reload Prometheus every time a new service is deployed or updated.

From the operational perspective, this solution is simpler than the previous solution we discussed. We do not need to find out the node it is running in, SSH into it, figure out the ID of the container, `exec` into it, and modify the config. Instead, we can alter the file on the network drive and send a reload request to Prometheus. While network drive simplifies the process, it does not make it as dynamic and independent from the services as it should be. We would need to make sure that the deployment pipeline of each of the services has the required steps that will reconfigure Prometheus. By doing that we would break one of our objectives. That is, our services would not contain all the information about themselves. Instead, we'd need to create a different pipeline for each and specify the targets, alerts, and other information we might need before reconfiguring Prometheus. We'll discard this solution as well.

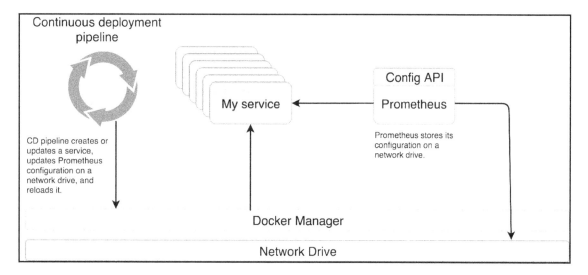

Figure 3-4: Updating Prometheus configuration stored on a network drive

What other options do we have? If we're looking for an out-of-the-box solution that uses the official Prometheus image, all our options are exhausted. But we are engineers. We are used to extending other people solutions and adapting them to suit our needs. Let's not limit our options and try to design a solution that would suit us well.

Designing a more dynamic monitoring solution

How can we improve Prometheus design to suit our purposes better? How can we make it more dynamic and more scheduler friendly?

One improvement we can make is the usage of environment variables. That would save us from having to create a new image every time we need to change its configuration. At the same time, environment variables would remove the need to use a network drive (at least for configuration).

> When using containers, environment variables are a preferable way of passing configuration information to the processes running inside them.

We can make a generic solution that will transform any environment variable into a Prometheus configuration entry or an initialization argument.

> We'll go through the code I created. It is written in Go and should be relatively straightforward to understand even if you are not a Go developer. The goal of the walkthrough is to get familiar with a potential solution that you could write yourself in your favorite language. That does not mean that you should not adopt *Docker Flow Monitor* as a ready to go solution and skip the coding part, but, rather, that you should evaluate your options and make your own choice.

To enable Prometheus configuration through environment variables, we need to distinguish those that should be used as command line arguments from those that will serve to create the configuration file. We'll define a naming convention stating that every environment argument with a name that starts with `ARG_` is a startup argument.

The code can be as follows:

```
func Run() error {
    cmdString := "prometheus"
    for _, e := range os.Environ() {
        if key, value := getArgFromEnv(e, "ARG"); len(key) > 0 {
            cmdString = fmt.Sprintf("%s -%s=%s", cmdString, key,
            value)
        }
    }
    cmd := exec.Command("/bin/sh", "-c", cmdString)
    return cmdRun(cmd)
}
```

It is a very simple function. It iterates through all the environment variables. If their names start with `ARG`, they will be added as arguments of the executable Prometheus. Once the iteration is done, binary is launched with arguments.

We made Prometheus more *Docker-friendly* with only a few lines of code that sits on top of it.

The full source code can be found in the `run.go` file at
`https://github.com/vfarcic/docker-flow-monitor/blob/master/prometheus/run.go`.

We should do something similar with the configuration file. Specifically, we can make the global section of the configuration use environment variables prefixed with `GLOBAL_`.

The logic of the code is similar to the `Run` function we explored. Please go through `config.go` for more details
(`https://github.com/vfarcic/docker-flow-monitor/blob/master/prometheus/config.go`). The `GetGlobalConfig` function returns global section of the config while the `WriteConfig` function writes the configuration to the file.

Please consult Prometheus configuration
(`https://prometheus.io/docs/operating/configuration/`) for more information about the available options.

By using environment variables, we managed to get rid of the network drive. As far as configuration is concerned, it will be fault tolerant. If the service fails and gets rescheduled with Swarm, it will not lose its configuration since it is part of the service definition. There is a downside though. Every time we want to change the configuration, we'll need to execute `docker service update` command or modify the stack file, and re-execute `docker stack deploy`. As a result, Docker will stop the currently running replica and start a new one thus producing a short downtime. However, since we are, at the moment, only dealing with global configuration and startup arguments, changes will be very uncommon. We'll deal with more dynamic parts of the configuration later.

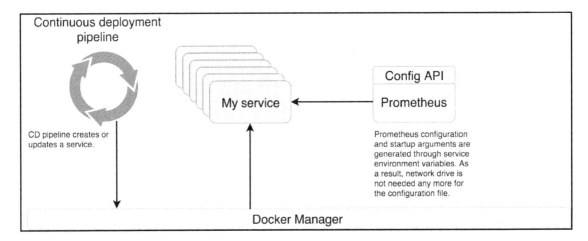

Figure 3-5: Prometheus configuration defined through environment variables

I have the code compiled and available as `vfarcic/docker-flow-monitor/` (`https://hub.docker.com/r/vfarcic/docker-flow-monitor/`). Let's give it a spin.

 Please note that you can choose not to use *Docker Flow Monitor* nor to create your own solution. What follows is still equally useful if you decide to use the "original" Prometheus. You will learn how to apply manually all the changes we'll perform in a more dynamic fashion.

Deploying Docker Flow Monitor

Deploying *Docker Flow Monitor* is easy (as almost all Docker services are). We'll start by creating a network called `monitor`. We could let Docker stack create it for us, but it is useful to have it defined externally so that we can easily attach it to services from other stacks:

```
docker network create -d overlay monitor
```

The stack is as follows:

```
version: "3"
services:
  monitor:
    image: vfarcic/docker-flow-monitor:${TAG:-latest}
    environment:
      - GLOBAL_SCRAPE_INTERVAL=10s
    networks:
      - monitor
    ports:
      - 9090:9090
networks:
    monitor:
        external: true
```

The environment variable `GLOBAL_SCRAPE_INTERVAL` shows the first improvement over the "original" Prometheus service. It allows us to define entries of its configuration as environment variables. That, in itself, is not a significant improvement but is a good start. More powerful additions will be explored later on.

Please visit environment variables section of the documentation for more information about configuration options at (`http://monitor.dockerflow.com/config/#environment-variables`).

Now we're ready to deploy the stack:

```
docker stack rm monitor
docker stack deploy \
    -c stacks/docker-flow-monitor.yml \
    monitor
```

Please wait a few moments until Swarm pulls the image and starts the service. You can monitor the status by executing `docker stack ps monitor` command.

Once the service is running, we can confirm that the environment variable indeed generated the configuration:

```
open "http://$(docker-machine ip swarm-1):9090/config"
```

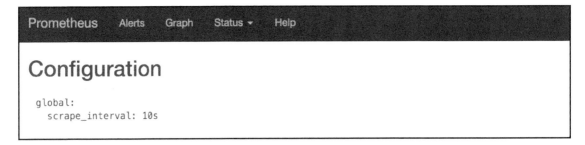

Figure 3-6: Prometheus configuration defined through environment variables

 Please note that you do not have to use Docker Flow Monitor to accomplish the same Prometheus configuration. We are using it mostly as a fast and dynamic way to configure it. You can choose to do the same by changing its configuration manually.

We are going to expose services url in pretty format, therefore we must get rid of port number (`9090`) in preceding url.

Integrating Docker Flow Monitor with Docker Flow Proxy

Having a port opened (other than `80` and `443`) is, often, not a good idea. If for no other reason, at least it's not user-friendly to remember a different port for each service. In general service might need to be accessible on its own subdomain, it might need SSL certificate, it might require some URL rewriting, it might need a basic authentication, and so on and so forth. I won't go into details since you probably already know all that and you are probably already using some proxy in your organization.

We'll integrate Docker Flow Monitor (`http://monitor.dockerflow.com/`) with **Docker Flow Proxy (DFP)** (`http://proxy.dockerflow.com/`). If you haven't used DFP before, please visit the official documentation (`http://proxy.dockerflow.com/`) for tutorials, setup, and configuration.

Before we apply the knowledge about new ways to configure Prometheus, we need to run the proxy:

```
docker network create -d overlay proxy
docker stack deploy \
    -c stacks/docker-flow-proxy.yml \
    proxy
```

We created the proxy network and deployed the `docker-flow-proxy.yml` stack. We won't go into details how Docker Flow Proxy works. The essence is that it will configure itself with each service that has specific labels. For any deeper explanation, please visit Docker Flow Proxy Stack Tutorial (`http://proxy.dockerflow.com/swarm-mode-stack/`) or any other tutorial available.

With the proxy up and running, we should redeploy our monitor.

We'll replace the current monitor stack with a new one with in order to achieve this. The major difference is that this time we'll define startup arguments as well as the labels that will allow the proxy to reconfigure itself to enable access to monitor. You'll also notice that we will not expose port 9090. It'll be accessible through the proxy on port 80, so there's no reason to open any other port.

The stack is as follows:

```
monitor:
  image: vfarcic/docker-flow-monitor:${TAG:-latest}
  environment:
    - GLOBAL_SCRAPE_INTERVAL=10s
    - ARG_WEB_ROUTE-PREFIX=/monitor
    - ARG_WEB_EXTERNAL-URL=http://${DOMAIN:-localhost}/monitor
  networks:
    - proxy
    - monitor
  deploy:
    labels:
      - com.df.notify=true
      - com.df.distribute=true
      - com.df.servicePath=/monitor
      - com.df.serviceDomain=${DOMAIN:-localhost}
      - com.df.port=9090


swarm-listener:
  image: vfarcic/docker-flow-swarm-listener
  networks:
    - monitor
```

```
      volumes:
        - /var/run/docker.sock:/var/run/docker.sock
      environment:
        - DF_NOTIFY_CREATE_SERVICE_URL=http://monitor:8080\
/v1/docker-flow-monitor/reconfigure
        - DF_NOTIFY_REMOVE_SERVICE_URL=http://monitor:8080\
/v1/docker-flow-monitor/remove
      deploy:
        placement:
          constraints: [node.role == manager]

networks:
  monitor:
    external: true
  proxy:
    external: true
```

This time we added a few additional environment variables. They will be used instead Prometheus' default startup arguments.

We are specifying the route prefix (`ARG_WEB_ROUTE-PREFIX`) as well as the full external URL (`ARG_WEB_EXTERNAL-URL`).

Please visit ARG variables section of the documentation (`http://monitor.dockerflow.com/config/#arg-variables`) for more information about environment variables that can be used as startup arguments.

We also used the `com.df.*` service labels that will tell the proxy how to reconfigure itself so that Prometheus is available through the path `/monitor`.

The second service is Docker Flow Swarm Listener (`http://swarmlistener.dockerflow.com/`) that will listen to Swarm events and send reconfigure and remove requests to the monitor. You'll see its usage later on. For now, just remember that we deployed it alongside the monitor service.

Let us deploy the new version of the monitor stack:

```
docker stack rm monitor

DOMAIN=$(docker-machine ip swarm-1) \
    docker stack deploy \
    -c stacks/docker-flow-monitor-proxy.yml \
    monitor
```

In the "real-world" situation, you should use your domain (for example `monitor.acme.com`) and would not need `ARG_WEB_ROUTE-PREFIX` and `com.df.servicePath` set to `/monitor`. However, since we do not have a domain for this exercise, we used the IP of `swarm-1` node instead.

Please execute, `docker stack ps monitor` to check the status of the stack. Once it's up-and-running, we can confirm that the monitor is indeed integrated with the proxy:

```
open "http://$(docker-machine ip swarm-1)/monitor/flags"
```

By opening the *flags* screen, not only that we confirmed that the integration with *Docker Flow Proxy* worked but also that the arguments we specified as environment variables are properly propagated. You can observe that through the values of the `web.external-url` and `web.route-prefix` flags:

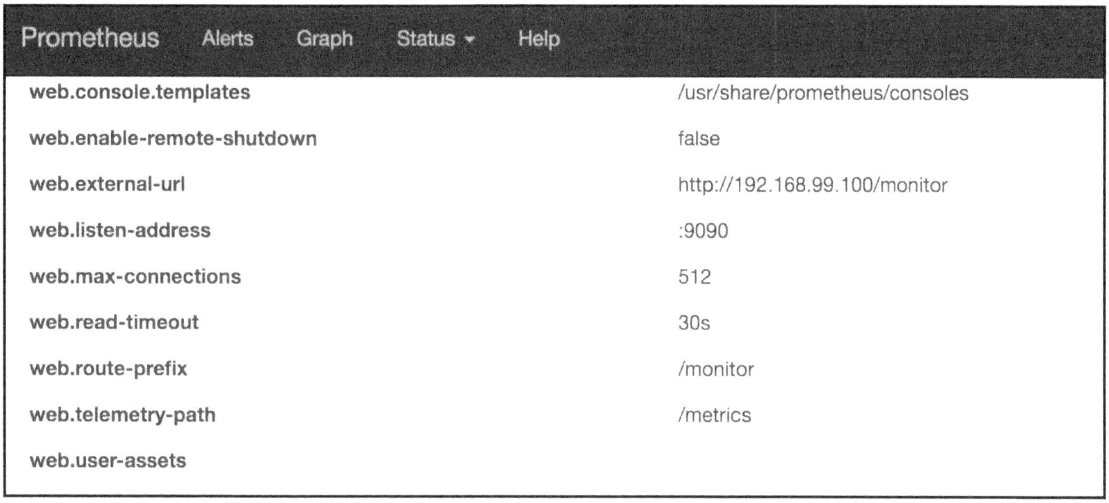

Prometheus	Alerts	Graph	Status ▾	Help	
web.console.templates					/usr/share/prometheus/consoles
web.enable-remote-shutdown					false
web.external-url					http://192.168.99.100/monitor
web.listen-address					:9090
web.max-connections					512
web.read-timeout					30s
web.route-prefix					/monitor
web.telemetry-path					/metrics
web.user-assets					

Figure 3-7: Prometheus flags screen with values passed through environment variables

Please note that we did not specify the port of the `monitor` service. As soon as the service was created, `swarm-listener` detected it and sent a request to the proxy to reconfigure itself. The information the proxy needs was obtained through the labels (for example `com.df.servicePath`).

There was a hidden reason behind the integration of the two. Apart from the need to have a proxy, I wanted to show you an existing implementation of the logic we are exploring. There was no need for a manual configuration of the proxy, nor we had to define the data proxy needs anywhere but inside the service definition itself. The `monitor` service contains all the information, and any other part of the system can fetch it. Everything related to the service is in a single location. By everything, I mean everything that we need for now. Later on, we'll extend the definition of this and many other services.

 Service labels are a precious asset that can be used as a single source of information for a service.

What now?

Soon we'll start exploring exporters and their integration with *Prometheus* and *Docker Flow Monitor*.

We'll take a break and remove the machines we created. Every chapter will start from scratch. Don't be scared. It'll take only a couple of minutes to get back to the previous state:

```
docker-machine rm -f \
    swarm-1 swarm-2 swarm-3
```

4
Scraping Metrics

Prometheus is a pull-based system. It requires targets from which it will get metrics. They can be exposed from inside your services or as generic exporters acting as intermediaries between Prometheus and other services or systems.

Services can be instrumented to provide metrics using one of the Client Libraries (`https://prometheus.io/docs/instrumenting/clientlibs/`). Many of the languages are supported. If no library is available for your programming language of choice to instrument by one of Prometheus data formats, or if you don't want to add one more dependency by using Prometheus data format, there is always the option of implementing one of the exposition formats (`https://prometheus.io/docs/instrumenting/exposition_formats/`).

The alternative to instrumentation of our services is to use exporters. The Exporters and Integrations (`https://prometheus.io/docs/instrumenting/exporters/`) page lists quite a few official and community maintained solutions.

Having both options in front of us, we should make a decision which type to use. Should we instrument our services or use exporters? The decision does not have to be binary. We can use both.

In some cases, we do not have a choice. With third-party software like, for instance, HAProxy, exporters might be the only option since it does not natively provide metrics in Prometheus format. On the other hand, if there is a very particular set of metrics that should be scraped from one of our services, instrumentation is the best option unless that service already exposes metrics in a different format.

More often than not, we do have a choice between using an exporter or instrumenting a service. In such a case, I have a strong preference towards exporters. Instrumentation, even though it is sometimes unavoidable, leads to undesirable coupling. Our services should do only what they are designed to do. If, for example, we have a service that acts as a shopping cart, adding instrumentation and, probably, dependency on Prometheus library introduces tight coupling. If we do that, our shopping cart is not focused on solving only that single business domain but has side functions as well. You might argue that adding instrumentation is not a significant effort. Still, keeping services focused exclusively on their business domain has multiple benefits, and we should avoid increasing their scope by adding any additional responsibilities. That is, as long as we can avoid doing that.

My advice is to always start with exporters, and instrument your services only if you require metrics that are not provided by one of the existing exporters. That way, your services will have clear responsibilities and be focused on a business domain while all infrastructure type of tasks will be delegated to vertical services like, in this case, exporters.

In this chapter, we'll use exporters as the only mean of providing targets that will be utilized by Prometheus to scrape metrics. If you realize that you do have to instrument your services, please consult Prometheus documentation (`https://prometheus.io/docs/instrumenting/clientlibs/`) for more information.

Later on in the book, we might instrument our demo service if we do realize that it provides a substantial advantage.

Now that we had a brief overview of the different ways to expose metrics, we can proceed towards a hands-on exploration of the subject.

Creating the cluster and deploying services

We'll start by recreating the cluster and deploying the stacks that we used in the previous chapter.

 All the commands from this chapter are available in the `04-exporters.sh` Gist at `https://gist.github.com/vfarcic/955690ba490ce4464fab11823eb61d97`.

```
chmod +x scripts/dm-swarm-04.sh./scripts/dm-swarm-04.sheval $(docker-
machine env swarm-1)
```

We executed the `dm-swarm-04.sh` script which, in turn, created a Swarm cluster composed of Docker Machines, created the networks and deployed the stacks. Now we should wait a few moments until all the services in the `monitor` stack are up and running. Please use `docker stack ps monitor` command to confirm that the status of all the services in the stack is *Running*.

Finally, we'll confirm that everything is deployed correctly by opening Prometheus in a browser.

```
open "http://$(docker-machine ip swarm-1)/monitor"
```

Now the state of our cluster is the same as it was at the end of the previous chapter and we can proceed towards deploying exporters.

Deploying exporters

Exporters provide data Prometheus can scrape and put into its database.

The stack we'll deploy is as follows:

```
version: "3"

services:

  ha-proxy:
    image: quay.io/prometheus/haproxy-exporter:${HA_PROXY_TAG:-\
latest}
    networks:
      - proxy
      - monitor
    deploy:
      labels:
        - com.df.notify=true
        - com.df.scrapePort=9101
    command: -haproxy.scrape-
uri="http://admin:admin@proxy/admin?stats;csv"

  cadvisor:
    image: google/cadvisor:${CADVISOR_TAG:-latest}
    networks:
      - monitor
    volumes:
      - /:/rootfs
      - /var/run:/var/run
```

```
            - /sys:/sys
            - /var/lib/docker:/var/lib/docker
        deploy:
          mode: global
          labels:
            - com.df.notify=true
            - com.df.scrapePort=8080

    node-exporter:
      image: basi/node-exporter:${NODE_EXPORTER_TAG:-v1.13.0}
      networks:
        - monitor
      environment:
        - HOST_HOSTNAME=/etc/host_hostname
      volumes:
        - /proc:/host/proc
        - /sys:/host/sys
        - /:/rootfs
        - /etc/hostname:/etc/host_hostname
      deploy:
        mode: global
        labels:
          - com.df.notify=true
          - com.df.scrapePort=9100
      command: '-collector.procfs /host/proc -collector.sysfs\
     /host/sys -collector.filesystem.ignored-mount-points\
     "^/(sys|proc|dev|host|etc)($$|/)" -collector.\
    textfile.directory /etc/node-exporter/ -\
     collectors.enabled="conntrack,diskstats,entropy,filefd,\
    filesystem,loadavg,mdadm,meminfo,netdev,netstat,stat,\
    textfile,time,vmstat,ipvs"'

    networks:
      monitor:
        external: true
      proxy:
        external: true
```

As you can see, the stack definition contains the node and haproxy exporters as well as cadvisor service. haproxy-exporter provides proxy metrics, node-exporter collects server data, while cadvisor outputs information about containers inside our cluster. You'll notice that cadvisor and node-exporter are running in the global mode. A replica will run on each server so that we can obtain an accurate picture of all the nodes that form the cluster.

The important parts of the stack definition are `com.df.notify` and `com.df.scrapePort` labels. The first one tells `swarm-listener` that it should notify the monitor when those services are created (or destroyed). The `scrapePort` labels are defining ports of the exporters that Prometheus will scrape metrics from.

Please visit `Scrape Parameters` section of the documentation for more information how to define scrape parameters.

Let's deploy the stack and see it in action.

```
docker stack deploy \
    -c stacks/exporters.yml \
    exporter
```

Please wait until all the services in the stack are running. You can monitor their status with `docker stack ps exporter` command.

Once confirmed the `exporter` stack is up-and-running, we can verify whether all the services were added to the `monitor` config.

```
open "http://$(docker-machine ip swarm-1)/monitor/config"
```

```
Prometheus    Alerts    Graph    Status ▾    Help

Configuration

global:
  scrape_interval: 10s

scrape_configs:
  - job_name: "exporter_cadvisor"
    dns_sd_configs:
      - names: ["tasks.exporter_cadvisor"]
        type: A
        port: 8080
  - job_name: "exporter_ha-proxy"
    dns_sd_configs:
      - names: ["tasks.exporter_ha-proxy"]
        type: A
        port: 9101
  - job_name: "exporter_node-exporter"
    dns_sd_configs:
      - names: ["tasks.exporter_node-exporter"]
        type: A
        port: 9100
```

Figure 4-1: Configuration with exporters

We can also confirm that all the targets are indeed working by accessing targets page.

```
open "http://$(docker-machine ip swarm-1)/monitor/targets"
```

There should be three targets. If they are still not registered, please wait a few moments and refresh your screen.

Two of the targets (`exporter_cadvisor` and `exporter_node-exporter`) are running as global services. As a result, each has three endpoints, one on each node. The last target is `exporter_ha-proxy`. Since we did not deploy it globally nor specified multiple replicas, in has only one endpoint.

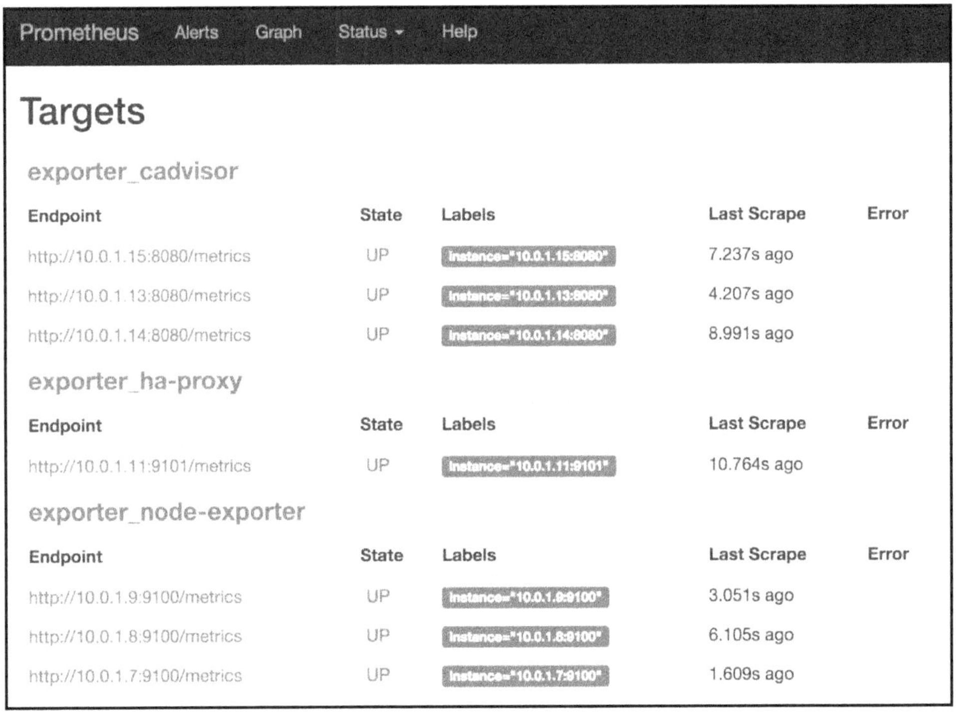

Figure 4-2: Targets and endpoints

If we used the "official" Prometheus image, setting up those targets would require an update of the config file and reload of the service. On top of that, we'd need to persist the configuration. Instead, we let *Swarm Listener* notify *Docker Flow Monitor* that there are new services that should, in this case, generate new scraping targets. Instead of splitting the initial information into multiple locations, we specified scraping info as service labels and let the system take care of the distribution of that data.

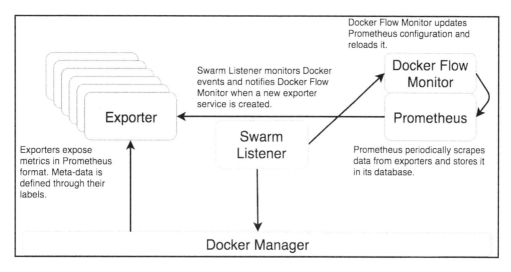

Figure 4-3: Prometheus scrapes metrics from exporters

Let's take a closer look into the exporters running in our cluster.

Exploring exporter metrics

All the exporters we deployed expose metrics in Prometheus format. We can observe them by sending a simple HTTP request. Since the services do not publish any ports, the only way we can communicate with them is through the `monitor` network attached to those exporters.

We'll create a new utility service and attach it to the `monitor` network.

```
docker service create \
    --name util \
    --network monitor \
    --mode global \
    alpine sleep 100000000
```

We created a service based on the `alpine` image, named it `util`, and attached it to the `monitor` network so that it can communicate with exporters we deployed. We made the service `global` so that it runs on every node. That guaranteed that a replica runs on the node we're in. Since `alpine` does not have a long running process, without `sleep`, it would stop as soon as it started, Swarm would reschedule it, only to detect that it stopped again, and so on. Without `sleep` it would enter a never ending loop of failures and rescheduling.

```
ID=$(docker container ls -q \
    -f "label=com.docker.swarm.service.name=util")

docker container exec -it $ID \
    apk add --update curl
```

Next, we found the `ID` of the container, entered it, and installed `curl`.

Now we're ready to send requests to the exporters:

```
docker container exec -it $ID \
    curl node-exporter:9100/metrics
```

Partial output of the request to the `node-exporter` is as follows.

```
...
# HELP process_cpu_seconds_total Total user and system CPU time\
spent in seconds.
# TYPE process_cpu_seconds_total counter
process_cpu_seconds_total 3.05
# HELP process_max_fds Maximum number of open file descriptors.
# TYPE process_max_fds gauge
process_max_fds 1.048576e+06
# HELP process_open_fds Number of open file descriptors.
# TYPE process_open_fds gauge
process_open_fds 7
# HELP process_resident_memory_bytes Resident memory size in bytes.
# TYPE process_resident_memory_bytes gauge
process_resident_memory_bytes 1.6228352e+07
# HELP process_start_time_seconds Start time of the process \
since unix epoch in seconds.
# TYPE process_start_time_seconds gauge
process_start_time_seconds 1.49505618366e+09
# HELP process_virtual_memory_bytes Virtual memory size in bytes.
# TYPE process_virtual_memory_bytes gauge
process_virtual_memory_bytes 2.07872e+07
...
```

As you can see, each metric contains a help entry that describes it, states the type, and displays metric name followed with a value.

We won't go into details of all the metrics provided by `node-exporter`. The list is quite big, and it would require a whole chapter (maybe even a book) to go through all of them. The important thing, at this moment, is to know that almost anything hardware and OS related is exposed as a metric.

Please note that Overlay network load-balanced our request and forwarded it to one of the replicas of the exporter. We don't know what the origin of those metrics is. It could be a replica running on any of the nodes of the cluster. That should not be a problem since, at this moment, we're interested only in observing how metrics look like. If you go back to the configuration screen, you'll notice that targets are configured to use `tasks.[SERVICE_NAME]` format for addresses. When a service name is prefixed with `tasks.`, Swarm returns the list of all replicas (or tasks) of a service.

Let's move to `cadvisor` metrics.

```
docker container exec -it $ID \
    curl cadvisor:8080/metrics
```

Partial output of the request to `cadvisor` metrics is as follows.

```
...
# HELP container_network_receive_bytes_total Cumulative count of bytes
received
# TYPE container_network_receive_bytes_total counter
container_network_receive_bytes_total{id="/",interface="dummy0"} 0
container_network_receive_bytes_total{id="/",interface="eth0"}
6.6461026e+07
container_network_receive_bytes_total{id="/",interface="eth1"}
1.3054141e+07
...
container_network_receive_bytes_total{container_label_com_docker_stack\
_namespace="proxy",container_label_com_docker_swarm_node_id="zvn1kazs\
toa12pu3rfre9j4sw",container_label_com_docker_swarm_service_id="gfoia\
s8w9bf1cve5dujzzlpfh",container_label_com_docker_swarm_service_name=\
"proxy_swarm-listener", container_label_com_docker_swarm_task="",\
container_label_com_docker_swarm_task_id="39hgd75s8vt051smew3ke4imw",\
container_label_com_docker_swarm_task_name="proxy_swarm-listener.1.39\
hgd75s8vt051smew3ke4imw", id="/docker/f2232d2ddf801b1ff41120bb1b9521\
3be15767fe0e6d45266b3b8bba149b3634",image="vfarcic/docker-flow-swarm-\
listener:latest@sha256:d67494f08aa3efba86d5231adba8ee7281c29fd401a5f6\
7377ee026cc436552b",interface="eth0",name="proxy_swarm-listener.1.39h\
gd75s8vt051smew3ke4imw"} 112764
...
```

The major difference, when compared to `node-exporter`, is that `cadvisor` provides a lot of labels. They help a lot when querying metrics, and we'll use them soon.

Just like with `node-exporter`, we won't go into details of each metric exposed through `cadvisor`. Instead, as we're progressing towards creating a *self-healing* system, we'll gradually increase the number of metrics we're using and comment on them as they come.

Now that we have the metrics and that Prometheus is scraping and storing them in its database, we can turn our attention to queries we can execute.

Querying metrics

Targets are up and running, and Prometheus is scraping their data. We should generate some traffic that would let us see Prometheus query language in action.

We'll deploy `go-demo` stack. It contains a service with an API and a corresponding database. We'll use it as a demo service that will allow us to explore better some of the metrics we can use.

```
docker stack deploy \
    -c stacks/go-demo.yml \
    go-demo
```

We should wait a few moments for the services from the `go-demo` stack to start running. Please execute `docker stack ps go-demo` to confirm that all the replicas are running.

Now that the demo service is running, we can explore some of the metrics we have at our disposal by opening graph page.

```
open "http://$(docker-machine ip swarm-1)/monitor/graph"
```

Please type `haproxy_backend_connections_total` in the **Expression** field, and press the **Execute** button. The result should be zero connections on the backend `go-demo_main-be8080`. Let's spice it up by creating a bit of traffic:

```
for ((n=0;n<200;n++)); do
    curl "http://$(docker-machine ip swarm-1)/demo/hello"
done
```

We sent 200 requests to the `go-demo` service.

If we go back to the Prometheus UI and repeat the execution of the `haproxy_backend_connections_total` expression, the result should be different. In my case, there are *200* backend connections from `go-demo_main-be8080`.

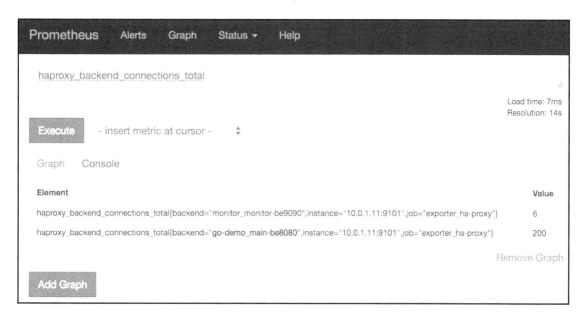

Figure 4-4: HA Proxy metrics

We could display the data as a graph by clicking the **Graph** tab.

 You might be tempted to make a Dashboard (or two) in Prometheus. Don't! I recommend using Grafana, even though it is out of the scope of this book.

How about memory usage? We have the data through `cadvisor` so we might just as well use it.

Please type `container_memory_usage_bytes{container_label_com_docker_swarm_service_name="go-demo_main"}` in the **Expression** field and click the **Execute** button.

The result is memory usage limited to the Docker service `go-demo_main`. Depending on the view, you should see three values in **Console** or three lines in the **Graph** tab. They represent memory usage of the three replicas of the `go-demo_main` service.

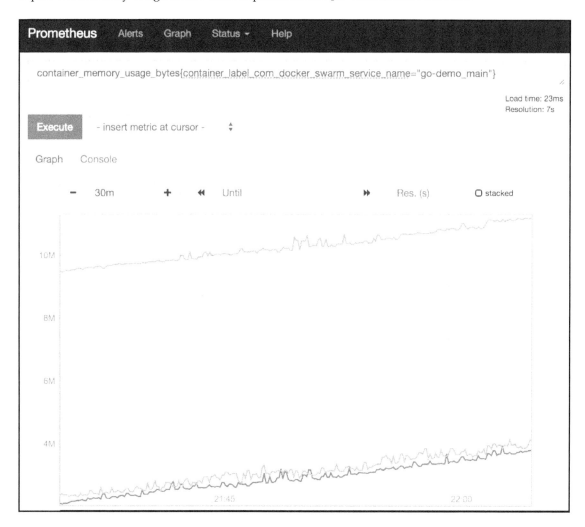

Figure 4-5: cAdvisor metrics

Finally, let's explore one of the `node-exporter` metrics. We can, for example, display the amount of available memory from each of the nodes.

Please type `sum by (instance) (node_memory_MemFree)` in the **Expression** field and click the **Execute** button.

The result is a representation of free memory for each of the nodes of the cluster:

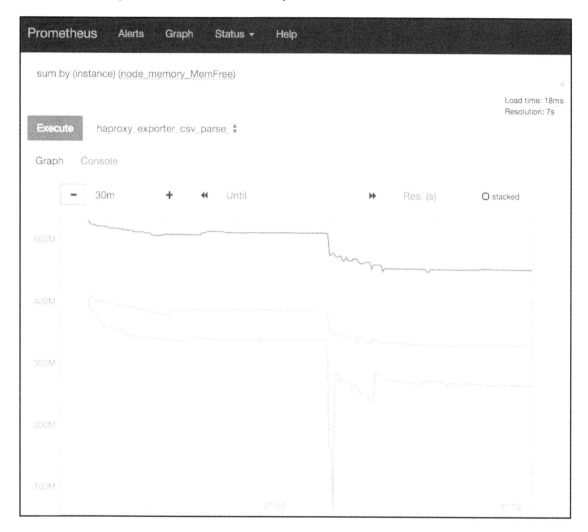

Figure 4-6: Graph with available memory

Now that we had a very brief overview of the ways we can query metrics, we should start using them.

Updating service constraints

The services we created so far are scheduled without any constraints, apart from those that tie some of the services to one of the Swarm managers.

Without constraints, Swarm will distribute service replicas evenly. It will place them on a node that has fewest containers. Such a strategy can be disastrous. For example, we might end up with Prometheus, ElasticSearch, and MongoDB on the same node. Since all three of them require a fair amount of memory, their performance can deteriorate quickly. At the same time, the rest of the nodes might be running very undemanding services like go-demo. As a result, we can end up with a very uneven distribution of replicas from the resource perspective.

We cannot blame Swarm for a poor distribution of service replicas. We did not give it any information to work with. As a minimum, we should have defined how much memory it should reserve for each service as well as memory limits.

Memory reservation gives Swarm a hint how much it should reserve for a service. If, for example, we specify that a replica of a service should reserve 1 GB of memory, Swarm will make sure to run it on a node that has that amount available. Bear in mind that it does not compare reservation with the actual memory usage but, instead, it compares it with the reservations made for other services and the total amount of memory allocated to each node.

 When a service defines how much memory should be reserved, it is only a hint to Swarm how much memory we expect it to use. The service will not get that memory assigned to it. Doing something like that would require a VM instead of a container.

Memory limit, on the other hand, should be set to the maximum amount we expect a service to use. If the actual usage surpasses it, the container will be shut down and, consequently, Swarm will reschedule it. Memory limit is, among other things, a useful protection against memory leaks and a way of preventing a single service abducting all the resources.

Let us revisit the services we are currently running and try to set their memory reservations and limits.

What should be the constraint values? How do we know how much memory should be reserved and what should be the limit? As it happens, there are quite a few different approaches we can take.

We could visit a fortune teller and consult a crystal ball, or we can make a lot of very inaccurate assumptions. Either of those is a bad way of defining constraints. You might be inclined to say that databases need more memory than backend services. We can assume that those written in Java require more resources than those written in Go. There is no limit to the number of guesses we could make. However, more often than not, they will be false and inaccurate. If those two would be the only options, I would strongly recommend visiting a fortune teller instead guessing. Since the result will be, more or less, the same, a fortune teller can, at least, provide a fun diversion from day to day monotony and lead to very popular photos uploaded to Instagram.

 When faced only with bad options, choose the one that is most pleasing to execute.

The correct approach is to let the services run for a while and consult metrics. Then let them run a while longer and revisit the metrics. Then wait some more and consult again. The point is that the constraints should be reviewed and, if needed, updated periodically. They should be redefined and adapted as a result of new data. It's a task that should be repeated every once in a while. Fortunately, we can create alerts that will tell us when to revisit constraints. However, you'll have to wait a while longer until we get there. For now, we are only concerned with the initial set of constraints.

While we should let the services run for at least a couple of hours before consulting metrics, my patience is reaching the limit. Instead, we'll imagine that enough metrics were collected and consult Prometheus.

The first step is to get a list of the stacks we are currently running:

```
docker stack ls
```

The output is as follows:

```
1   NAME      SERVICES
2   exporter  3
3   go-demo   2
4   monitor   2
5   proxy     2
```

Let us consult the current memory usage of those services.

Please open Prometheus' graph screen.

```
open "http://$(docker-machine ip swarm-1)/monitor/graph"
```

Type
`container_memory_usage_bytes{container_label_com_docker_stack_namespace`
`="exporter"}` in the **Expression** field, click the **Execute** button, and switch to the **Graph** view.

If you hover over the lines in the graph, you'll see that one of the labels is `container_label_com_docker_swarm_service_name`. It contains the name of a service allowing you to identify how much memory it is consuming.

While the exact numbers will differ from one case to another, `exporter_cadvisor` should be somewhere between 20 MB and 30 MB, while `exporter_node-exporter` and `exporter_ha-proxy` should have lower usage that is around 10 MB.

With those numbers in mind, our `exporter` stack can be as follows (limited to relevant parts).

```
    ...

    ha-proxy:
      ...
      deploy:
        ...
        resources:
          reservations:
            memory: 20M
          limits:
            memory: 50M
      ...

    cadvisor:
      ...
      deploy:
        ...
        resources:
          reservations:
            memory: 30M
          limits:
            memory: 50M

    node-exporter:
```

```
...
deploy:
  ...
  resources:
    reservations:
      memory: 20M
    limits:
      memory: 50M
  ...
```

We set memory reservations similar to the upper bounds of the current usage. That will help Swarm schedule the containers better, unless they are global and have to run everywhere. More importantly, it allows Swarm to calculate future schedules by excluding these reservations from the total available memory.

Memory limits, on the other hand, will provide limitations on how much memory containers created from those services can be used. Without memory limits, a container might "go wild" and abduct all the memory on a node for itself. Good example are in-memory databases like Prometheus. If we would deploy it without any limitation, it could easily take over all the resources leaving the rest of the services running on the same node struggling.

Let's deploy the updated version of the `exporter` stack.

```
docker stack deploy \
    -c stacks/exporters-mem.yml \
    exporter
```

Since most of the stack are global services, we will not see much difference in the way Swarm schedules them. No matter the reservations, a replica will run on each node when the mode is global. Later on, we'll see more benefits behind memory reservations. For now, the important thing to note is that Swarm has a better picture about the reserved memory on each node and will be able to do future scheduling with more precision.

We'll continue with the rest of the stacks. The next in line is `go-demo`.

Please go back to Prometheus' Graph screen, type `container_memory_usage_bytes{container_label_com_docker_stack_namespace ="go-demo"}` in the **Expression** field, and click the **Execute** button.

The current usage of `go-demo_db` should be between 30 MB and 40 MB while `go-demo_main` is probably below 5 MB. We'll update the stack accordingly.

The new `go-demo` stack is as follows (limited to relevant parts).

```
...
  main:
    ...
    deploy:
      ...
      resources:
        reservations:
          memory: 5M
        limits:
          memory: 10M

  db:
    ...
    deploy:
      resources:
        reservations:
          memory: 40M
        limits:
          memory: 80M
...
```

Now we can deploy the updated version of the `go-demo` stack.

```
docker stack deploy \
    -c stacks/go-demo-mem.yml \
    go-demo
```

Two stacks are done, and two are still left to be updated. The `monitor` and `proxy` stacks should follow the same process. I'm sure that by now you can query Prometheus by yourself. You'll notice that `monitor_monitor` service (Prometheus) is the one that uses the most memory (over 100 MB). Since we can expect Prometheus memory usage to rise with time, we should be generous with its reservations and set it to 500 MB. Similarly, a reasonable limit could be 800 MB. The rest of the services are very moderate with their memory consumption.

Once you're done exploring the rest of the stacks through Prometheus, the only thing left is to deploy of the updated versions.

```
DOMAIN=$(docker-machine ip swarm-1) \
    docker stack deploy \
    -c stacks/docker-flow-monitor-mem.yml \
    monitor

docker stack deploy \
    -c stacks/docker-flow-proxy-mem.yml \
    proxy
```

 Memory limits and reservations need to be reviewed periodically. With time, the system will grow both in size as well as in the load it is experiencing. Service definitions need to be adapted to those and other changes.

Now that our stacks are better-defined thanks to metrics, we can proceed and try to improve our queries through memory reservations and limits.

Using memory reservations and limits in Prometheus

Metrics obtained through cAdvisor are not restricted to actual usage. We have, among others, metrics based on container specs. We can, for example, retrieve memory limits with the metric `container_spec_memory_limit_bytes`.

Please type `container_spec_memory_limit_bytes{container_label_com_docker_stack_name space!=""}` in the **Expression** field and click the **Execute** button. The result should be straight lines that represent memory limits we defined in our stacks.

The usage of the `container_label_com_docker_stack_namespace` label is important. We used it to filter the metrics so that only those that come from the stacks are included. That way, we excluded root metrics from cAdvisor that provide summarized totals.

In Prometheus, memory limits are not very useful in themselves. However, if we combine them with the actual memory usage, we can get percentages that can provide indications of the health of our system.

Please type
```
container_memory_usage_bytes{container_label_com_docker_stack_namespace
!=""} /
container_spec_memory_limit_bytes{container_label_com_docker_stack_name
space!=""} * 100
```
in the **Expression** field and click the **Execute** button.

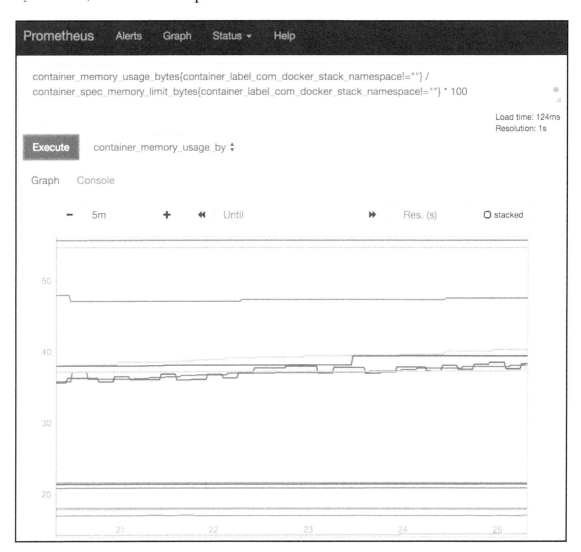

Figure 4-7: Graph percentages based on memory limits and the actual usage

The result consists of percentages based on memory limits and the actual usage. These should all be below 60%. We will leverage this information later when we start working on alerts.

What now?

We did not go deep into metrics and queries. There are too many of them. Listing each metric would be the repetition of the HELP entries that already explain them (even though often not in much detail). More importantly, I believe that the best way to learn something is through a practical usage. We'll use those metrics soon when we start creating alerts, and you will have plenty of opportunities to get a better understanding how they work. The same holds true for queries. They will be indispensable for creating alerts and will be explained in more details in the next chapter. Still, even though we'll go through quite a few metrics and queries, the book will not provide a detailed documentation of every combination you can apply. Querying Prometheus (https://prometheus.io/docs/prometheus/latest/querying/basics/) is a much better place to learn how queries work. Instead, we'll focus on practical hands-on experience.

Now it's time for another break. Remove the VMs, grab a coffee, do something fun, and come back fresh. Alerts are coming next.

```
docker-machine rm -f \
    swarm-1 swarm-2 swarm-3
```

5
Defining Cluster-Wide Alerts

A common mistake is to focus on dashboards as the primary means of noticing when something is wrong. Dashboards have their place in the big scheme of things and are an indispensable part of any monitoring solution. However, they are not as critical as we think.

Monitoring systems are not meant to be a substitute for Netflix. They are not supposed to be watched. Instead, they should collect data and, if certain conditions are met, create alerts. Those alerts should try to communicate with the system and trigger a set of actions that will correct the problem automatically. Notifications should be sent to humans only if the system does not know how to fix the issue. In other words, we should strive to create a self-healing system that consults doctors (us, humans) only when it cannot fix itself.

Dashboards come in handy when we know that there is a problem. If the system is working as expected, looking at dashboards is a waste of time that could be better spent on improving the system.

Imagine a Slack notification that would say that "there is no available memory in the cluster and the system failed to create additional VMs." Please notice the second part of that sentence. The system detected a problem and failed to correct it. Something went wrong, and it could not scale up. It failed to create new VMs. That was a good example of a type of notification that should be sent to a human operator. If the system managed to heal itself, there would be no need for that Slack notification.

We should consult dashboards only after we receive a message stating that the system failed to heal itself. Until that moment, everything is fine, and we can work on the next big improvement of the system. After receiving the message, we should visit a dashboard or two. We should try to get the high-level picture of the system. Sometimes, information from a dashboard is all we need. More often than not, we need more. We need to visit Prometheus and start querying it for additional information. Finally, once the culprit is found, we can create a fix, test it, employ it in production, improve the self-healing system so that the problem is fixed automatically the next time it happens, and write "post-mortem" report.

As you can see, it all starts with a single alert, and that will be the focus of this chapter. For now, we will not distinguish alerts fired to a system that will auto-correct itself from those that are sending notifications to human operators. That will come later. For now, we'll focus on creating alerts without defining events they should fire.

Creating the cluster and deploying services

We'll start by recreating the cluster and deploying the stacks that we used in the previous chapter.

 All the commands from this chapter are available in the `05-alerts.sh` Gist at https://gist.github.com/vfarcic/cc5b51283a2555b8d5963c41afdf097d .

```
chmod +x scripts/dm-swarm-05.sh

./scripts/dm-swarm-05.sh

eval $(docker-machine env swarm-1)
```

We executed the `dm-swarm-05.sh` script which, in turn, created a Swarm cluster composed of Docker machines, created the networks, and deployed the stacks. Now we should wait a few moments until all the services in the `monitor` stack are up and running. Please use `docker stack ps monitor` command to confirm that the status of all the services in the stack is *Running*.

Finally, we'll confirm that everything is deployed correctly by opening Prometheus in a browser:

```
open "http://$(docker-machine ip swarm-1)/monitor"
```

Now the state of our cluster is the same as it was at the end of the previous chapter and we can proceed towards deploying exporters.

Creating alerts based on metrics

Let us create the first alert. We'll update our `go-demo_main` service by adding a few labels:

```
docker service update \
    --label-add com.df.alertName=mem \
    --label-add com.df.alertIf='container_memory_usage_\
bytes{container_label_com_docker_swarm_service_name=\
"go-demo_main"} > 20000000' \
    go-demo_main
```

Normally, we should have labels defined inside our stack file. However, since we'll do quite a few iterations with different values, we'll be updating the service instead modifying the stack file. That way we'll be able to iterate faster.

The label `com.df.alertName` is the name of the alert. It will be prefixed with the name of the service stripped from underscores and dashes (`godemomem`). That way, a unique alert name is guaranteed.

The second label (`com.df.alertIf`) is more important. It defines the expression. Translated to plain words, it takes the memory usage limited to the `go-demo_main` service and checks whether it is bigger than 20 MB (20000000 bytes). An alert will be launched if the expression is true.

For more info about *Docker Flow Monitor* alert parameters, please visit **Alert Parameters** (`http://monitor.dockerflow.com/usage/#alert-parameters`) section of the documentation.

Let's take a look at the Prometheus configuration.

```
open "http://$(docker-machine ip swarm-1)/monitor/config"
```

As you can see, `alert.rules` file was added to the `rule_files` section.

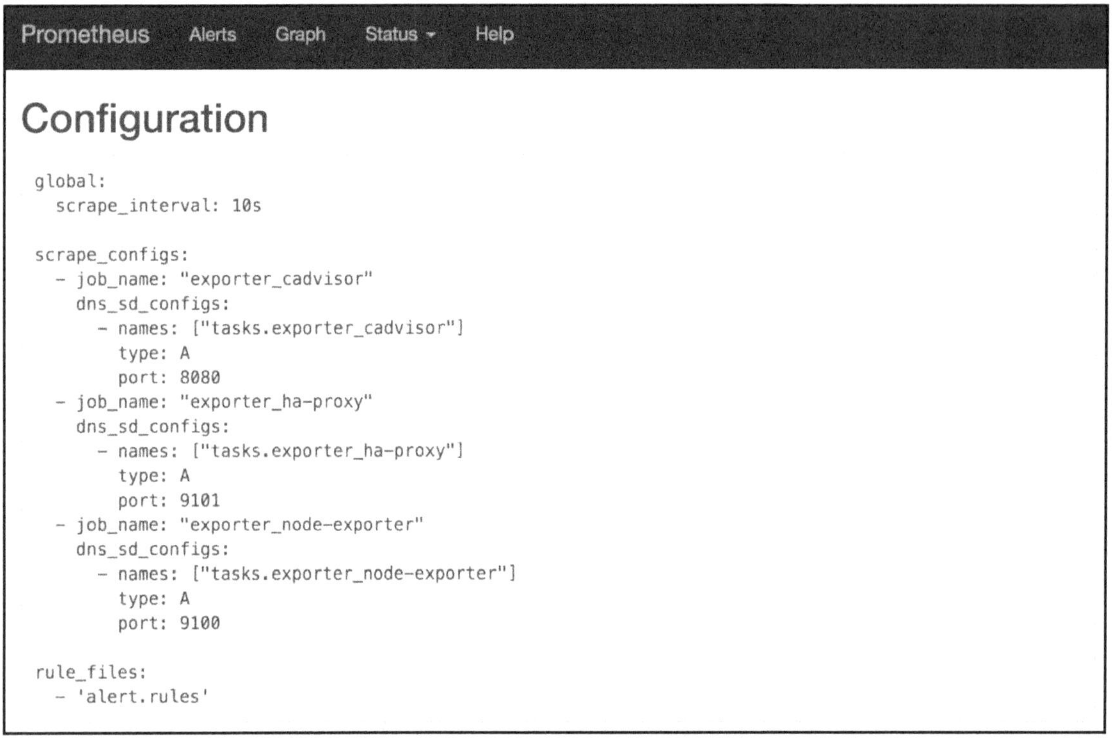

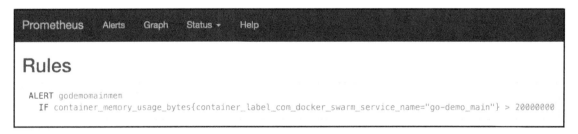

Figure 5-1: Prometheus configuration with alert rules

Let us explore the rules we created so far.

```
open "http://$(docker-machine ip swarm-1)/monitor/rules"
```

As you can see, the expression we specified with the `com.df.alertIf` label reached *Docker Flow Monitor*.

Figure 5-2: Prometheus rule with go-demo memory usage

Finally, let's take a look at the alerts.

```
open "http://$(docker-machine ip swarm-1)/monitor/alerts"
```

The **godemomainmem** alert is green meaning that none of the go-demo_main containers are using over 20 MB of memory. Please click the **godemomainmem** link to expand the alert definition.

Figure 5-3: Prometheus alerts with go-demo memory usage

The alert is green meaning that the service uses less than 20 MB of memory. If we'd like to see how much memory it uses, we need to go back to the graph screen.

```
open "http://$(docker-machine ip swarm-1)/monitor/graph"
```

Once inside the graph screen, please type the expression that follows, and press the **Execute** button.

```
container_memory_usage_bytes{container_label_com_docker_swarm_service_\
name="go-demo_main"}
```

The exact value will vary from one case to another. No matter which one you got, it should be below 20 MB.

Let's change the alert so that it is triggered when go-demo_main service uses more than 1 MB.

```
docker service update \
    --label-add com.df.alertName=mem \
    --label-add com.df.alertIf='container_memory_usage_\
bytes{container_label_com_docker_swarm_service_name=\
"go-demo_main"} > 1000000' \
    go-demo_main
```

Since we are updating the same service and using the same `alertName`, the previous alert definition was overwritten with the new one.

Let's go back to the alerts screen.

```
open "http://$(docker-machine ip swarm-1)/monitor/alerts"
```

This time, the alert is red, meaning that the condition is fulfilled. If it is still green, please wait for a few moments and refresh your screen.

Our service is using more than 1 MB of memory and, therefore, the `ALERT IF` statement is fulfilled, and the alert is firing.

Please click the **godemomainmem** link to expand the alert and see more details:

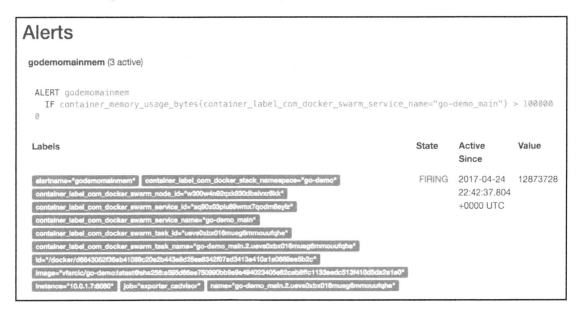

Figure 5-4: Prometheus alerts screen with go-demo memory usage in firing state

The flow of the events can be described through the following figure:

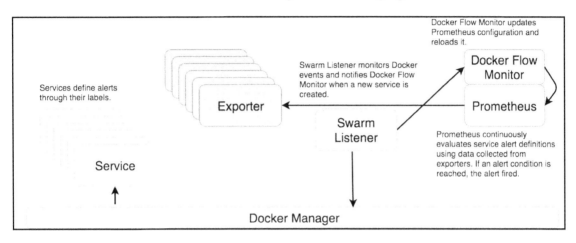

Figure 5-5: The flow of the events that result in a service alert being fired

Let's take a look at the graph screen.

```
open "http://$(docker-machine ip swarm-1)/monitor/graph"
```

Let us quickly review `go-demo_main` service memory reservations and limits. They might be useful in defining alerts.

Please type the expression that follows, and press the **Execute** button.

```
container_spec_memory_limit_bytes{container_label_com_docker_swarm_\
service_name="go-demo_main"}
```

As you can see, memory metric is set to 10 MB. Soon, we'll use those metrics to our benefit.

Next, we'll check the metrics of the "real" memory usage of the service.

Please type the expression that follows, and press the **Execute** button.

```
container_memory_usage_bytes{container_label_com_docker_swarm_service_\
name="go-demo_main"}
```

Memory consumption will vary from one case to another. In my case it ranges from 1 MB to 3.5 MB:

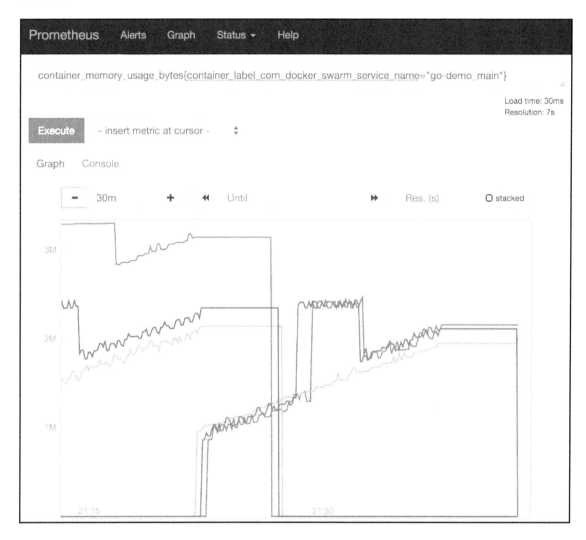

Figure 5-6: go-demo memory usage

If we go back to the `alertIf` label we specified, there is an apparent duplication of data. Both the `alertIf` label and the service reservations are defining the thresholds of the service. As you probably already know, duplication is not a good idea because it increases the chances of an error and complicates future updates that would need to be performed in multiple places.

A better definition of the `alertIf` statement is as follows:

```
docker service update \
    --label-add com.df.alertName=mem_limit \
    --label-add com.df.alertIf='container_memory_usage_bytes\
{container_label_com_docker_swarm_service_name="go\
-demo"}/container_spec_memory_limit_bytes\
{container_label_com_docker_swarm_service_name="go-demo"} > 0.8' \
    go-demo_main
```

This time we defined that the `mem_limit` alert should be triggered if memory usage is higher than 80% of the memory limit. We avoided duplicating the value that is already defined as service' memory limit. That way, if, at some later stage, we change the value of the `--limit-memory` argument, the alert will continue working properly.

Let's confirm that *Docker Flow Swarm Listener* sent the notification and that *Docker Flow Monitor* was reconfigured accordingly.

```
open "http://$(docker-machine ip swarm-1)/monitor/alerts"
```

Please click the **godemo_main_mem_limit** link to see the new definition of the alert:

```
godemo_main_mem_limit (0 active)

 alert: godemo_main_mem_limit
 expr: container_memory_usage_bytes{container_label_com_docker_swarm_service_name="go-demo_main"}
   / container_spec_memory_limit_bytes{container_label_com_docker_swarm_service_name="go-demo_main"}
   > 0.8
 for: 5m
 labels:
   receiver: system
   service: go-demo_main
 annotations:
   summary: Memory of the service go-demo_main is over 0.8
```

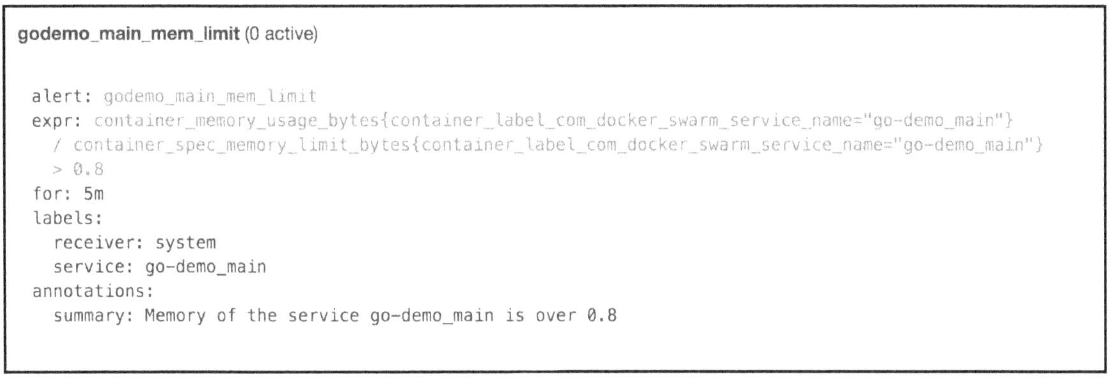

Figure 5-7: go-demo alert based on memory limit and usage

Defining multiple alerts for a service

In many cases, one alert per service is not enough. We need to be able to define multiple specifications. *Docker Flow Monitor* allows us that by adding an index to labels. We can, for example, define labels com.df.alertName.1, com.df.alertName.2, and com.df.alertName.3. As a result, *Docker Flow Monitor* would create three alerts.

Let's see it in action.

We'll update the node-exporter service in the exporter stack so that it registers two alerts.

```
docker service update \
    --label-add com.df.alertName.1=mem_load \
    --label-add com.df.alertIf.1='(sum by
(instance)\(node_memory_MemTotal)\
- sum by (instance) (node_memory_MemFree +\
node_memory_Buffers + node_memory_Cached)) / sum by (instance)\
(node_memory_MemTotal) > 0.8' \
    --label-add com.df.alertName.2=diskload \
    --label-add com.df.alertIf.2='(node_filesystem_size{fstype="aufs"}\  -
node_filesystem_free{fstype="aufs"}) / node_filesystem_\
size{fstype="aufs"} > 0.8' \
    exporter_node-exporter
```

This time, alertName and alertIf labels got an index suffix (for example .1 and .2). The first one (mem_load) will create an alert if memory usage is over 80% of the total available memory. The second alert will fire if disk usage is over 80%.

Let's explore the *alerts* screen.

```
open "http://$(docker-machine ip swarm-1)/monitor/alerts"
```

As you can see, two new alerts were registered:

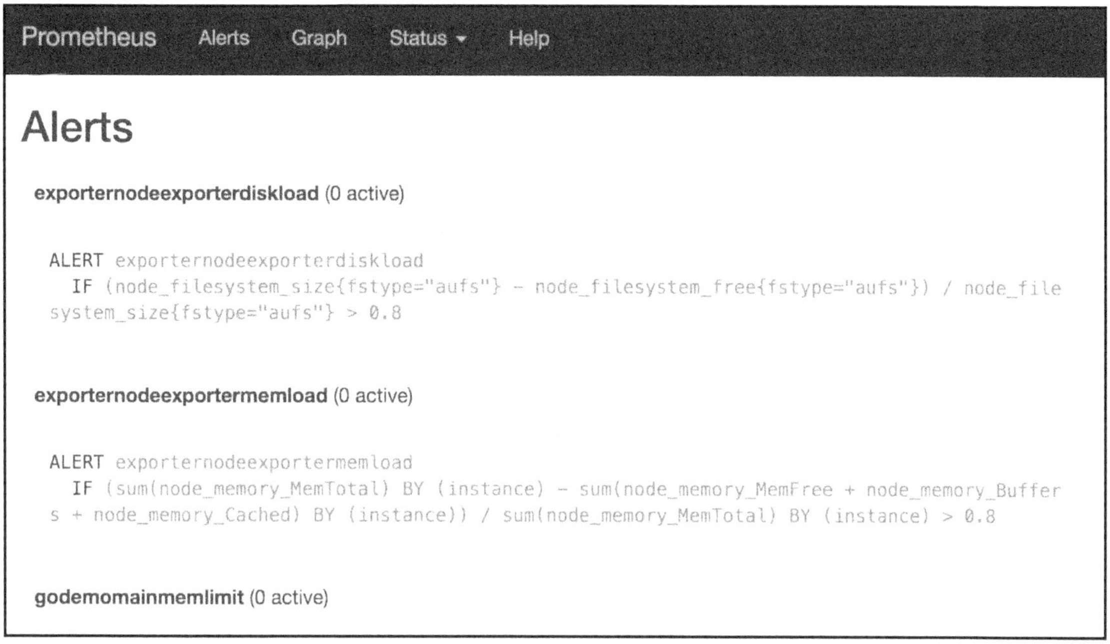

Prometheus
Alerts
Graph
Status
Help
Alerts
exporternodeexporterdiskload (0 active)
ALERT exporternodeexporterdiskload
IF (node_filesystem_size{fstype="aufs"} - node_filesystem_free{fstype="aufs"}) / node_file
system_size{fstype="aufs"} > 0.8
exporternodeexportermemload (0 active)
ALERT exporternodeexportermemload
IF (sum(node_memory_MemTotal) BY (instance) - sum(node_memory_MemFree + node_memory_Buffer
s + node_memory_Cached) BY (instance)) / sum(node_memory_MemTotal) BY (instance) > 0.8
godemomainmemlimit (0 active)

Figure 5-8: Node exporter alerts

The flow of the events can be described through the following figure:

Exporters define alerts through their labels.
Docker Flow Monitor updates Prometheus configuration and reloads it.
Docker Flow Monitor
Swarm Listener monitors Docker events and notifies Docker Flow Monitor when a new exporter is created.
Exporter
Prometheus
Swarm Listener
Prometheus continuously evaluates exporter alert definitions using data collected from exporters. If an alert condition is reached, the alert fired.
Service
Docker Manager

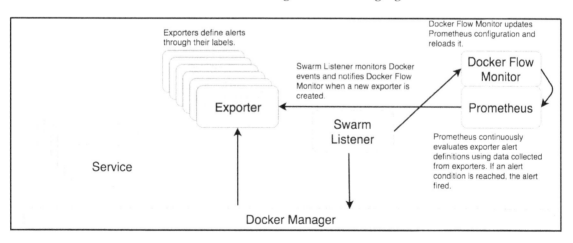

Figure 5-9: The flow of the events that result in an exporter alert being fired

Postponing alerts firing

Firing an alert as soon as the condition is met is often not the best idea. The conditions of the system might change temporarily and go back to "normal" shortly afterward. A spike in memory is not bad in itself. We should not worry if memory utilization jumps to 95% only to go back to 70% a few moments later. On the other hand, if it continues being over 80% for, let's say, five minutes, some actions should be taken.

We'll modify the go-demo_main service so that it fires an alert only if memory threshold is reached and the condition continues for at least one minute.

The relevant parts of the go-demo stack file are as follows:

```
services:

  main:
    ...

    deploy:
      ...
      labels:
        ...
        - com.df.alertName=mem_limit
        -  com.df.alertIf=container_memory_usage_\
bytes{container_label_com_docker_swarm_service_name="go-\
demo"}/container_spec_memory_limit_bytes{container_label_com_docker_sw\
arm_service_name="go-demo"} > 0.8
        - com.df.alertFor=30s
...
```

We set the com.df.alertName and com.df.alertIf labels to the same values as those we used to update the service. The new addition is the com.df.alertFor label that specifies the period Prometheus should wait before firing an alert. In this case, the condition would need to persist for thirty seconds before the alert is fired. Until then, the alert will be in the pending state.

Let's deploy the new stack.

```
docker stack deploy \
    -c stacks/go-demo-alert-long.yml \
    go-demo
```

After a few moments, the `go-demo_main` service will be rescheduled, and the `alert` labels will be propagated to the Prometheus instance. Let's take a look at the alerts screen.

```
open "http://$(docker-machine ip swarm-1)/monitor/alerts"
```

The `go-demo` memory limit alert with the `FOR` statement set to thirty seconds is registered:

Figure 5-10: go-demo memory limit alert with the FOR statement

We should test whether the alert indeed works. We'll temporarily decrease the threshold to five percent. That should certainly trigger the alert.

```
docker service update \
    --label-add com.df.alertIf='container_memory_usage_\
bytes{container_label_com_docker_swarm_service_name="go-demo_main\
"}/container_spec_memory_limit_bytes{container_label_com_docker_swarm_\
 service_name="go-demo_main"} > 0.05' \
    go-demo_main
```

Let us take another look at the alerts screen.

```
open "http://$(docker-machine ip swarm-1)/monitor/alerts"
```

If you opened the screen within thirty seconds since the update, you should see that there are three alerts in the **PENDING** state. Once thirty seconds expire, the status will change to **FIRING**. Unfortunately, there is no destination Prometheus can fire those alerts. We'll fix that in the next chapter. For now, we'll have to be content by simply observing the alerts from Prometheus:

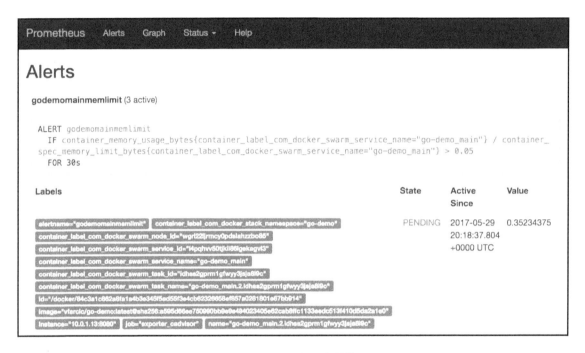

Figure 5-11: go-demo alerts in the PENDING state

Defining additional alert information through labels and annotations

We might want to specify supplementary information to our alerts. We can accomplish that through the usage of alert labels and annotations.

Alert labels clause allows specifying a set of additional labels to be attached to the alert. The annotations clause specifies another set of labels that are not identifying for an alert instance. They are used to store longer additional information such as alert descriptions or runbook links.

We can, for example, update our `go-demo` stack by adding service labels that follow:

```
...
services:

  main:
    ...
    deploy:
      ...
      labels:

        ...
        - com.df.alertLabels=severity=high,receiver=system
        - com.df.alertAnnotations=summary=Service memory is \
high,description=Do something or start panicking
        ...
```

Let's deploy the updated stack.

```
docker stack deploy \
    -c stacks/go-demo-alert-info.yml \
    go-demo
```

A few moments later, the alert definition reached Prometheus, and we can explore it from a browser.

```
open "http://$(docker-machine ip swarm-1)/monitor/alerts"
```

Please expand the **godemo_main_mem_limit** alert, and you'll see that it contains the labels and annotations we specified through service labels.

Besides serving as additional information, alert labels and annotations can be used with *Alertmanager* which we'll explore in the next chapter. For now, just remember that they are available:

```
Prometheus    Alerts    Graph    Status ▾    Help

Alerts

exporternodeexporterdiskload (0 active)

exporternodeexportermemload (0 active)

godemomainmemlimit (0 active)

ALERT godemomainmemlimit
  IF container_memory_usage_bytes{container_label_com_docker_swarm_service_name="go-demo_main"}
 / container_spec_memory_limit_bytes{container_label_com_docker_swarm_service_name="go-demo_mai
n"} > 0.8
  FOR 5s
  LABELS {receiver="system", severity="high"}
  ANNOTATIONS {description="Do something or start panicking", summary="Service memory is high"}
```

Figure 5-12: go-demo alerts with labels and annotations

Using shortcuts to define alerts

Setting alerts as service labels is great but, as you probably noticed, a bit cumbersome. Alert conditions can get pretty long and repetitive. I, for one, got tired of writing the same statement over and over again. So, I created shortcuts that accomplish the same functionality. Let's see them in action.

The modified version of the `go-demo` stack definition is as follows (restricted to relevant parts).

```
version: '3'

services:

  main:
    ...
    deploy:
```

```
...
labels:
  - com.df.alertIf=@service_mem_limit:0.8
  ...
```

We simplified the definition by replacing the expression that follows with
`com.df.alertIf=@service_mem_limit:0.8`.

```
com.df.alertIf=container_memory_usage_bytes{container_label_com_\
docker_swarm_service_name="go-demo_main"}/container_spec_memory_limit_\
bytes{container_label_com_docker_swarm_service_name="go-demo_main"}\
> 0.8
```

Similarly, the modified version of the `exporter` stack definition is as follows (limited to relevant parts).

```
version: "3"

services:

  ...
  node-exporter:
    ...
    deploy:
      ...
      labels:
        ...
        - com.df.alertIf.1=@node_mem_limit:0.8
        ...
        - com.df.alertIf.2=@node_fs_limit:0.8
      ...
```

Just as with the `go-demo`, we simplified the stack definition by replacing `alertIf` labels with shortcut values.

Now we can deploy the modified stacks:

```
docker stack deploy \
    -c stacks/exporters-alert.yml \
    exporter

docker stack deploy \
    -c stacks/go-demo-alert.yml \
    go-demo
```

Let's check the outcome in the Prometheus *Alerts* screen:

```
open "http://$(docker-machine ip swarm-1)/monitor/alerts"
```

If you check the details of the alerts, you'll notice that they are the same as they were before. The shortcuts were sent to Prometheus and expanded into their full syntax.

 For more info about *Docker Flow Monitor* alert shortcuts, please visit **AlertIf Parameter Shortcuts** (http://monitor.dockerflow.com/usage/#alertif-parameter-shortcut s) section of the documentation.

What now?

We are moving forwards. Alerts are an important step towards a self-healing system. However, at this moment, we can only see them. They are not firing any events. Prometheus is aware of the conditions that should create an alert but is unaware what to do with them. We'll fix that in the next chapter.

Take another break. Remove the machines we created, do something fun, and come back fresh. A brain needs a rest every once in a while:

```
docker-machine rm -f \
    swarm-1 swarm-2 swarm-3
```

6
Alerting Humans

While Prometheus alerts are great by themselves, they are not very useful unless you're planning to spend all your time in front of the *alerts* screen. There are much better things to stare. For example, you can watch Netflix instead. It is much more entertaining than watching Prometheus screen. However, before you start watching Netflix during your working hours, we need to find a way so that you do get notified when an alert is fired.

Before we proceed, I must stress that alerts to humans (operators and sysadmins) are the last resort. We should receive them only if the system was not capable of fixing the problem. However, in the beginning, we do not have a self-healing system. The approach we'll take is to send each alert to a human. That's a quick fix. From there on, we'll try to build the system that will receive those alerts instead us. It will be per use-case. We'll create a system that sends us all alerts and then we'll start exploring each of the scenarios. If we can make the system accept that alert and self-heal, we'll stop sending it to a human. On the other hand, if we cannot add that scenario into the system, it will continue alerting us. In other words, all alerts will be sent to humans except those integrated into the self-healing system we'll build.

Where should we send alert messages? Slack is probably a good candidate to start. Even if you do not use Slack, the principles we'll explore will be the same no matter whether your end-point will be email, Hangouts, Messenger, HipChat, SMS, or pigeon couriers. As long as that end-point has an API, we should be able to utilize it. That might be easier for some than others. Pigeon couriers might not yet have an API.

Creating the cluster and deploying services

We'll start by recreating the cluster and deploying the stacks that we used in the previous chapter.

 All the commands from this chapter are available in the `06-alert-humans.sh` Gist at https://gist.github.com/vfarcic/2cdd86977b22288313345a2ca0416fe9 .

```
chmod +x scripts/dm-swarm-06.sh
./scripts/dm-swarm-06.sh
eval $(docker-machine env swarm-1)
```

We executed the `dm-swarm-06.sh` script which, in turn, created a Swarm cluster composed of Docker machines, created the networks and deployed the stacks. Now we should wait a few moments until all the services in the `monitor` stack are up and running. Please use `docker stack ps monitor` command to confirm that the status of all the services in the stack is *Running*.

Finally, we'll confirm that everything is deployed correctly by opening Prometheus in a browser.

```
open "http://$(docker-machine ip swarm-1)/monitor"
```

Now the state of our cluster is the same as it was at the end of the previous chapter and we can proceed towards deploying exporters.

Setting up Alertmanager

Since we are already using Prometheus, it makes sense to deploy Prometheus' companion *Alertmanager*. It will receive alerts, filter and forward them to the end-points we'll define. Slack will be the first.

Alertmanager Docker image expect us to define a configuration file that defines routes, receivers, and a few other things. One possible configuration can be as follows.

```
route:
  receiver: "slack"
  repeat_interval: 1h

receivers:
    - name: "slack"
```

```
    slack_configs:
        - send_resolved: true
          text: "Something horrible happened! Run for your lives!"
          api_url: "https://hooks.slack.com/services\
/T308SC7HD/B59ER97SS/S0KvvyStVnIt3ZWpIaLnqLCu"
```

The configuration defines the `route` with `slack` as the receiver of the alerts. In the `receivers` section, we specified that we want resolved notifications (besides alerts), creative text, and the Slack API URL. As a result, alerts will be posted to the *df-monitor-tests* channel in DevOps20 team slack. Please sign up through the DevOps20 registration page (`http://slack.devops20toolkit.com/`) and make sure you join the *df-monitor-tests* channel. This configuration should be more than enough for demo purposes.

Please consult the alerting documentation (`https://prometheus.io/docs/alerting/configuration/`) for more information about *Alertmanager* configuration options.

Next, we'll take a quick look at the `alert-manager-slack.yml` (`https://github.com/vfarcic/docker-flow-monitor/blob/master/stacks/alert-manager-slack.yml`)stack.

```
version: "3"

services:

  alert-manager:
    image: prom/alertmanager
    ports:
      - 9093:9093
    networks:
      - monitor
    secrets:
      - alert_manager_config
    command: -config.file=/run/secrets/alert_manager_\
config -storage.path=/alertmanager

networks:
  monitor:
    external: true

secrets:
  alert_manager_config:
    external: true
```

The stack is very straightforward. The only thing worth noting is that we are exposing port 9093 only for demo purposes. Later on, when we integrate it with *Docker Flow Monitor*, they will communicate through the `monitor` network without the need to expose any ports. We need the port 9093 to demonstrate manual triggering of alerts through *Alertmanager*. We'll get rid of it later on.

If you take a look at the `command`, you'll notice that it specifies the configuration file that resides in the `/run/secrets/` directory. It is an in-memory file system where Docker stores secrets. We defined `alert_manager_config` as the external secret. Please visit Alerting Rules (`https://prometheus.io/docs/alerting/rules/`) for more information.

Let's create the secret.

```
echo 'route:
  receiver: "slack"
  repeat_interval: 1h

receivers:
  - name: "slack"
    slack_configs:
      - send_resolved: true
        text: "Something horrible happened! Run for your lives!"
        api_url: "https://hooks.slack.com/services/T308SC7HD\
/B59ER97SS/S0KvvyStVnIt3ZWpIaLnqLCu"
' | docker secret create alert_manager_config -
```

Now that the secret with the *Alertmanager* configuration is created, we can deploy the `alert-manager-slack.yml` stack.

```
docker stack deploy \
    -c stacks/alert-manager-slack.yml \
    alert-manager
```

Please wait a few moments until the service is deployed. You can monitor the status through the `docker stack ps alert-manager` command.

Now we can send a manual request to the Alertmanager.

```
curl -H "Content-Type: application/json" \
    -d '[{"labels":{"alertname":"My Fancy Alert"}}]' \
    $(docker-machine ip swarm-1):9093/api/v1/alerts
```

Before you execute the request, please change the `My Fancy Alert` name to something else. That way you'll be able to recognize your alert from those submitted by other readers.

The output should be as follows.

```
{
  "status": "success"
}
```

Please open *df-monitor-tests* channel in *DevOps20* Slack team and observe that a new notification was posted.

Now that we confirmed that `alert-manager` works when triggered manually, we'll remove the stack and deploy the version integrated with *Docker Flow Monitor*.

```
docker stack rm alert-manager
```

We'll deploy the `docker-flow-monitor-slack.yml` stack. It contains `monitor` and `swarm-listener` services we're already familiar with and adds `alert-manager`. The only change to the `monitor` service is the addition of the environment variable `ARG_ALERTMANAGER_URL=http://alert-manager:9093`. It defines the address and the port of the `alert-manager`.

The definition of the `alert-manager` service is as follows.

```
monitor:
  image: vfarcic/docker-flow-monitor
  environment:
    ...
    - ARG_ALERTMANAGER_URL=http://alert-manager:9093
    ...

alert-manager:
  image: prom/alertmanager
  networks:
    - monitor
  secrets:
    - alert_manager_config
  command: -config.file=/run/secrets/
alert_manager_config -storage.path=/alertmanager
  ...
```

We added the environment variable `ARG_ALERTMANAGER_URL` to the `monitor` service. Prometheus will use it as the address to which to send alerts. Since both services are connected through the same `monitor` network, all we had to specify is the name of the service and the internal port.

The `alert-manager` service is the same as the one we deployed earlier except that the ports are removed. There's no need to publish them when services communicate through Overlay network.

Let's deploy the new stack.

```
DOMAIN=$(docker-machine ip swarm-1) \
    docker stack deploy \
    -c stacks/docker-flow-monitor-slack.yml \
    monitor
```

We should confirm that the `alert-manager` is correctly configured through the environment variable `ARG_ALERTMANAGER_URL`.

```
open "http://$(docker-machine ip swarm-1)/monitor/flags"
```

As you can see from the *flags* screen, the *alertmanager.url* is now part of the Prometheus configuration. Since both are connected through the same network (`monitor`), the address is the name of the service:

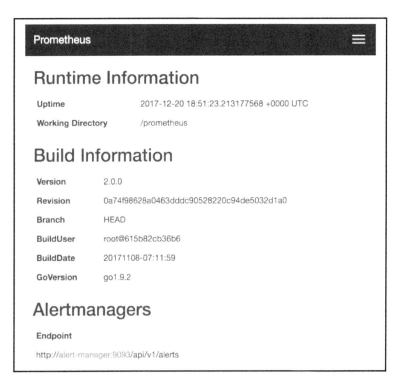

Figure 6-1: Prometheus flags screen with values passed through environment variables

Let us generate an alert.

```
docker service update \
    --label-add com.df.alertIf=@service_mem_limit:0.1 \
    go-demo_main
```

We updated the `main` service from the `go-demo` stack by adding the `alertIf` label. It defines `mem_limit` alert that will be triggered if the service exceeds 10% of the memory limit. In other words, it will almost certainly fire the alert.

Let's open the alerts screen.

```
open "http://$(docker-machine ip swarm-1)/monitor/alerts"
```

As you can see, the alert is red (if it isn't, wait a few moments and refresh your screen). Since we configured *Alertmanager*, the alert was already sent to it and, from there, forwarded to Slack. Please open the *df-monitor-tests* channel in the *DevOps20* Slack team and observe that a new notification was posted:

[FIRING:3] godemomainmemlimit (go-demo gr0u3kyyrews0b0innx82ytfe go-demo_main vfarcic/go-demo:latest@sha256:a595d66ee750990bb9e9e494023405e62cab8ffc1133eedc5 13f410d5da2a1e0 exporter_cadvisor system go-demo_main)
Something horrible happened! Run for your lives!

Figure 6-2: Slack message generated by Alertmanager

As you can see, the message is not very well defined. The title is anything but understandable, the text of the message is the same no matter which alert was fired, and the link does not lead back to Prometheus but to the internal address. We'll fix all those problems soon. For now, the important thing is that we managed to send alert to Slack.

The flow of the events is described through the following figure.

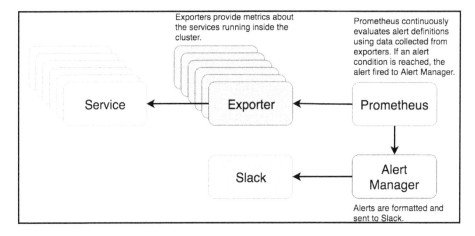

Figure 6-3: The flow of the events that results in a Slack message being created

We'll restore the `go-demo` alert to its original state (used memory over 80%).

```
docker service update \
    --label-add com.df.alertIf=@service_mem_limit:0.8 \
    go-demo_main
```

A few moments later, we can observe that the alert is green again.

```
open "http://$(docker-machine ip swarm-1)/monitor/alerts"
```

If the alert is still not green, please wait for a while and refresh the screen.

Since we specified `send_resolved: true` in the `alert-manager` config, we got another notification. This time, the message states that the issue is resolved.

The only thing left is to create your own *Alertmanager* configuration. You'll need Webhook URL if you choose to send alerts to your team's Slack. The instructions for obtaining it are as follows.

Please login to your team Slack channel, open the settings menu by clicking the team name, and select *Apps & integrations*.

Figure 6-4: Team setting Slack menu

You will be presented with the *App Directory* screen. Click the **Manage** link located in the top-right corner of the screen followed by the **Custom Integrations** item in the left-hand menu. Select **Incoming WebHooks** and click the **Add Configuration** button. Choose the channel where alerts will be posted and click the **Add Incoming WebHooks integration** button. Copy the *Webhook URL*. You'll need it when you customize the solution to your needs.

Now that you know how to get the *Webhook URL*, feel free to replace the one from the examples that follow. That does not mean that you cannot run them as they are. You're free to use *DevOps20* team Slack if that suits you better.

Using templates in Alertmanager configuration

Defining *Alertmanager* configuration using static text is not very useful if we're running more than one service. Instead, we should employ templates that will help us customize messages. While we're at it, we can also fix the broken link from the message and customize the title.

Before we proceed, let us remove the `monitor_alert-manager` service and the `alert_manager_config` secret. That will allow us to deploy it again with better-defined messages.

```
docker service rm monitor_alert-manager
```

```
docker secret rm alert_manager_config
```

We'll create a new secret with the complete Alertmanager configuration.

```
echo "route:
  group_by: [service]
  receiver: 'slack'
  repeat_interval: 1h

receivers:
  - name: 'slack'
    slack_configs:
      - send_resolved: true
        title: '[{{ .Status | toUpper }}] {{ .GroupLabels.service }}\
service is in danger!'
        title_link: 'http://$(docker-machine ip \
swarm-1)/monitor/alerts'
```

```
        text: '{{ .CommonAnnotations.summary}}'
        api_url: 'https://hooks.slack.com/services/T308SC7HD\
/B59ER97SS/S0KvvyStVnIt3ZWpIaLnqLCu'
"  | docker secret create alert_manager_config -
```

Previously, we specified only `text` and `api_url` and let *Alertmanager* fill in the blanks. This time, we added `title` and `title_link` to the mix.

We used `{{ .GroupLabels.service }}` to specify the name of the service inside the `title`. Group labels are defined in the `route` section. Even though we could use "normal" labels, group labels are easier since they are unique for all the alerts coming from, in this case, the same service. The title is prefixed with the alert `status` in the upper case. That should give us clear indication whether the alert is fired or resolved.

The previous configuration produced a link that did not work. That was to be expected since the communication goes through internal networking. This time, we made sure that the `title_link` is correct and points to one of the servers in the cluster.

Finally, the `text` is the same as the alert summary defined as one of the alert `ANNOTATIONS`.

Please visit Notification Template Reference (`https://prometheus.io/docs/alerting/notifications/`)for more info about the templates that can be used when configuring Alertmanager.

If everything works as expected, the new Alertmanager config will result in clearer messages customized for each service.

Let us deploy the stack and, with it, `alert-manager` with the new configuration.

```
DOMAIN=$(docker-machine ip swarm-1) \
    docker stack deploy \
    -c stacks/docker-flow-monitor-slack.yml \
    monitor
```

We'll test the alert in the same way as before by decreasing the threshold.

```
docker service update \
    --label-add com.df.alertIf=@service_mem_limit:0.1 \
    go-demo_main
```

A few moments later, Prometheus will change the state of the alert to *pending* and, a while later to *firing*. We can observe those changes by opening the *Alerts* screen.

```
open "http://$(docker-machine ip swarm-1)/monitor/alerts"
```

If you open Slack channel *#df-monitor-tests* you'll notice that the message is much better this time.

The only thing left is to confirm that we're receiving the correct message when an issue is resolved. We'll change the alert threshold back to 80%.

```
docker service update \
    --label-add com.df.alertIf=@service_mem_limit:0.8 \
    go-demo_main
```

After a while, Prometheus will change the alert status to *resolved*, send a notification to Alertmanager which, in turn, will communicate the news to Slack. The result will be the RESOLVED message.

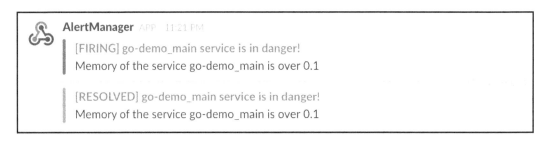

Figure 6-5: Customized Slack alert messages

What now?

We're done. We have a system that will alert us whenever there's something wrong inside the cluster. The next step is to start alerting the system so that it can self-heal and leave our Slack channel only for emergencies that cannot be auto-fixed.

The next chapter will explore the options for alerting the system. For now, the time has come for both us and our laptops to take a rest.

```
docker-machine rm -f \
    swarm-1 swarm-2 swarm-3
```

7
Alerting the System

Our alerting is already set up. Alertmanager is configured to send notifications to Slack. While that was a good step forward, it is still far from having alerting that serves as the base of a self-adapting and self-healing system. What we did by now can be considered a fallback strategy. If the system cannot detect changed conditions and, when needed, adapt or heal itself, notifying humans through Slack is a good solution. In some cases, Slack notifications will be temporary and replaced with requests to the system that will autocorrect itself. In other situations, the system will not be able to fix itself, so notifications will have to be sent to doctors (us, humans, engineers).

We already built the initial solution for an alerting system. Alertmanager can fulfill some of our needs. It is not alone, and there is another one that we used throughout the book, even though we never mentioned it in this context. I'm sure that you can guess which one it is. If you can't, I'll leave you in suspense for a while longer.

Before we proceed and start building the system that will receive the alerts, we should discuss the types of actions a system might need to perform.

The four quadrants of a dynamic and self-sufficient system

Any system that intends to be fully automated and self-sufficient must be capable of self-healing and self-adaptation. As a minimum, it needs to be able to monitor itself and perform certain actions both on service and infrastructure levels.

Two axes can represent the set of actions a system might execute. One group of actions be represented through the differences between infrastructure and services. The other axis can be explained by the type of activities, with self-healing on one end, and self-adaptation on the other.

The most common type of self-healing, when applied to infrastructure, is to recreate a failed or a faulty node. When infrastructure needs to be adapted to changed conditions, nodes are scaled. Self-healing is mostly about rescheduling failed services. When system's conditions change, it should self-adapt by scaling some of the services.

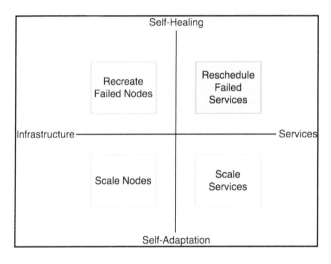

Figure 7-1: The types of system actions

How does the system distinguish self-adaptation from self-healing? When should it choose to perform one action over the other?

Every system has a design. It might stay unchanged for a long time, or it can be redesigned every few minutes. The frequency of a change of a system design distinguishes static from dynamic systems. Throughout most of the short history of the software industry, we favored long lasting designs. We would spend a long time planning and even longer time designing a system before implementing it. It was no wonder that we were not very eager to spend months, or even years, in doing all that only to change it the week after launch. We worked using waterfall model where everything is planned in advance and executed in very long phases. Most of the time the result would be a failure, but we won't enter into that discussion right now. If you worked in this industry for a while, you probably know what waterfall is. Hopefully, your company changed, or you changed the company. Waterfall is dead, and long lasting static designs are gone with it.

Dynamic systems are characterized by very frequent, not to say continuous, change in design. We would design a service that would run five replicas, only to change that number to seven a week later. We would design infrastructure that is composed of twenty-seven nodes, only to change it to thirty short while later. Every time we make a conscious decision to change something inside a system, we are changing the design. Each of those changes is a result of either the initial miscalculation or the modification in the external conditions that are affecting the system. A steady increase in traffic requires a change in design. It demands that we scale the number of replicas of one or more services. Everything else being equal, an increase in the number of replicas requires an increase of infrastructure resources. We need to add more nodes that will host that increase. If that's not the case, we over-provisioned the system. We had idle resources that can be put to use when scaling up the services.

Self-adaptation is an automated way to change a design of a system. When we (humans) change it, we do it by evaluating metrics. At least, we should do it like that. Otherwise, we are consulting a crystal ball, employing a fortune teller, or purely guessing. If we can make decisions based on metrics, so can the system. No matter who changes the system, every change is a modification of the design. If we automate the process, we get self-adaptation.

Self-healing does not impact the design. Quite the contrary, it follows it. If the design is to have five replicas and only four are running, the system should do its best to add another replica. And it's not always about increasing numbers. If there are more replicas than designed, some should be removed. The same logic applies to nodes or any other quantifiable part of the system. Long story short, self-healing is about making sure that the design is always followed.

Self-adaptation is about having an automated way to apply changes to the design of a system. The objective behind self-healing is to make sure that the design is followed at any given moment. When we combine self-adaptation with self-healing, the result is a truly dynamic, resilient, and fault tolerant system with high availability.

A system can adapt or heal services or infrastructure. The most common action behind healing is to recreate things that failed while adaptation is often about scaling. They are the four quadrants that represent a dynamic and self-sufficient system.

We are about to start building an (almost) autonomous system using those four quadrants. Everything we did until this point were prerequisites for such a system. We have the metrics inside Prometheus, and we can manage alerts through Alertmanager. The time has come to put those to good use and extend their reach.

The first quadrant we'll explore converges on self-healing and services.

8
Self-Healing Applied to Services

The job of a system that self-heals services is to make sure that they are (almost) always running according to the design. Such a system needs to monitor the state of the cluster and continuously ensure that all the services are running the specified number of replicas. If one of them stops, the system should start a new one. If a whole node goes does, all the replicas that were running on that node should be scheduled to run across the healthy nodes. As long as the capacity of the cluster can host all the replicas, such a system should be able to maintain the defined specifications.

Having a system that self-heals services does not mean that it provides high-availability. If a replica stops being operational, the system will bring it back into the running state. However, there will be a (very) short period between a failure and until the system is restored to the desired state. If we're running only one replica of a service, during that time there will be downtime. The best way to remedy this problem is to run at least a couple of replicas of each service. That way, when one of them goes down, the others will handle the requests until the failed one is restored to its desired state.

Assuming that the conditions of the cluster do not change (nodes do not go down) and that the load on the cluster is constant, the system capable of self-healing services should provide near 100% up-time. Unfortunately, nodes do go down, and the load on the cluster is (almost) never constant. We'll explore how to remedy those problems later. For now, we'll focus on how to build the part of the system that will make sure that the services are healing automatically.

Creating the cluster and deploying services

We'll start by setting up a Swarm cluster and deploying the stacks that we'll use in this chapter.

A note to *The DevOps 2.1 Toolkit* readers
You should be very familiar with Docker Swarm, and the rest of this chapter will not provide any information that you do not already know. You are free to skip to the *Is it enough to have self-healing applied to services?* section in this chapter. If, on the other hand, you feel a bit forgetful and would like to refresh your memory, I'll do my best to be as brief as possible and provide only the bare minimum.

All the commands from this chapter are available in the `08-self-healing-services.sh` Gist at `https://gist.github.com/vfarcic/99325930813d7e25375b982c7e2498d2`.

```
chmod +x scripts/dm-swarm-08.sh

./scripts/dm-swarm-08.sh

eval $(docker-machine env swarm-1)

docker stack ls
```

We executed the `dm-swarm-08.sh` script which, in turn, created a Swarm cluster composed of Docker machines, created the networks and deployed the stacks. The last command listed all the stacks in the cluster. We are running only `go-demo` and `proxy` stacks. Where are `prometheus` and `exporter` stacks we deployed in the previous chapters? Why are we missing them? The reason is quite simple. We don't need them to demonstrate self-healing applied to services. We have everything we need.

Before we proceed, please confirm that all the replicas that compose the `go-demo` stack are running. You can check their statuses by executing `docker stack ps go-demo` command. You might see a few failed replicas of the `go-demo_main` service. The reason is in its design. It fails if it cannot connect to the database running inside the `go-demo_db` service. Since the database is a bigger image, it takes more time to pull it. Ignore the failed replicas and confirm that there are three instances of `go-demo_main` running.:

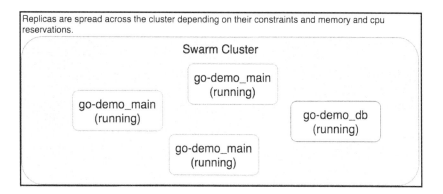

Figure 8-1: Replicas spread across the cluster

Using Docker Swarm for self-healing services

Docker Swarm already provides almost everything we need from a system that self-heals services.

What follows is a short demonstration of some of the scenarios the system might encounter when facing failed service replicas. I already warned you that at least basic knowledge of operating Swarm is the pre-requirement for this book so I chose to skip a lengthy discussion about the features behind the scheduler. I won't go into details but only prove that Swarm guarantees that the services will (almost) always be healthy.

Let's see what happens when one of the three replicas of the go-demo_main service fails. We'll simulate it by stopping the primary process inside one of the replicas.

The first thing we need to do is find out the node where one of the replicas are running.

```
NODE=$(docker service ps \
    -f desired-state=Running \
    go-demo_main | tail -n 1 \
    | awk '{print $4}')

eval $(docker-machine env $NODE)
```

We listed all the processes of the `go-demo_main` service and used a filter to limit the output only to those that are running. The output was sent to tail so that only one result is returned. Further on, we used `awk` to print only the fourth column which contains the name of the node. The result was assigned to the environment variable `NODE`.

The second command changed our local Docker client to point to the node with one of the replicas.

Next, we need to find the ID of one of the replicas running on the node we selected.

```
CONTAINER_ID=$(docker container ls -q \
    -f "label=com.docker.swarm.service.name=go-demo_main" \
    | tail -n 1)
```

We listed all the containers in quiet mode so that only IDs are returned. We used filtering so that only containers labeled as the service `go-demo_main` are retrieved. Since we need only one container (there might be more on that node), we sent the output to tail that returned only the last row.

Now we can stop the main process inside the container and observe what happens.

```
docker container exec -it \
    $CONTAINER_ID pkill go-demo
```

We killed the `go-demo` process inside the container. That was the main and the only process inside that container. As soon as it stopped, container stopped as well.

Let's list the processes of the `go-demo` stack.

```
docker stack ps go-demo
```

The output, limited to the replica we killed, is as follows (IDs are removed for brevity):

```
NAME                  IMAGE                        NODE     DESIRED STATE CURRENT STATE    \
    ERROR                        PORTS
go-demo_main.3     vfarcic/go-demo:latest swarm-2 Running         Running 1 second\
  ago
  \_ go-demo_main.3 vfarcic/go-demo:latest swarm-2 Shutdown        Failed 11 second\
s ago "task: non-zero exit (2)"
```

As you can see, Swarm detected that one of the replicas failed, and scheduled a new one. It made sure that the specification (the design) is followed. When we deployed the go-demo stack, we told Swarm that we want to have three replicas of the go-demo_main service and Swarm is continuously monitoring the cluster making sure that our desire is always fulfilled. There were a few seconds between the failure and until the new replica was running. If we'd run only one replica, that would mean a short downtime. However, since we are running three, the other two took over the requests, and there was no downtime. High availability is preserved:

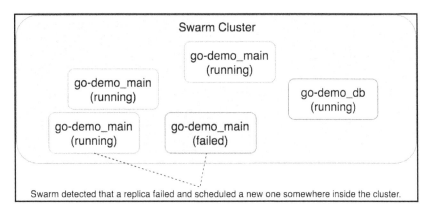

Figure 8-2: The failed replica was re-scheduled

What happens when a whole node is destroyed? I'm sure you already know the answer, but I'll go through a small demonstration never the less.

We'll repeat the command that we executed earlier and find a node with at least one of the go-demo_main replicas.

```
NODE=$(docker service ps \
    -f desired-state=Running \
    go-demo_main | tail -n 1 \
    | awk '{print $4}')
```

Let's be destructive and delete the node:

```
docker-machine rm -f $NODE
```

To be on the safe side, we'll list all the machines and confirm that one was indeed removed.

`docker-machine ls`

The output is as follows:

```
1   NAME        ACTIVE    DRIVER      STATE     URL                         SWARM   DO\
2   CKER          ERRORS
3   swarm-1     -         virtualbox  Running   tcp://192.168.99.100:2376           v1\
4   7.03.1-ce
5   swarm-3     *         virtualbox  Running   tcp://192.168.99.102:2376           v1\
6   7.03.1-ce
```

Next, we'll have to change our environment variables to ensure that our local Docker client is not pointing to the node we just removed.

```
NODE=$(docker-machine ls -q | tail -n 1)

eval $(docker-machine env $NODE)
```

Now we can, finally, list the processes of the `go-demo` stack and see the result.

`docker stack ps go-demo`

The output, limited to the relevant parts, is as follows (IDs are removed for brevity).

```
1   NAME                IMAGE                    NODE     DESIRED STATE CURRENT STATE   \
2           ERROR                        PORTS
3   ...
4   go-demo_main.3      vfarcic/go-demo:latest swarm-1 Running        Running 2 minute\
5   s ago
6    \_ go-demo_main.3 vfarcic/go-demo:latest swarm-2 Shutdown       Running 7 minute\
7   s ago
8   ...
```

Docker Swarm detected that `swarm-2` node is not available and changed the desired state of the replicas that were running there to Shutdown. Unlike the case when a container fails, the current state stayed unchanged. Swarm still assumes that the replicas are running inside `swarm-2`. We know that the node is destroyed and that no replicas are running inside it. Swarm, on the other hand, is not aware of that. It just knows what the last known state of that replica is. The node, from Swarm's point of view, might still be operational and only lost the connection with the cluster. Theoretically, the connection could be reestablished later. There could be many other explanations besides the destruction of the node, so Swarm keeps the last known state. Never the less, if the node rejoins the cluster, that replica is scheduled for shutdown and will be destroyed immediately as a way to preserve the desired state:

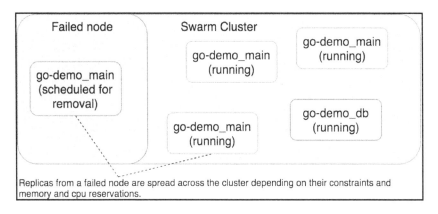

Figure 8-3: Replicas from a failed node are spread across the cluster

Is it enough to have self-healing applied to services?

Self-healing applied to services is only the beginning. It is by no means enough. The system, as it is now, is far from being autonomous. At best, it can recuperate from a few types failures. If one replica of a service goes down, Swarm will do the right thing. Even a simultaneous failure of a few replicas should not be a cause for alarm. However, self-healing applied to services by itself does not contemplate many of the common circumstances.

Let us imagine that the sizing of a cluster is done in a way that around 80 percent of CPU and memory is utilized. Such a number, more or less, provides a good balance between having too many unused resources and under-provisioning our cluster. With greater resource utilization we are running a risk that even a failure of a single node would mean that there are no available resources to reschedule the replicas that were running inside it. On the other hand, if we have more than twenty percent of available resources, we are paying for more hardware than we need.

Assuming that we do aim for eighty percent of resource utilization, without self-healing applied to infrastructure, a failure of more than one node could have a devastating effect. Swarm would not have enough available resources to reschedule replicas from the failed servers. While it is not common, an availability zone (to use AWS terms) can go down. Assuming that our infrastructure is spread over three availability zones, such a failure would mean that our capacity is reduced by thirty-three percent. When we do the math, that would mean that we would be missing sixteen percent of resources. It is even worse than that since Swarm cannot schedule services so that hundred percent is used. Somewhere around ninety to ninety-five percent is more likely. So, a failure of an availability zone would mean that we would be missing quite a lot of resources and some replicas could not be rescheduled. At best, we would have reduced performance. Self-healing applied to infrastructure is a must, and we will explore it soon.

Even if nothing failed, our system would not function autonomously for long. We should expect that the load will increase with time. After all, we want our business to expand and that, in most cases, results in increased load. We need to build a system that will adapt to those changes. We need it to expand when the load increases thus providing high availability and low response times. At the same time, we need it to contract when the load decreases and save money from paying for unused resources. We need the system not only to self-heal but also self-adapt to the changed conditions. We need it to redesign itself.

There are many other things that we are missing, and we won't discuss them just yet. Patience is a virtue, and you'll have to wait for a while longer.

What now?

We're done with a brief exploration of self-healing capabilities provided with Docker Swarm. We have a system that will reschedule failed services as long as there is enough capacity inside our cluster. The next step is to apply self-adaptation to our services.

Please remove the machines we created. We'll recreate the cluster in the next chapter:

```
docker-machine rm -f \
    swarm-1 swarm-2 swarm-3
```

9
Self-Adaptation Applied to Services

We saw how services could self-heal. It was relatively easy to set up a system that would make sure that the desired number of replicas of each service is (almost) always running. Docker Swarm does all the work. As long as there are enough available hardware resources, our services will (almost) always run the specified number of replicas. All we have to do is specify `replicas: [NUMBER_OF_REPLICAS]` in the YAML file that defines our stack.

The problem with self-healing is that it does not take into account changes that affect our systems. We'll run the same number of replicas even if there is a huge spike in their memory utilization. The same applies if, for example, network traffic increases. Docker Swarm will not make sure that our system adapts to changed conditions. It will follow the blueprint blindly. While that is a vast improvement compared to how we operated the system in the past, it is, by no means, enough. We need the system both to self-heal and self-adapt.

In this chapter, we'll expand on the knowledge we obtained by now and start exploring ways we can make the system self-adapt. For now, we'll limit ourselves to services and ignore that hardware needs to heal and adapt as well. That will come later.

Choosing the tool for scaling

We already adopted a few tools. We have metrics stored in Prometheus. We deployed Swarm Listener that propagates information to Prometheus. We have Alertmanager that receives notifications whenever a certain threshold is reached. While those tools allowed us to move forward towards our goals, they are not enough. Now we need to figure out what to do with those alerts. Receiving them in Slack is only the last resort. We need a tool that will be capable of receiving an alert, process the data that comes with it, apply certain logic, and decide what to do.

In most cases, self-adaptation is all about scaling. Since we are limiting ourselves to services, the system, when it receives an alert, needs to be capable of deciding whether to scale up, or down, or do nothing. We need a tool that can accept remote requests, that is capable of running code that will determine what should be done, and that can interact with Docker.

If you read the book, *The DevOps 2.1 Toolkit: Docker Swarm* (`https://www.amazon.com/dp/1542468914`), you know that I suggested Jenkins for our continuous deployment processes. We can also use it as the tool that will perform actions that will result in self-adaptation. After all, the real power behind Jenkins is not for running (only) continuous integration/delivery/deployment pipelines but for running tasks of any kind. Its jobs can be triggered remotely from Alertmanager. It has a potent, yet simple scripting language through Pipeline DSL. If we expose Docker Socket in Jenkins agents, they can easily interact with Docker and execute any command available.

Even if you prefer some other tool, the examples we'll implement in Jenkins can easily be adapted to anything else as long as the before mentioned requirements are fulfilled.

Let's get going.

Creating the cluster and deploying services

Just as in (almost) any other chapter, we'll start the practical part by setting up a Swarm cluster and deploying the stacks that we used previously.

All the commands from this chapter are available in the `09-self-adapting-services.sh` Gist at `https://gist.github.com/vfarcic/4a7253f5aaff4c2b7a55170ebbb48cbd`.

```
chmod +x scripts/dm-swarm-09.sh

./scripts/dm-swarm-09.sh

eval $(docker-machine env swarm-1)

docker stack ls
```

We executed the `dm-swarm-09.sh` script which, in turn, created a Swarm cluster composed of Docker machines, created the networks, and deployed the stacks. The last command listed all the stacks in the cluster. We are running `proxy`, `monitor`, `exporter`, and `go-demo` stacks. Those four comprise the whole toolkit we used by now.

Preparing the system for alerts

We'll deploy the stack defined in `stacks/jenkins.yml` (`https://github.com/vfarcic/docker-flow-monitor/blob/master/stacks/jenkins.yml`). The definition is as follows.

```yaml
version: '3.1'

services:

  master:
    image: vfarcic/jenkins
    ports:
      - 50000:50000
    environment:
      - JENKINS_OPTS="--prefix=/jenkins"
    networks:
      - proxy
      - default
    deploy:
      labels:
        - com.df.notify=true
        - com.df.distribute=true
        - com.df.servicePath=/jenkins
        - com.df.port=8080
    extra_hosts:
      - "${SLACK_HOST:-devops20.slack.com}:${SLACK_IP:-54.192.78.227}"
    secrets:
```

```
      - jenkins-user
      - jenkins-pass

  agent:
    image: vfarcic/jenkins-swarm-agent
    environment:
      - USER_NAME_SECRET=/run/secrets/${JENKINS_USER_SECRET:-\
jenkins-user}
      - PASSWORD_SECRET=/run/secrets/${JENKINS_PASS_SECRET:-\
jenkins-pass}
      - COMMAND_OPTIONS=-master http://master:8080/jenkins -labels\
 'prod' -executors 4
    networks:
      - default
    volumes:
      - /var/run/docker.sock:/var/run/docker.sock
    secrets:
      - jenkins-user
      - jenkins-pass
  deploy:
    placement:
      constraints: [node.role == manager]

networks:
  proxy:
    external: true
  default:
    external: false

secrets:
  jenkins-user:
    external: true
  jenkins-pass:
    external: true
```

The stack contains two services. The first one is Jenkins master. We are running
`vfarcic/jenkins` instead the official Jenkins image (`https://hub.docker.com/_/
jenkins/`). The `vfarcic/jenkins` image is already built with an administrative user and
has all the plugins we'll need. With it, we'll be able to skip Jenkins' setup process. I won't go
into more detail about the image. If you're curious, please read the Automating Jenkins
Docker Setup (`https://technologyconversations.com/2017/06/16/automating-jenkins-
docker-setup/`) article.

The `master` service from the stack publishes port `50000` so that other agents from this, or other clusters, can connect to it. If all the agents run inside the same cluster, there would be no need for this port. Instead, they would be attached to the same Overlay network. Since, in most cases, Jenkins agents tend to be spread across multiple clusters, having the port open is a must.

Environment variable `JENKINS_OPTS` defines `/jenkins` as the prefix so that Docker Flow Proxy (`http://proxy.dockerflow.com/`) can distinguish requests meant for Jenkins from those that should be forwarded to the other services inside the cluster. The service will be attached to the proxy and default networks. The first one will be used for communication with *Docker Flow Proxy* while the second is meant to connect it to the agent. Labels are there to provide sufficient information to the proxy so that it can reconfigure itself.

We had to add the Slack address as the extra host. Otherwise, Jenkins would not know the address of the `devops20.slack.com` domain. Finally, we specified two secrets (`jenkins-user` and `jenkins-pass`) that will define the credentials of the administrative user.

The `agent` follows a similar logic. We're using `vfarcic/jenkins-swarm-agent` image that contains Docker, Docker Compose, and Jenkins Swarm Plugin (`https://wiki.jenkins.io/display/JENKINS/Swarm+Plugin`). The latter allows us to connect to the master automatically. The alternative would be to use the "traditional" approach of adding agents manually through Jenkins' UI.

Please note that the environment variable `COMMAND_OPTIONS` has the `-labels` argument set to `prod`. Since this agent will run on the production cluster, we need to identify it as such. Even though in this chapter we won't use Jenkins for continuous deployment processes, it is important to label agents from the start so that, later on, we can add others that will serve a different purpose.

Just as the `main` service, the agent uses `jenkins-user` and `jenkins-pass` secrets to provide credentials that will be used to connect to Jenkins master.

Finally, we need the agent to communicate with one of the Docker managers, so we set the `node.role == manager` constraint. Without this constraint, agents would not be able to spin new services since only managers are allowed to perform such actions. Containers that form Jenkins agents have Docker socket mounted so that Docker commands executed inside them spin containers on one of the nodes, not inside the container. The later would produce **Docker-in-Docker** (**DinD**) which is, in most cases, not a good idea. If you do not want to take my word for granted, please read Jerome's post Using Docker-in-Docker for your CI or testing environment? Think twice (`http://jpetazzo.github.io/2015/09/03/do-not-use-docker-in-docker-for-ci/`).

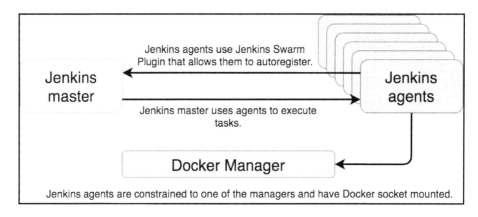

Figure 9-1: Jenkins agents connected to a master and Docker managers

Now that we have a general idea about the services inside the `jenkins` stack, we can deploy it:

```
echo "admin" | \
    docker secret create jenkins-user -

echo "admin" | \
    docker secret create jenkins-pass -

export SLACK_IP=$(ping \
    -c 1 devops20.slack.com \
    | awk -F '[()]' '/PING/{print $2}')

docker stack deploy \
    -c stacks/jenkins.yml jenkins
```

We created the secrets and deployed the stack. The value of the environment variable `SLACK_IP` was obtained by pinging `devops20.slack.com` domain.

All that is left, before we start using Jenkins, is a bit of patience. We need to wait until Docker pulls the images. Please execute `docker stack ps jenkins` to confirm that the services are running.

Let's open Jenkins UI in a browser:

```
open "http:// $(docker-machine ip swarm-1)/jenkins"
```

If Jenkins does not open, please wait a few moments and refresh the screen. The fact that Docker service is running does not mean that the process inside it is initialized. Jenkins needs ten to fifteen seconds (depending on hardware) to start.

Once you see the Jenkins home screen, please click the **Log in** link located in the top-right corner of the screen, and use `admin` as both username and password. Click the **log in** button to authenticate.

We should confirm that the agent was added to the master by observing the *computer* screen.

```
open "http://$(docker-machine ip swarm-1)/jenkins/computer"
```

You should see two agents. The *master* agent is set up by default with each Jenkins instance. The second agent identified with a hash name was added through the agent service in the stack.

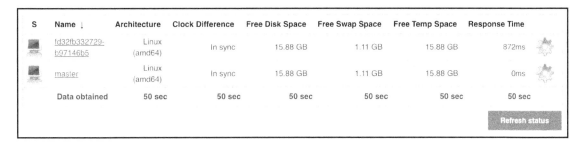

S	Name ↓	Architecture	Clock Difference	Free Disk Space	Free Swap Space	Free Temp Space	Response Time	
	fd32fb332729-b97146b5	Linux (amd64)	In sync	15.88 GB	1.11 GB	15.88 GB	872ms	
	master	Linux (amd64)	In sync	15.88 GB	1.11 GB	15.88 GB	0ms	
	Data obtained	50 sec	50 sec	50 sec	50 sec	50 sec	50 sec	

Refresh status

Figure 9-2: Jenkins agent automatically added to the master

Creating a scaling pipeline

Now comes the exciting part. We're about to start writing a Pipeline job that will serve as the base for the first self-adaptation script.

```
open "http://$(docker-machine ip swarm-1)/jenkins/newJob"
```

Once inside the *New Job* screen, please type `service-scale` as the item name. Select **Pipeline** as job type and click the **OK** button.

Since Jenkins service we created comes with enabled authorization, we need an authentication mechanism for triggering builds. We could use the administrative *username* and *password*. A better option is to make a trigger that will be independent of any particular user. That can be accomplished with tokens.

Please select the **Trigger builds remotely** checkbox from the *Build Trigger* section of the job configuration screen. Type `DevOps22` as the *Authentication Token*. We'll use it to authenticate remote requests which will trigger a build of this job.

Now we can start writing a Pipeline script. There are quite a few things that it should do so we'll go step by step. The first thing we need is parameters.

As a minimum, we need to know which service should be scaled and how many replicas to add or remove. We'll assume that if the number of replicas is positive, we should scale up. Similarly, if the value is negative, we should scale down.

Please type the script that follows inside the **Pipeline Script** field.

```
pipeline {
  agent {
    label "prod"
  }
  parameters {
    string(
      name: "service",
      defaultValue: "",
      description: "The name of the service that should be scaled"
    )
    string(
      name: "scale",
      defaultValue: "",
      description: "Number of replicas to add or remove."
    )
  }
  stages {
    stage("Scale") {
      steps {
        echo "Scaling $service by $scale"
      }
    }
  }
}
```

If you do not like typing, feel free to copy and paste the contents of the `service-scale-1.groovy` Gist at (`https://gist.github.com/vfarcic/98778e9f414f1af1ab30cd07e39b015a`).

Don't forget to click the **Save** button.

Since we're trying to scale services running in production, we defined the agent as such.

Next, we set the parameters service and scale.

Finally, we have only one stage (Scale) with a single step that prints a message. Each pipeline has one or more stages, and each stage is a collection of steps. A step (in this case echo) is a task or logic that should be executed.

Please note that we are using Declarative (`https://jenkins.io/doc/book/pipeline/syntax/#declarative-pipeline`) instead Scripted (`https://jenkins.io/doc/book/pipeline/syntax/#scripted-pipeline`) Pipeline syntax. Both have pros and cons. Declarative is a more opinionated and structured syntax while Scripted provides more freedom. The main reason we're using Declarative flavor is that it has better support for the new Blue Ocean (`https://jenkins.io/projects/blueocean/`) UI. Moreover, I happen to know the Jenkins roadmap and Declarative Pipeline is at its center.

The default Jenkins UI is not among the prettiest in town. It, kind of, hurts the eyes if you look at it for more than a couple of seconds. Since I do not want your health to deteriorate as a result of reading this book, we'll switch to *Blue Ocean*. It is available as the alternative UI (soon to become the default) and we already have it installed as one of the plugins.

Please click the **Open Blue Ocean** link located in the left-hand menu.

And Lo and behold. We just jumped through time from the 80s to the present tense (at least from the aesthetic perspective).

Now we can see our simple pipeline script in action.

Since we did not yet run this Pipeline, you will be presented with the **This job has not been run** message and the **Run** button. Please click it.

The job will fail the first time we run it. You can consider it a bug that will, hopefully, be fixed shortly. It failed because it got confused with the parameters we specified. I'll skip the debate about the reasons behind this bug since the workaround is straightforward. Just rerun it by pressing the **Run** button located in the top-left corner.

You'll be presented with a screen that contains the input parameters we specified in the script. Please type `go-demo_main` as *the name of the service that should be scaled* and *2* as the *number of replicas to add or remove*. Click the **Run** button.

This time the Pipeline worked, and we can observe the result by clicking on the row of the last build which, in this case, should be *2*.

We specified only one stage that contains a single step that prints the message. Please click the **Print Message** row to see the result. The output should be as follows:

```
Scaling go-demo_main by 2
```

Figure 9-3: Jenkins Pipeline with a simple Print Message step

Even though Blue Ocean UI is very pleasing, our goal is not to use it to execute builds. Instead, we should invoke it through an HTTP request. That way, we can be confident that Alertmanager will be capable of invoking it as well.

Please execute the command that follows:

```
curl -X POST "http://$(docker-machineip swarm-1)/jenkins/job\
/service-scale/buildWithParameters?token=DevOps22&service=\
go-demo_main&scale=2"
```

The request we sent is very straightforward. We invoked `buildWithParameters` endpoint of the job and passed the token and required inputs as query parameters.

We received no response and can consider that no news is good news. The job was run, and we can confirm that through the UI.

```
open "http://$(docker-machineip swarm-1)\
/jenkins/blue/organizations/jenkins/service-scale/activity"
```

You'll see the list of builds (there should be three). While the *admin* user executed the first two through the UI, the last one was triggered remotely. We can see that by observing the *started by the remote host* message.

Please click the row of the last build and observe that the *Print Message* is the same as when we executed the job through UI.

Similarly, we can change the scale parameter to a negative value if we'd like to scale down.

```
curl -X POST "http://$(docker-machine ip swarm-1)\
/jenkins/job/service-scale/buildWithParameters?token=DevOps22&service=\
go-demo_main&scale=-1"
```

If you repeat the steps from before, the output of the *Print Message* should be **Scaling go-demo_main by -1**.

The Pipeline we have does not do anything but accept parameters and print a message that confirms that parameters are passed correctly. As you probably guessed, we are missing the main ingredient.

We need to tell Docker to scale the service. The problem is that Swarm does not accept relative scale values. We cannot instruct it to increase the number of replicas by two nor to decrease it by, let's say, one. We can overcome this limitation by finding out the current number of replicas and adding or subtracting the value of the scale parameter.

First things first. How can we find out the current number of replicas? The answer lies in the `docker service inspect` command.

Let's see the output Docker provides if we inspect the `go-demo_main` service.

```
docker service inspect go-demo_main
```

The output is too long to be presented here. Instead, we'll focus on the part that interests us. In particular, we need the `Replicas` value. The relevant part of the output is as follows.

```
[
    {
        ...
        "Spec": {
            ...
            "Mode": {
                "Replicated": {
                    "Replicas": 3
                }
            },
            ...
```

As you can see, we got the information that the service runs three replicas.

We can execute the same command from Jenkins pipeline, capture the output, and filter it in a way that only the value of the `Replicas` key is retrieved.

In the spirit of brevity, we'll go only through the stages section of the Pipeline. The whole scripts are available as Gist in case you want to copy and paste them in their entirety.

```
...
stages {
  stage("Scale") {
    steps {
      script {
          def inspectOut = sh script: "docker service inspect\ $service",
returnStdout: true
          def inspectJson = readJSON text: inspectOut.trim()
          def currentReplicas =\
inspectJson[0].Spec.Mode.Replicated.Replicas
          def newReplicas = currentReplicas + scale.toInteger()
          echo "We should scale from $currentReplicas to\
 $newReplicas replicas"
      }
    }
  }
}
...
```

Due to Declarative Pipeline's decision not to allow an easy way to declare variables, we coded everything as one `script` step.

The script is executing `docker service inspect` as an `sh` step. The `returnStdout` argument is mandatory if we want to be able to capture the output of a command. Later on, we're using the `readJSON` step that converts plain text to JSON map. The current number of replicas is retrieved by filtering JSON array. We limited the output to the first element and navigated through `Spec`, `Mode`, `Replicated`, and `Replicas` items. The result is stored in the variable `currentReplicas`.

From there on, it is a simple math of subtracting the current number of replicas with the `scale` parameter. Since it is a string, we had to convert it to an integer.

Finally, we are outputting the result using the `echo` step.

The complete code can be found in the `service-scale-2.groovy` Gist at (`https://gist.github.com/vfarcic/77bc5baae1b19d13a7d048f27d03eaff`).

Let's open the *service-scale* configure screen and modify the script.

```
open "http://$(docker-machine ip swarm-1)/jenkins/job\
/service-scale/configure"
```

Feel free to replace the current script with the one from the `service-scale-2.groovy` Gist (`https://gist.github.com/vfarcic/77bc5baae1b19d13a7d048f27d03eaff`). Personally, I learn better when I write code instead of copying and pasting snippets. No matter the choice, please click the **Apply** button once the Pipeline is updated.

Let us repeat the build request and see the outcome.

```
curl -X POST "http://$(docker-machine ip swarm-1)/jenkins/job\
/service-scale/buildWithParameters?token=DevOps22&service=\
go-demo_main&scale=2"
```

We'll go to the *job activity* screen and observe the result.

```
open "http://$(docker-machine ip\
swarm-1)/jenkins/blue/organizations/jenkins/service-scale/activity"
```

Please click the row of the top-most (most recent) build followed with the click on the last (bottom) step with the **Print Message** label.

The output should be as follows:

```
We should scale from 3 to 5 replicas
```

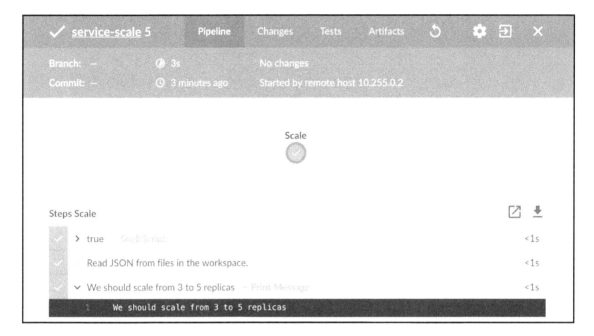

Figure 9-4: Jenkins Pipeline with a Print Message stating that we should scale to five replicas

Let us confirm that de-scaling calculation works as well.

```
curl -X POST "http://$(docker-machine ip swarm-1)/jenkins/job\
/service-scale/buildWithParameters?token=DevOps22&service=\
go-demo_main&scale=-1"
```

If we open the details of the last build and expand the last step, the message should be as follows:

```
We should scale from 3 to 2 replicas
```

We are still not performing scaling but, at this moment, we are capable of discovering the current number of replicas and performing a simple calculation that provides us with the number of replicas our system should have.

Now we are ready to expand the script and truly scale the service.

Equipped with the desired number of replicas stored in the variable `newReplicas`, all we have to do is execute `docker service scale` command. The updated Pipeline script, limited to the relevant parts, is as follows:

```
...
  script {
      def inspectOut = sh script: "docker service inspect $service",
                          returnStdout: true
      def inspectJson = readJSON text: inspectOut.trim()
      def currentReplicas = inspectJson[0].Spec.Mode.Replicated.Replicas
      def newReplicas = currentReplicas + scale.toInteger()
      sh "docker service scale $service=$newReplicas"
      echo "$service was scaled from $currentReplicas to $newReplicas\
replicas"
  }
  ...
```

The only addition is the `sh "docker service scale $service=$newReplicas"` line. It should be pretty obvious what it does so we'll just go ahead and modify it in Jenkins.

```
open "http://$(docker-machine ip swarm-1)/jenkins/job/service\
-scale/configure"
```

Please update the current script or replace it with the `service-scale-3.groovy` Gist (`https://gist.github.com/vfarcic/2b160b93c6cc08320be80d284eb03017`). When finished, please press the **Apply** button.

Let us run the build one more time and observe the result:

```
curl -X POST "http://$(docker-machine ip swarm-1)/jenkins/job\
/service-scale/buildWithParameters?token=DevOps22&service=\
go-demo_main&scale=2"
```

This time, we do not need to open Jenkins UI to see the outcome. If everything went as planned, we should see that the `go-demo_main` service is scaled from three to five replicas.

```
docker stack ps \
    -f desired-state=Running go-demo
```

We listed all the processes that belong to the `go-demo` stack. As a way to reduce noise from those that previously failed or were shut down, we used the filter that limited the output only to those with Running as the desired state.

The output is as follows (IDs are removed for brevity):

```
1   NAME              IMAGE                    NODE     DESIRED STATE  CURRENT STATE        \
2     ERROR PORTS
3   go-demo_main.1 vfarcic/go-demo:latest swarm-1 Running        Running 2 hours ago
4   go-demo_db.1    mongo:latest            swarm-1 Running        Running 2 hours ago
5   go-demo_main.2 vfarcic/go-demo:latest swarm-3 Running        Running 2 hours ago
6   go-demo_main.3 vfarcic/go-demo:latest swarm-2 Running        Running 2 hours ago
7   go-demo_main.4 vfarcic/go-demo:latest swarm-2 Running        Running 2 minutes ago
8   go-demo_main.5 vfarcic/go-demo:latest swarm-1 Running        Running 2 minutes ago
```

As you can see, the number of `go-demo_main` replicas is now five. Two of them are running for only a few minutes.

Since I am a paranoid person, I like testing at least a few combinations of any code or script I write. Let's see whether it works if we choose to scale by a negative number.

```
curl -X POST "http://$(docker-machine ip swarm-1)/jenkins/job\
/service-scale/buildWithParameters?token=DevOps22&service=\
go-demo_main&scale=-1"
```

After a few moments, the number of replicas should scale down from five to four. Let's double-check it.

```
docker stack ps \
    -f desired-state=Running go-demo
```

The output is as follows (IDs are removed for brevity):

```
1   NAME              IMAGE                    NODE     DESIRED STATE  CURRENT STATE        \
2     ERROR PORTS
3   go-demo_main.1 vfarcic/go-demo:latest swarm-1 Running        Running 2 hours ago
4   go-demo_db.1    mongo:latest            swarm-1 Running        Running 2 hours ago
5   go-demo_main.2 vfarcic/go-demo:latest swarm-3 Running        Running 2 hours ago
6   go-demo_main.3 vfarcic/go-demo:latest swarm-2 Running        Running 2 hours ago
7   go-demo_main.4 vfarcic/go-demo:latest swarm-2 Running        Running 25 minutes a\
8   go
```

As you can see, the replica number five disappeared, proving that the script works in both directions. We can use it to scale or de-scale services.

As a side note, don't get alarmed if some other replica disappeared. There is no guarantee that, when we scale down by one replica, it will be the last one that is removed from the system. For example, replica number two could have been removed instead of the replica five. Indexes are not of importance. What matters is that only four replicas are running inside the cluster:

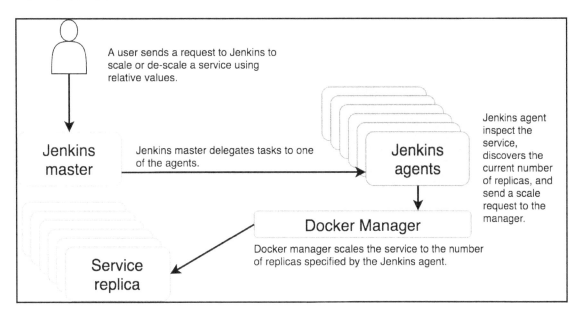

Figure 9-5: Manual scaling through Jenkins

Preventing the scaling disaster

On the first look, the script we created works correctly. Doesn't it?. I've seen similar scripts in other places, and there is only one thing I have to say. **Do not run this pipeline in production!!!** It is too dangerous. It can easily crash your entire cluster or make your service disappear. Can you guess why?

Let us imagine the following situation. Prometheus detects that certain threshold is reached (for example, memory utilization, response time, and so on) and send a notification to Alertmanager. It sends a build request to Jenkins which, in turn, scales the service by increasing the number of replicas by one. So far, so good.

What happens if scaling does not resolve the problem? What if the threshold reached in Prometheus persists? After a while, the process will be repeated, and the service will be scaled up one more time. That might be correct. Maybe there was a significant increase in requests. Maybe that new feature convinced a huge number of new users to start using our service. In such a situation, scaling twice is a legitimate operation. But, what if the second round of scaling did not produce results. What if the system continues scaling up until all the resources are used, and the nodes start failing one by one? The whole cluster could be destroyed.

If you think that scenario is bad, let me tell you that it can get much worse. Let's assume that there is a system in place that would create new nodes when resources are over certain threshold. In that scenario, scaling up indefinitely would result in infinite addition of new nodes. As a result, the bill from AWS could ruin your company. Fortunately, there is a limit to how many nodes an account can create. Still, the unlimited increase in the number of replicas together with the growth of nodes up to a limit would only produce a massive bill, and the cluster would still fail at the end.

As you can imagine, neither of those scenarios is pretty.

What happens if the system decides to de-scale? Maybe you set up a lower threshold for a memory limit or for response time. When that boundary is reached, the system should scale-down. Following the similar logic from the previous examples, scaling-down could continue until the number of replicas reaches zero. At that moment, the service is as good as if it would be removed from the system. As a result, we'd have downtime. The major difference is that we would not get a huge bill from our hosting vendor and only a part of the system would experience downtime. The rest of the services should work correctly unless they also start experiencing the same fate.

 Automated scaling must be tamed with hard-coded lower and upper limits. Without them, we can experience unlimited scaling that will crash any cluster. Equally, de-scaling might result in a complete removal of a service from the cluster.

What we need to do is set some limits. We should define what the minimum and the maximum number of replicas of a service is.

However, the trick is not only to know what information should be defined but also where to put that information. Jenkins needs to know what are those limits and I can think of a few ways to provide that information.

We could add two new input parameters to the `service-scale` Pipeline job. They could be `scaleMin` and `scaleMax`. The problem, in that case, is that Alertmanager would need to pass those parameters when sending requests to Jenkins. But, Alertmanager does not have that information. It would need to rely on Prometheus which could get it from the labels scraped from cAdvisor. However, that would assume that all alerts are generated with data that come from cAdvisor. That might not be the case.

So, if neither Alertmanager nor Prometheus are the right places to define (or discover) the scaling limits of a service, the only option left is for Jenkins job to discover it directly from the service. Since Pipeline code has, through its agents, access to Docker Manager, it could, simply, request that information. That should be the optimum solution since it would follow the pattern we used before. We would continue specifying all the information related to a service inside the service itself. To be more precise, we could add a few additional labels and let Jenkins "discover them".

The `stacks/go-demo-scale.yml` (`https://github.com/vfarcic/docker-flow-monitor/blob/master/stacks/go-demo-scale.yml`) is a slightly modified version of the one we used by now. It defines two new labels.

The relevant parts of the stack are as follows:

```
version: '3'

services:

  main:
    image: vfarcic/go-demo
    ...
    deploy:
      ...
      labels:
        ...
        - com.df.scaleMin=2
        - com.df.scaleMax=4
      ...
```

We used the `com.df.scaleMin` and `com.df.scaleMax` labels to define that the minimum number of replicas is two and the maximum four.

Let's update the stack with the new definition.

```
docker stack deploy \
    -c stacks/go-demo-scale.yml \
    go-demo
```

Please note that the `go-demo-scale.yml` stack has the number of replicas set to three, so the deployment of the stack will remove any extra replicas we created previously.

Let us update the Pipeline script. The new version is as follows.

```
...
script {
  def inspectOut = sh script: "docker service inspect $service",
                      returnStdout: true
  def inspectJson = readJSON text: inspectOut.trim()
  def currentReplicas = inspectJson[0].Spec.Mode.Replicated.Replicas
  def newReplicas = currentReplicas + scale.toInteger()
  def minReplicas =\
  inspectJson[0].Spec.Labels["com.df.scaleMin"].toInteger()
  def maxReplicas =\
  inspectJson[0].Spec.Labels["com.df.scaleMax"].toInteger()
  if (newReplicas > maxReplicas) {
    error "$service is already scaled to the maximum number of\
    $maxReplicas replicas"
  } else if (newReplicas < minReplicas) {
    error "$service is already descaled to the minimum number of\
    $minReplicas replicas"
  } else {
    sh "docker service scale $service=$newReplicas"
    echo "$service was scaled from $currentReplicas to $newReplicas
    replicas"
  }
}
...
```

Let us go through the new additions to the script.

We are extending the usage of JSON obtained through `docker service inspect` command. In addition to the number of replicas, we are retrieving the values of the labels `com.df.scaleMin` and `com.df.scaleMax`.

Further on, we have a simple conditional. If the new number of replicas is more than the maximum allowed, throw an error. Similarly, if the number of replicas is less than the minimum allowed, throw an error as well. We are scaling the service only if neither of those conditions is met. The script is still relatively simple and straight forward.

Let's go back to the job configuration screen.

```
open "http://$(docker-machine ip swarm-1)/jenkins/job/service\
-scale/configure"
```

Please replace the current pipeline with the contents of the `service-scale-4.groovy` Gist (`https://gist.github.com/vfarcic/fd15bcae2278d3a5ca223d67fe2f2e64`) or edit it manually and test your ability to type while reading a book. Either way, press the **Apply** button when finished.

Now we can test whether our scaling process can destroy the cluster.

```
curl -X POST "http://$(docker-machine ip swarm-1)/jenkins/job/service\
-scale/buildWithParameters?token=DevOps22&service=go-demo_main&scale=1"
```

Let us open the job activity screen and check the result of the last build.

```
open "http://$(docker-machine ip swarm\
-1)/jenkins/blue/organizations/jenkins/service-scale/activity"
```

As before, please navigate to the details of the last build and expand the last step. The output should be as follows.

```
go-demo_main was scaled from 3 to 4 replicas
```

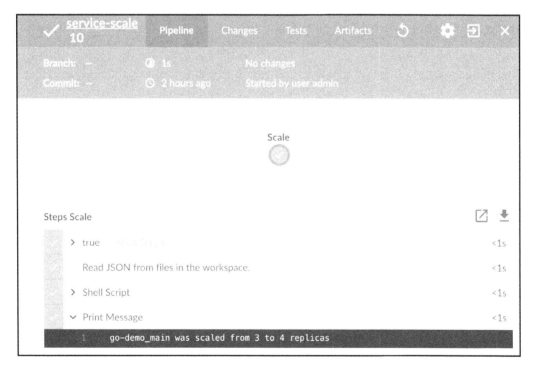

Figure 9-6: Jenkins job scaled the service

We'll confirm the same result by listing the running processes of the `go-demo` stack.

```
docker stack ps \
    -f desired-state=Running go-demo
```

The output is as follows (IDs are removed for brevity):

```
1   NAME            IMAGE               NODE     DESIRED STATE CURRENT STATE        \
2       ERROR PORTS
3   go-demo_db.1    mongo:latest        swarm-1 Running          Running about an hou\
4   r ago
5   go-demo_main.1 vfarcic/go-demo:latest swarm-1 Running          Running 6 hours ago
6   go-demo_main.2 vfarcic/go-demo:latest swarm-3 Running          Running 6 hours ago
7   go-demo_main.3 vfarcic/go-demo:latest swarm-2 Running          Running 6 hours ago
8   go-demo_main.4 vfarcic/go-demo:latest swarm-2 Running          Running 16 seconds a\
9   go
```

As expected, the service scaled from three to four replicas.

And now comes the moment of truth. Will our service continue scaling indefinitely or the limits will be respected? I know you know the answer, but I like being melodramatic every once in a while.

```
curl -X POST "http://$(docker-machine ip swarm-1)/jenkins/job/service\
-scale/buildWithParameters?token=DevOps22&service=go-demo_main&scale=1"
```

If everything worked as planned, the last build threw an error. Feel free to check it yourself. If there is a purpose in UIs, that's to announce in red color that something failed.

More importantly than the error message in Jenkins, we should confirm that the number of replicas is still four.

```
docker stack ps \
    -f desired-state=Running go-demo
```

The output is as follows (IDs are removed for brevity):

```
1  NAME            IMAGE              NODE     DESIRED STATE CURRENT STATE        \
2      ERROR PORTS
3  go-demo_db.1    mongo:latest        swarm-1 Running       Running about an hou\
4  r ago
5  go-demo_main.1 vfarcic/go-demo:latest swarm-1 Running       Running 6 hours ago
6  go-demo_main.2 vfarcic/go-demo:latest swarm-3 Running       Running 6 hours ago
7  go-demo_main.3 vfarcic/go-demo:latest swarm-2 Running       Running 6 hours ago
8  go-demo_main.4 vfarcic/go-demo:latest swarm-2 Running       Running 17 minutes a\
9  go
```

I'll skip the instructions for scaling down and observing that the lower limit is maintained. Feel free to play with it yourself, or just take my word for granted and trust me blindly. Either way, there is one more important thing missing.

Notifying humans that scaling failed

We made significant progress by creating upper and lower limit for scaling. From now on, the script will not exceed them. However, the fact that we will stay within those limit does not mean that the problem that initiated the procedure is gone. Whichever process decided that a service should be scaled probably did that based on some metrics. If, for example, the average response time was slow and the system failed to scale up, the problem will persist unless there is some dark magic involved. We can categorize this situation as "the body tried to self-adapt, it failed, it's time to consult a doctor." Since we live in the 21st century, we won't call him but send him a Slack message.

Before we proceed and modify the script one more time, we need to configure Slack in Jenkins:

```
open "http://$(docker-machine ip swarm-1)/jenkins/configure"
```

Once inside the *Configure System* screen, please scroll down to the *Global Slack Notifier Settings* section. Please enter devops20 in the Team Subdomain field and 2Tg33eiyB0PfzxII2srTeMbd in the Integration Token field.

Now there is another bug or an undocumented feature. I guess it all depends on who you ask. We cannot test the connection before clicking the **Apply** button. There is an explanation for that, but we won't go through it now. Once you applied the configuration, please click the **Test Connection** button. If everything worked as expected, you should see the Success message.

At the same time, the *#df-monitor-tests* channel inside DevOps20 team (`https://devops20.slack.com/`) should have received a message similar to `Slack/Jenkins plugin: you're all set on http://192.168.99.100/jenkins/.`

Feel free to change the subdomain and the token to match your own Slack channel. You'll find the token in **Slack | App & Integrations | Manage | Jenkins CI screen**.

All that's left is to *Save* the changes to the config and update the Pipeline script. We'll add post section.

```
...
post {
   failure {
     slackSend(
       color: "danger",
       message: """$service could not be scaled.
Please check Jenkins logs for the job ${env.JOB_NAME}\ #${env.BUILD_NUMBER}
${env.RUN_DISPLAY_URL}"""
     )
   }
}
```

Post sections in Declarative Pipeline are always executed no matter the outcome of the build steps. We can fine tune it by adding conditions. In our case, we specified that it should be executed only on `failure`. Inside it, we used the `slackSend` step from the Slack Notification Plugin (`https://jenkins.io/doc/pipeline/steps/slack/`). There are quite a few arguments we could have specified but, in this case, we constrained ourselves to only two. We set the color to danger and the mandatory message. Please consult the plugin for more information if you'd like to fine-tune the behavior to your needs.

Now we can open the job configuration page and apply the changes.

```
open "http://$(docker-machine ip swarm-1)/jenkins/job/service\
-scale/configure"
```

Please modify the script yourself or replace it with the `service-scale-5.groovy` Gist (`https://gist.github.com/vfarcic/aeb332b2ab889a81377833f904148d10`). When finished, please press the **Apply** button.

We can quickly confirm whether notifications to Slack work by sending a request that would scale way below the limit.

```
curl -X POST "http://$(docker-machine ip swarm-1)/jenkins/job\
/service-scale/buildWithParameters?token=DevOps22&service=\
go-demo_main&scale=-123"
```

Please open the *#df-monitor-tests* channel in `https://devops20.slack.com/` and confirm that the message was sent:

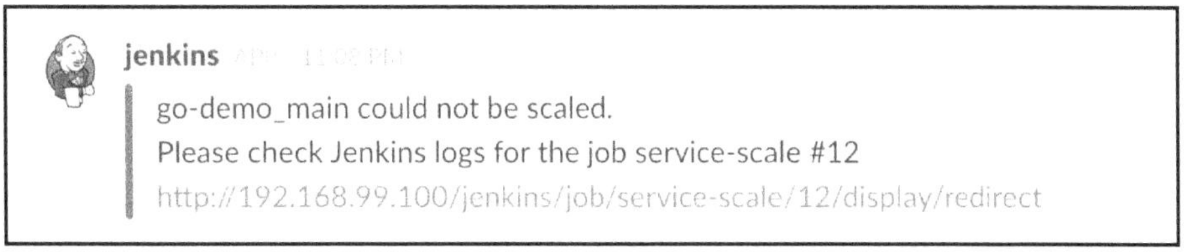

 jenkins

go-demo_main could not be scaled.

Please check Jenkins logs for the job service-scale #12

http://192.168.99.100/jenkins/job/service-scale/12/display/redirect

Figure 9-7: Jenkins notification in Slack

Now that we have a Jenkins job that is in charge of scaling our services, we should make sure that the system can execute it when certain thresholds are met.

Integrating Alertmanager with Jenkins

At the moment, we are running Alertmanager configured in the previous chapter. It creates a Slack notification on all alerts. Let's try to change it so that alerts trigger a remote invocation of the Jenkins job service-scale.

Since Alertmanager configuration is stored as a Docker secret and they are immutable (we cannot update them), we need to remove the service and the secret and create them again.

```
docker service rm monitor_alert-manager

docker secret rm alert_manager_config
```

Let us define a Slack config that will send build requests to the *service-scale* job. The command that creates the service with the configuration is as follows.

```
echo "route:
  group_by: [service]
  repeat_interval: 1h
  receiver: 'jenkins-go-demo_main'

receivers:
  - name: 'jenkins-go-demo_main'
    webhook_configs:
      - send_resolved: false
        url: 'http://$(docker-machine ip swarm-1)/jenkins/job\
/service-scale/buildWithParameters?token=DevOps22&service=\
go-demo_main&scale=1'
" | docker secret create alert_manager_config -
```

Unlike the previous configuration, this time we're using `webhook_config` (https://prometheus.io/docs/alerting/configuration/#%3Cwebhook_config%3E). The URL is the same as the one we used before. If the alert is executed, it will send a `buildWithParameters` request that will build `service-scale` job with `go-demo_main` as the service.

You'll notice that the parameters of the request are hard-coded. This time we are not using templating to customize the config. The problem is that url cannot use templated fields. For good or bad, that is part of the design. Instead, it sends all the fields of the alert as payload and expects the endpoint to translate it for its own needs. That would be great except for the fact that Jenkins does not accept job input fields in any other but its own format. All in all, both Alertmanager and Prometheus expect the other to adapt. So, we're in a bit of a trouble and have to specify an entry for each service. That is far from optimum.

Later on, we might discuss alternatives to this approach. We might come to the conclusion that Alertmanager should be extended with `jenkins_config`. Maybe we'll extend Alertmanager with our own custom code that reconfigures it using labels. It could be Docker Flow Alertmanager. We might choose a different tool altogether. We are engineers, and we should not accept limitations of other tools but extend them to suit our needs or build our own. Everything in this book is based on open source, and we should contribute back to the community.

However, we will not do any of those. For now, we'll just accept the limitation and move on. The important thing to note is that you'd need a receiver for every service that should be scaled. It's not the best solution, but it should do until a better solution emerges.

If you're interested in a discussion about the decision not to allow templates in url fields, please explore the Alertmanager issue 684 (https://github.com/prometheus/alertmanager/issues/684).

Since we removed the `monitor_alert-manager` service, we should redeploy the monitor stack. This time, we'll use a slightly modified version of the stack. The only difference is that we'll (temporarily) publish Alertmanager's port `9093`. That will allow us to test the configuration by sending HTTP requests to it.

```
DOMAIN=$(docker-machine ip swarm-1) \
    docker stack deploy \
    -c stacks/docker-flow-monitor-slack-9093.yml \
    monitor
```

Please wait a few moments until `monitor_alert-manager` service is up and running. You can check the status by listing processes of the monitor stack (for example, `docker stack ps monitor`).

Before we test the integration with Alertmanager, we should reset the number of replicas of `go-demo_main` service back to three.

```
docker service scale go-demo_main=3
```

Now that Alertmanager with the new configuration is running, we'll send it a request that will help us validate that everything works as expected.

```
curl -H "Content-Type: application/json" \
    -d '[{"labels":{"service":"it-does-not-matter"}}]' \
    $(docker-machine ip swarm-1):9093/api/v1/alerts
```

Please note that this time we did not specify `go-demo_main` as the service. Since all alerts are forwarded to the same Jenkins job and with the same parameters, it does not matter what we put in the request. We'll fix that soon. For now, we should open Jenkins and see the activity of the `service-scale` job.

```
open "http://$(docker-machineip\
swarm-1)/jenkins/blue/organizations/jenkins/service-scale/activity"
```

Alertmanager sent a request to Jenkins which, in turn, run a new build of the `service-scale` job. As a result, `go-demo_main` service should be scaled from three to four replicas. Let us confirm that.

```
docker service ps \
    -f desired-state=Running go-demo_main
```

The output is as follows (IDs are removed for brevity):

```
NAME            IMAGE                   NODE    DESIRED STATE CURRENT STATE       \
  ERROR PORTS
go-demo_main.1 vfarcic/go-demo:latest swarm-1 Running       Running 3 hours ago
go-demo_main.2 vfarcic/go-demo:latest swarm-2 Running       Running 3 hours ago
go-demo_main.3 vfarcic/go-demo:latest swarm-3 Running       Running 3 hours ago
go-demo_main.4 vfarcic/go-demo:latest swarm-1 Running       Running 3 minutes ago
```

As you can see from the output, the service is scaled to four replicas.

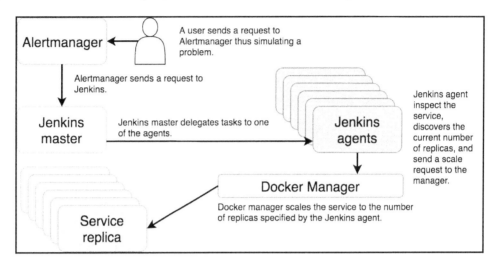

Figure 9-8: Alertmanager triggering of a Jenkins job that results in scaling of a service

Being able to send requests from Alertmanager to Jenkins works fine if all the alerts are the same. However, that is almost never the case. We should start distinguishing alerts. One easy improvement we can do is to create a default receiver. We can, for example, say that by default all alerts are sent to Slack and specify explicitly those that should be forwarded somewhere else.

Let us remove the secret and the service and discuss the new configuration.

```
docker service rm monitor_alert-manager
```

```
docker secret rm alert_manager_config
```

The configuration that envelops both Slack and Jenkins as receivers is as follows.

```
echo "route:
  group_by: [service]
  repeat_interval: 1h
  receiver: 'slack'
  routes:
  - match:
      service: 'go-demo_main'
    receiver: 'jenkins-go-demo_main'

receivers:
  - name: 'slack'
```

```
      slack_configs:
        - send_resolved: true
          title: '[{{ .Status | toUpper }}]\
{{ .GroupLabels.service }} service is in danger!'
          title_link: 'http://$(docker-machine ip\
 swarm-1)/monitor/alerts'
          text: '{{ .CommonAnnotations.summary}}'
          api_url: 'https://hooks.slack.com/services/T308SC7HD\
/B59ER97SS/S0KvvyStVnIt3ZWpIaLnqLCu'

    - name: 'jenkins-go-demo_main'
      webhook_configs:
        - send_resolved: false
          url: 'http://$(docker-machine ip\
 swarm-1)/jenkins/job/service-scale\
/buildWithParameters?token=DevOps22&service=go-demo_\
main&scale=1'
" | docker secret create alert_manager_config -
```

The route section defines slack as the receiver. Further down, the routes section uses match to filter alerts. We specified that any alert with the service label set to `go-demo_main` should be sent to the `jenkins-go-demo_main` receiver. In other words, every alert will be sent to Slack unless it matches one of the routes.

The receivers section defines slack and `jenkins-go-demo_main` entries. They are the same as those we used in previous configurations.

We should be able to test the whole system now. We should generate a situation that will create an alert in Prometheus, fire it to Alertmanager, and, depending on the alert type, see the result in Slack or Jenkins. But, first things should come first. We should create the new `monitor_alert-manager` service by redeploying the stack.

```
DOMAIN=$(docker-machine ip swarm-1) \
    docker stack deploy \
    -c stacks/docker-flow-monitor-slack.yml \
    monitor
```

As before, please execute `docker stack ps monitor` to confirm that all the services in the stack are running.

We'll also revert the number of replicas of the `go-demo_main` service to three. Since we set the maximum to four, an intent to scale up would fail if we do not put it back to three.

```
docker service scale go-demo_main=3
```

Finally, we'll simulate the "disaster" scenario by changing the `alertIf` conditions of our services. The first we'll play with is node-exporter service from the exporter stack. We'll set its node memory limit to one percent. That is certain to be lower than the actual usage.

```
docker service update \
    --label-add com.df.alertIf.1=@node_mem_limit:0.01 \
    exporter_node-exporter
```

If everything went as planned, the chain of the events is about to unfold. The first stop is Prometheus. Let's open the alerts screen.

```
open "http://$(docker-machine ip swarm-1)/monitor/alerts"
```

The `exporter_nodeexporter_mem_load` alert should change its status to pending (orange color) and then to firing (red). If it's still green, please wait a few moments and refresh the screen.

Prometheus fired the alert to Alertmanager. Since it does not match any of the routes (service is not `go-demo_main`), it falls into "default" category and will be forwarded to Slack. That is the logical flow of actions. Since we do not (yet) have a mechanism that scales nodes, the only reasonable action is to notify humans through Slack and let them solve this problem.

Feel free to visit the *#df-monitor-tests* channel inside `devops20.slack.com` (https:// devops20.slack.com/). The message generated with the alert from your system should be waiting for you.

Before we proceed, we'll revert the `exporter_node-exporter` service to its original state.

```
docker service update \
    --label-add com.df.alertIf.1=@node_mem_limit:0.8 \
    exporter_node-exporter
```

Soon, another message will appear in Slack stating that the problem with the `exporter_node-exporter` is resolved.

Let's see what happens when an alert is generated and matches one of the routes. We'll simulate another "disaster".

```
docker service update \
    --label-add com.df.alertIf=@service_mem_limit:0.01 \
    go-demo_main
```

You should know the drill by now. Wait until Prometheus fires the alert, wait a bit more, and, this time, confirm it by opening the `service-scale` activity screen in Jenkins.

```
open "http://$(docker-machine ip \
swarm-1)/jenkins/blue/organizations/jenkins/service-scale/activity"
```

Alertmanager filtered the alert, deduced that it matches a specific route and sent it to the matching receiver. This time, that receiver was `webhook_config` that sends requests to build `service-scale` Jenkins job using `go-demo_main` as the input parameter.

All in all, our service was scaled one more time, and we'll confirm that by listing all the running processes of the service.

```
docker service ps \
    -f desired-state=Running go-demo_main
```

The output is as follows (IDs are removed for brevity):

```
NAME            IMAGE                   NODE    DESIRED STATE CURRENT STATE        \
  ERROR PORTS
go-demo_main.1 vfarcic/go-demo:latest swarm-1 Running       Running 3 seconds ago
go-demo_main.2 vfarcic/go-demo:latest swarm-2 Running       Running 3 hours ago
go-demo_main.3 vfarcic/go-demo:latest swarm-3 Running       Running 3 hours ago
go-demo_main.4 vfarcic/go-demo:latest swarm-1 Running       Running 16 minutes a\
go
```

A new replica (with index 1) was created three seconds ago. We averted the "disaster" that could be caused by an imaginary increase in traffic that resulted in the increase in memory usage of the service.

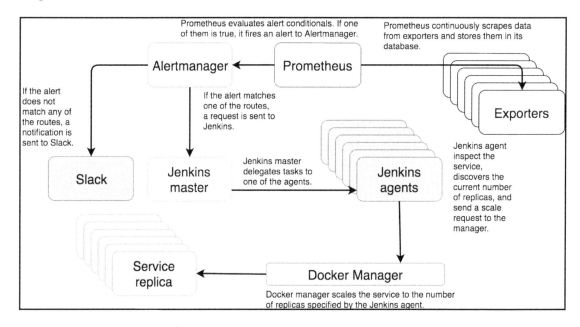

Figure 9-9: The full self-adaptive system applied to services

Unfortunately, we do not have a mechanism in place to scale down. The good news is that we will have it soon.

What now

We explored how we can add Jenkins to the mix and make it scale any service. We used relative scaling and made sure that there are some limits so that the service will always be within some boundaries.

Jenkins, by itself, proved to be very flexible and allowed us to set up a reasonably bullet-proof scaling mechanism with only a few lines of Declarative Pipeline code. Unfortunately, we hit some limits when integrating Alertmanager with Jenkins. As a result, Alertmanager config is not as generic as we'd like it to be. We might revisit that subject later and apply some alternative strategy. We might want to extend it. The solution might be called *Docker Flow Alertmanager*. Or, we might choose to replace Jenkins with our own solution. Since I'm fond of names that start with *Docker Flow*, we might add *Scaler* to the mix. We might opt for something completely unexpected, or we might say that the current solution is good enough. Time will tell. For now, the important thing to note is that we made a very important step towards having a *Self-Adapting* system that works on Swarm's out-of-the-box *Self-Healing* capabilities.

There are still a few critical problems we need to work on. Our *Self-Adapting* system applied to services does not scale down. The reason is simple. We need more data. Using memory as a metric is very important but not very reliable. Having memory below some threshold hardly gives us enough reason to scale up, and it definitely does not provide a valid metric that would let us decide to scale down. We need something else, and I'll leave you guessing what that is.

Another major missing piece of the puzzle is hardware. We are yet to build a system that *Self-Heals* and *Self-Adapts* servers. For now, we were concentrated only on services.

That was the longest chapter by now. You must be wasted. If you're not, I am, and this is where we'll make a break. As always, hardware needs to rest as much as we do so we'll destroy the machines we created in this chapter and start the next one fresh.

```
docker-machine rm -f swarm-1 swarm-2 swarm-3
```

10
Painting the Big Picture – The Self-Sufficient System Thus Far

A self-sufficient system is a system capable of healing and adaptation. Healing means that the cluster will always be in the designed state. As an example, if a replica of a service goes down, the system needs to bring it back up again. Adaptation, on the other hand, is about modifications of the desired state so that the system can deal with changed conditions. A simple example would be increased traffic. When it happens, services need to be scaled up. When healing and adaptation are automated, we get self-healing and self-adaptation. Together, they both a self-sufficient system that can operate without human intervention.

How does a self-sufficient system look? What are its principal parts? Who are the actors?

We'll limit the scope of the discussion to services and ignore the fact that hardware is equally important. With such a limitation in mind, we'll paint a high-level picture that describes a (mostly) autonomous system from the services point of view. We'll elevate ourselves from the details and have a birds-view of the system.

In case you are know-it-all type of person and want to see everything at once, the system is summarized in the following figure:

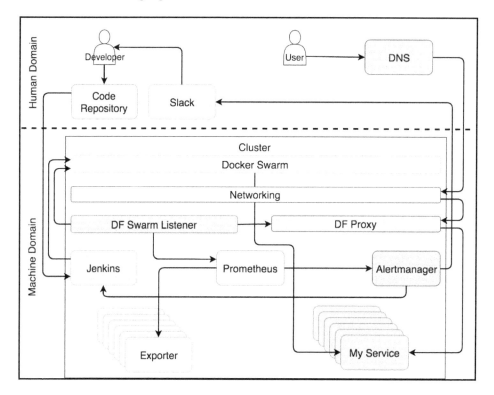

Figure 10-1: The system with self-healing and self-adapting services

> If everything in the diagram is clear and you do not have any doubts, the rest of this chapter will be boring, and you are welcome to skip it. If you continue reading, I will assume that you would benefit from a more detailed explanation.

A diagram like that one is probably too much to process at once. Throwing it into your face might make you think that empathy is not one of my strengths. If that's the case, you're not alone. My wife shares that impression even without any diagrams. This time I'll do my best to change your opinion and start over with a blank slate.

We can separate the system into two major domains; human and machine. Think of them as Matrix (http://www.imdb.com/title/tt0133093/). If you haven't seen the movie, stop reading the book right away, make some popcorn, and watch it.

In Matrix, the world is overtaken by machines. Humans don't do much except the few that realized what's going on. Most are living in a dream that reflects past events of human history. They are physically in the present, but their minds are in the past. The same situation can be observed with modern clusters. Most people still operate them as if it's 1999. Almost everything is manual, the processes are cumbersome, and the system is surviving due to a brute force and wasted energy. Some understood that the year is 2017 (at least at the time of this writing) and that a well-designed system is a system that does most of the work autonomously. Almost everything is run by machines, not human operators.

That does not mean that there is no place for us (humans). There is, but it is more related to creative and non-repetitive tasks. Therefore, if we focus only on cluster operations, the human domain is shrinking and being taken over by the machine domain.

The system can be divided into different roles. As you will see, a tool or a person can be very specialized and perform only a single role, or it can be in charge of multiple aspects of the operations.

Developer's role in the system

The human domain consists of processes and tools that are operated manually. We are trying to move away from that domain all the actions that are repeatable. That does not mean that the goal is for that domain to disappear. Quite the contrary. By pushing repetitive tasks away from it, we are freeing ourselves from mundane tasks and increasing the time we spend with those that bring real value. The less we do the tasks that can be delegated to machines, the more time we can spend with those that require creativity. This philosophy is in line with strengths and weaknesses of each actor in this drama. Machines are good at crunching numbers. They know how to execute predefined operations very fast. They are much better and more reliable at that than us. Unlike machines, we are capable of critical thinking. We can be creative. We can program those machines. We can tell them what to do and when.

I designated a developer as the leading actor of a human domain. I intentionally avoided using the word coder. A developer is everyone working on a software development project. It does not matter whether you're a coder, a tester, an operations guru, or a scrum master. I'm putting you all in the group labeled as developer. The result of your work is to push something to a code repository. Until it gets there, it's as if it does not exist. It does not matter whether it sits on your laptop, in a notebook, on your desk, or on a tiny piece of paper attached to a pigeon messenger. From the point of view of the system, it does not exist until it gets into a code repository. That repository is hopefully Git but, for the sake of argument, it can be any other place where you can store and version something.

That code repository is also part of the human domain. Even though it is a piece of software, it belongs to us. We operate it. We are pushing commits, pulling code, merging, and, sometimes, staring at it out of despair produced by too many merge conflicts. That does not mean that it does not have automated operations, nor that some parts of the machine domain are not operating it without any human involvement. Still, as long as something is mostly hands-on, we'll consider it being part of the human domain. Code repository definitely qualifies as a piece of the system that requires a lot of human intervention:

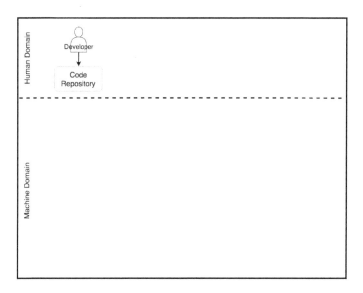

Figure 10-2: A developer commits code to a code repository

Let's see what happens when a commit is pushed to a code repository.

Continuous deployment role in the system

The continuous deployment process is fully automated. No exceptions. If your pipeline is not automated, it is not continuous deployment. You might require a manual action to deploy to production. If that action consists of pressing a single button that says, in bold letters, **deploy**, your process is continuous delivery. I can accept that. There might be business reasons for having such a button. Still, the level of automation is the same as with continuous deployment. You are only a decision maker. If there are any other manual operations, you are either doing continuous integration or, more likely, something that should not have a word continuous in its name.

No matter whether it is continuous deployment or delivery, the process is fully automated. You are excused from having manual parts of the process only if your system is a legacy system that your organization choose not to touch (typically a Cobol application). It just sits on top of a server and does something. I'm very fond of "nobody knows what it does, do not touch it" type of rules. It is a way to show utmost respect while still keeping the safe distance. However, I will assume that's not your case. You want to touch it. The desire is burning within you. If that's not the case and you are unfortunate enough to work on one of those stay-away-from-it types of systems, you are reading the wrong book, and I'm surprised you did not realize that yourself.

Once a code repository receives a commit or a pull request, it triggers a Webhook that sends a request to a CD tool which initiates the continuous deployment process. In our case, that tool is Jenkins (`https://jenkins.io/`). The request starts a build of the pipeline that performs all sorts of continuous deployment tasks. It checks out the code and runs unit tests. It builds an image and pushes it to a registry. It runs functional, integration, performance, and other types of tests that require a live service. The very end of the process (excluding production tests) is a request to a scheduler to deploy or update the service in the production cluster. Our choice for a scheduler is Docker Swarm.

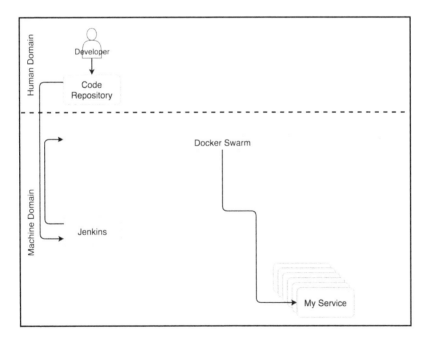

Figure 10-3: Deployment of a service through Jenkins

In parallel with continuous deployment, another set of processes is running and trying to keep the configurations of the system up-to-date.

Service configuration role in the system

Parts of the system needs to be reconfigured whenever any aspect of the cluster changes. A proxy might need an update of its configuration, metrics collector might require new targets, logs parser might need an update to it's rules.

No matter which parts of the system require changes, those changes need to be applied automatically. Hardly anyone disputes that. The bigger question is where to find those pieces of information that should be incorporated into the system. The most optimum place is in the service itself. Since almost all schedulers use Docker, the most logical place for the information about a service is inside it, in the form of labels. Setting the information anywhere else would prevent us from having a single source of truth and would make auto-discovery a hard thing to accomplish.

Having information about a service inside it does not mean that the same information should not reside in other places inside the cluster. It should. However, the service is where master information must be and, from there on, it should be propagated towards other services. Docker makes that very easy. It already has an API that anyone can hook into and discover any information about any service.

The choice of a tool that discovers service information and propagates it to the rest of the system is **Docker Flow Swarm Listener** (**DFSL**) (http://swarmlistener.dockerflow.com/). You might choose something else or build your own solution. The goal of such a tool, and *Docker Flow Swarm Listener* in particular, is to listen to Docker Swarm events. If a service contains a specific set of labels, the listener will fetch the information as soon as a service is deployed or updated and pass it to all interested parties. In this case, that is **Docker Flow Proxy** (**DFP**) (with HAProxy inside) and **Docker Flow Monitor** (**DFM**) (with Prometheus inside). As a result, both are having configurations that are always up-to-date. The proxy has the routes of all the publicly available services while Prometheus has the information about the exporters, alerts, the address of *Alertmanager*, and quite a few other things.

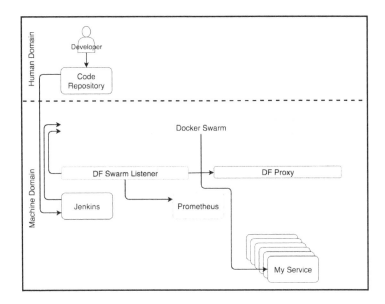

Figure 10-4: Reconfiguration of the system through Docker Flow Swarm Listener

While deployments and reconfigurations are going on, users must be able to access our services without downtime.

Proxy role in the system

Every cluster needs a proxy that will receive requests coming to a single port and forward them to destination services. The only exception is when we have only one public-facing service. In that case, it is questionable not only whether we need a proxy but whether we need a cluster at all.

When a request comes to the proxy, it is evaluated and, depending on its path, domain, or a few other headers, forwarded to one of the services.

Docker made quite a few aspects of proxies obsolete. There is no reason for load balancing. Docker's Overlay network does that for us. There's no need to maintain IPs of the nodes where services are hosted. Service discovery does that for us. Evaluation of headers and forwarding is pretty much everything that a proxy should do.

Since Docker Swarm utilizes rolling updates whenever an aspect of a service is changed, the **continuous deployment** (**CD**) process should not produce any downtime. For that statement to be true, a few requirements need to be fulfilled. Among others, a service needs to run at least two replicas, preferably more. Otherwise, any update of a service with a single replica will, unavoidably, create downtime. It does not matter whether that is a minute, a second, or a millisecond.

Downtime is not always disastrous. It all depends on the type of a service. If Prometheus is updated to a newer release, there will be downtime since it cannot scale. But, it is not a public facing service unless you count a few operators. A few seconds of downtime is not a big deal.

A public facing service like an online retail store where thousands or even millions of users are shopping can quickly lose good reputation if it goes down. We are so spoiled as consumers that a single glitch can change our mind and make us go to the competition. If that "glitch" is repeated over and over, loss of business is almost guaranteed. Continuous deployment has many advantages but, since it is executed fairly often, it also amplifies potential deployment problems, downtime being one of them. One second downtime produced many times a day is, indeed, not acceptable.

The good news is that rolling updates combined with multiple replicas will allow us to avoid downtime, as long as the proxy is always up-to-date.

The combination of rolling updates with a proxy that dynamically reconfigures itself results in a situation where a user can send a request to a service at any time without being affected by continuous deployment, failures, and other changes to the state of the cluster.

When a user sends a request to a domain, that request enters a cluster through any of the healthy nodes and is taken over by Docker's *Ingress* network. The network, in turn, detects that a request uses a port published by the proxy and forwards it. The proxy, on the other hand, evaluates the path, domain, or some other aspect of the request and forwards it to the destination service.

We're using **Docker Flow Proxy** (**DFP**) (`http://proxy.dockerflow.com/`) that adds the required level of dynamism on top of HAProxy.

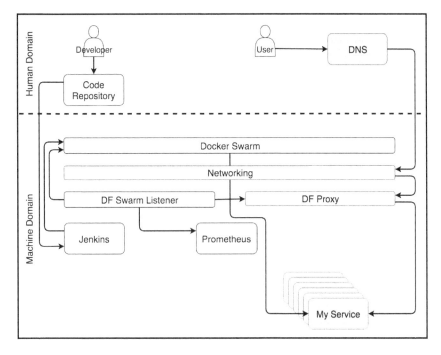

Figure 10-5: The flow of a request to the destination service

The next role we'll discuss is about collecting metrics.

Metrics role in the system

The crucial part of any cluster, especially those that are aiming towards self-adaptation, is data. Hardly anyone will dispute the need to have the past and present metrics. Without them, we'd run like a headless chicken when things go wrong. The central question is not whether they are required but what we do with them. Traditionally, operators would spend endless hours watching dashboards. That is far from efficient. Watch Netflix instead. It is, at least, more entertaining. The system should use metrics. The system generates them, it collects them, and it should decide what actions to perform when they reach some thresholds. Only then, the system can be self-adaptive. Only when it acts without human intervention can it be self-sufficient.

A system that implements self-adaptation needs to collect data, store them, and act upon them. I will skip the discussion of pros and cons between pushing and scraping data. Since we chose to use Prometheus (`https://prometheus.io/`) as a place where data is stored and evaluated and as the service that generates and fires alerts, the choice is to scrape data. That data is available in the form of exporters. They can be generic (for example, Node Exporter, cAdvisor, and so on), or specific to a service. In the latter case, services must expose metrics in a simple format Prometheus expects.

Independently of the flows we described earlier, exporters are exposing different types of metrics. Prometheus periodically scrapes them and stores them in its database. In parallel with scraping, Prometheus is continuously evaluating the thresholds set by alerts and, if any of them is reached, it is propagated to Alertmanager (`https://prometheus.io/docs/alerting/alertmanager/`). Under most circumstances, those limits are reached as a result of changed conditions (for example, increased load on the system).

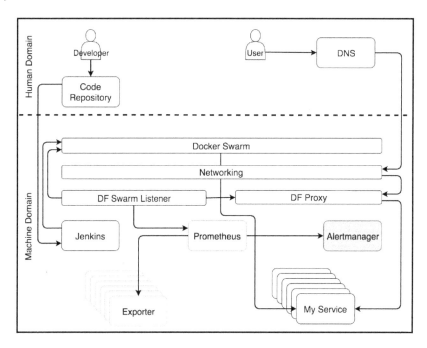

Figure 10-6: Data collection and alerting

Alert receivers are what makes the difference.

Alerting role in the system

The alerts are split into two general groups depending on alert receivers. It can be forwarded to the system or to humans. When an alert qualifies as the type that should be sent to the system, a request is usually forwarded to a service that is capable of evaluating the situation and executing tasks that will adapt the system. In our case, that service is *Jenkins* which executes one of the predefined jobs.

The most common set of tasks Jenkins performs is to scale (or de-scale) a service. However, before it attempts to scale, it needs to discover the current number of replicas and compare it with the upper and lower limits we set through service labels. If scaling would result in a number of replicas that is outside those boundaries, it sends a notification to Slack so that a human can decide what should be the correct set of actions that will remedy the problem. On the other hand, when scaling would keep the number of replicas within the limits, Jenkins sends a request to one of Swarm managers which, in turn, increases (or decreases) the number of replicas of a service. We're calling the process self-adaptation because the system is adapting to changed conditions without human intervention.

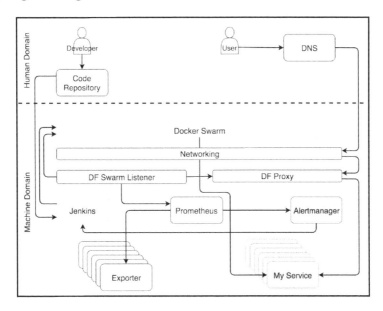

Figure 10-7: A notification to the system to self-adapt

Even though the goal is to make the system fully autonomous, it is almost sure that in some cases human intervention is needed. The cases are, in their essence, those that could not be predicted. When something expected happens, let the system fix it. On the other hand, call humans when unexpected occurs. In those cases, Alertmanager sends a message to the human domain. In our case, that is a Slack (`https://slack.com/`) message, but it could be any other communication service.

When you start designing a self-healing system, most of the alerts will fall into the "unexpected" category. You cannot predict all the situations that can happen to the system. What you can do is make sure that each of those cases is unexpected only once. When you receive an alert, your first set of tasks should be to adapt the system manually. The second, and equally important, group of actions would be to improve the rules in Alertmanager and Jenkins so that the next time the same thing happens, the system can handle it automatically.

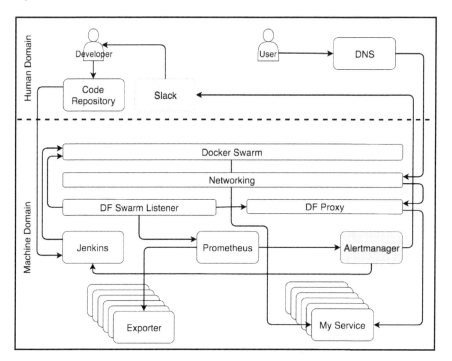

Figure 10-8: A notification to a human when something unexpected happens

Setting up a self-adapting system is hard, and it is something that never truly ends. It will need continuous improvements. How about self-healing? Is that equally hard to accomplish?

Scheduler role in the system

Unlike self-adaptation, self-healing is relatively easy to accomplish. As long as there are available resources, a scheduler will make sure that the specified number of replicas is always running. In our case, that scheduler is Docker Swarm (`https://docs.docker.com/engine/swarm/`).

Replicas can fail, they can be killed, and they can reside inside an unhealthy node. It does not really matter since Swarm will make sure that they are rescheduled when needed and (almost) always up-and-running. If all our services are scalable and we are running at least a few replicas of each, there will never be downtime. Self-healing processes inside Docker will make sure of that while our own self-adaptation processes aim to provide high-availability. The combination of the two is what makes the system almost fully autonomous and self-sufficient.

Problems begin piling up when a service is not scalable. If we cannot have multiple replicas of a service, Swarm cannot guarantee that there will be no downtime. If a replica fails, it will be rescheduled. However, if that replica is the only one, the period between a failure and until it is up and running results in downtime. It's a similar situation like with us. We get sick, stay in bed, and, after a while, return to work. The problem is if we're the only employee in the company and there's no one to take over the business while we're out. The same holds true for services. Two replicas is a minimum for any service that hopes to avoid any downtime.

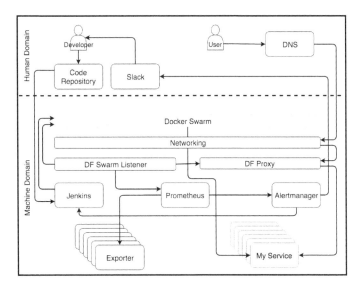

Figure 10-9: Docker Swarm ensures no downtime

Unfortunately, your services might not be designed with scalability in mind. Even when they are, the chances are that some of the third-party services you're using are not. Scalability is an important design decision, and it is an essential requirement we should evaluate whenever we're choosing the next tool we'll use. We need to make a clear distinction between services that must never have downtime and those that would not put the system at risk when they are not available for a few seconds. Once you make that distinction, you will know which ones must be scalable. Scalability is a requirement for no-downtime services.

Cluster role in the system

Finally, everything we do is inside one or more clusters. There are no individual servers anymore. We do not decide what goes where. Schedulers do. From our (human) perspective, the smallest entity is a cluster which is a collection of resources like memory and CPU.

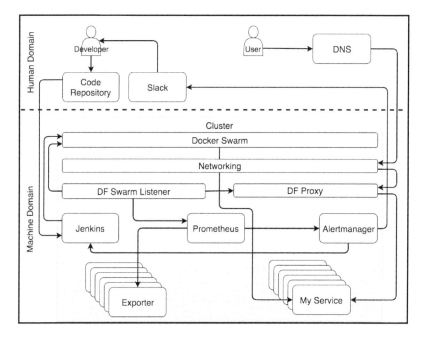

Figure 10-10: Everything is a cluster

What now?

We made a short break. I hope it was useful to get to a higher level and see what we did from afar. I hope this intermezzo made the picture clearer and that you recharged your batteries. There's still a lot to do, and I hope you're ready for new challenges.

11
Instrumenting Services

In the previous chapters, we used data from cAdvisor to scale services automatically. Specifically, Prometheus was firing alerts if memory limits were reached. When memory utilization was over the limit, we were scaling the service associated with the data. While that approach is a good start, it is far from enough for the type of the system we're building. As a minimum, we need to measure response times of our services. Should we look for an exporter that would provide that information?

The chances are that your first thought would be to use *haproxy_exporter* (`https://github.com/prometheus/haproxy_exporter`). If all public requests are going through it, it makes sense to scrape response times and set some alerts based on collected data. That model would be in line with the most of the other monitoring systems. The only problem with that approach is that it would be almost useless.

Not all requests are going through the proxy. Services that do not need to be accessed publicly are not hooked into the proxy. For example, Docker Flow Swarm Listener cannot be accessed. It does not publish any port, nor it has an API. It listens to Docker Socket and sends information to other services (for example, Docker Flow Proxy, Docker Flow Monitor, and so on). It is entirely invisible to the proxy. We could overlook this lack of information if that were the only problem behind the idea of monitoring the proxy.

When a request enters the proxy, it is forwarded to a service based on request paths, domains, and a few other criteria. By scraping metrics from the proxy, we would know only response times of those requests. In many cases, a service that receives a request forwarded from the proxy is making other requests. For example, go-demo communicates with MongoDB. A service that receives a request from the proxy might make many requests to other services. The proxy does not know about any of those. It receives a request, forwards it, waits for a response, and re-sends it to the client that initiated the communication. It is oblivious of any other processes or requests happening in the middle. As a result, we would know the duration of a request that enters the proxy but would be oblivious what are response times of each service involved in serving those requests.

Without the knowledge about response times of each service, we cannot deduce which one needs to be scaled. If a response time of a backend is high, should we scale that same backend or the database it uses?

To make things more complicated, response times are not the only metrics we need. We might be interested in failure rates, paths, methods, and a few other pieces of additional data. And all that needs to be related to a particular service, or even a concrete replica of a service

If your memory serves you well, you might remember that I said that my advice is to always start with exporters, and instrument your services only if you require metrics that are not provided by one of the existing exporters. Well... We reached that point when exporters are not enough. We need to instrument our services and gather more detailed metrics.

We'll limit the focus to only a few metrics. Specifically, we'll explore ways to collect error counts, response times, status codes, and a few other metrics. Do not take that as a sign that other types are not needed. They are. However, we need to keep the scope limited and produce tangible results within a decent number of pages. Otherwise, we could just as well start competing with *Encyclopedia Britannica* (`https://en.wikipedia.org/wiki/Encyclop%C3%A6dia_Britannica`). I will assume that you will take those examples for what they are and use them as a base for your own system. Error rates, response times, and status codes might be the most common types of metrics, but they are almost certainly not the only ones you need.

With the scope limited to only a few metrics, we should spend a bit of time discussing the data we would need.

Defining requirements behind service specific metrics

We might need different types of metrics. Some of them could be simple counters. A good example is errors. We might want to count them and react when their numbers reach certain thresholds. That in itself might not be enough, and we should be able to differentiate errors depending on a function or part of the service that produced them.

How about more complex metrics? Response times are another good example.

We might need a metric that will provide request response times. That might lead us towards having something like `resp_time 0.043` as the metric. It has a name (`resp_time`) and value in seconds (0.043). If we'd implement a metric like that, we'd soon discover that we need more. Having the information that the system responses are slow does not give us a clue which part of it is misbehaving. We need to know the name of the service.

We might not be able to instrument all the services in our clusters. If we take go-demo stack as an example, it consists of two services. It has a backend and a MongoDB. The backend is in our control, and we can easily extend it by adding instrumentation. The database is a different story. While we can (and should) use *MongoDB Exporter* (`https://github.com/dcu/mongodb_exporter`), it provides data related to the server status. What we need are metrics that we can relate to the backend service. We need to know whether a request sent to the go-demo stack is slow because of an issue in the backend or the database. Assuming that we are not going to "adapt" MongoDB to our own needs, we should try to answer that and few other questions by extending metrics inside services we're controlling.

We can use request path and method. If we add it to our metric, it should give us fairly good granularity of information. Depending on the path and the method, we can know whether the metric is related to the database or is limited to the internal processes of the service. We could also add query, but that would go too far. It would record almost each request separately and might result in too much memory and CPU usage when stored in Prometheus. Our updated metric could be as follows.

```
resp_time{method="GET",path="/demo/hello",service="go-demo"} 0.611446292
```

Through those labels, we would know which service the metric belongs to, the path of the request, and the method.

In the sea of possible additional labels we could add, there is one more that could be considered critical. We should know the status code. If we adopt standard HTTP response codes, the same ones our backend provides with the rest of the response, we can easily filter metrics and, for example, retrieve only those that are related to server errors.

Our updated metric could be as follows:

```
resp_time{code="200",method="GET",path="/demo/hello",service="go-demo"}
0.611446292
```

That is surely it. Right? Well, that's not quite what we truly need. A few other critical things are missing but we will not comment on them just yet. Since the libraries used to instrument code add a few additional features, we'll comment on them once we reach the hands-on part. For now, it is enough to know that we can instrument services to generate metrics to count (for example, errors) or observe (for example, response times). Any additional information can be provided through labels.

Differentiating services based on their types

Before we start instrumenting our services, we should discuss services we're deploying. They can be divided into three categories: online services, offline services, and batch processes. While there is overlap between each of those types and it is often not that easy to place a service into only one of them, such a division will provide us with a good understanding of the types of metrics we should implement.

We can define online services as those that accept requests from another service, a human, or a client (for example, browser). Those who send requests to online services often expect an immediate response. Front-end, APIs, and databases are only a few of the examples of such services. Due to the expectations we have from them, the key metrics we are interested in are the number of requests they served, the number of errors they produced, and latency.

Offline services are those that do not have a client that is waiting for a response. Something, or someone, instructs those services to do some tasks without waiting until they are finished. A good example of such a service would be Jenkins. Even though it does have it's UI and API and can fall in the category of online services, most of the work it does is offline. An example would be builds triggered by a Webhook from a code repository. Those Webhooks do not wait until Jenkins finishes building the jobs initiated by them. Instead, they announce that there is a new commit and trust that Jenkins will know what to do and will do it well. With offline services, we usually want to track the number of tasks being executed, the last time something was processed, and the length of queues.

Finally, the last group of services is batch processes. The significant difference when compared with offline services is that batch jobs do not run continuously. They start execution of a task or a group of tasks, terminate, and disappear. That makes them very difficult to scrape. Prometheus would not know when a batch job started nor when it should end. We cannot expect a system (Prometheus or any other) to pull metrics from a batch job. Our best bet is to push them instead. With such services, we usually track how long it takes to complete them, how long each stage of a job lasted, the time a job finished executing, and whether it produced an error or it was successful.

I prefer avoiding batch jobs since they are very hard to track and measure. Instead, when possible, we should consider converting them into offline services. A good example is, again, Jenkins. It allows us to schedule execution of a job thus providing a similar functionality as a batch process while still providing easy to scrape metrics and health checks.

Now that we divided services into groups, we can discuss different types of metrics we can define when instrumenting our services.

Choosing instrumentation type

Prometheus supports four major metric types. We can make a choice between counters, gauges, summaries, and histograms. We will see them in action soon. For now, we'll limit the discussion to a brief overview of each.

A counter can only go up. We cannot decrease its value. It is useful for accumulating values. An example would be errors. Each error in the system should increase the counter by one.

Unlike counters, gauge values can go both up and down. A good example of a gauge is memory usage. It can increase, only to decrease a few moments later.

Histograms and summaries are more complex types. They are often used to measure duration of requests and sizes of responses. They track both summaries and counts. When those two are combined, we can measure averages over time. Their data is usually placed in buckets that form quantiles.

We'll go deeper into each of the metric types through practical examples starting with a counter as the simplest of all. But, before we do that, we need to create a cluster that will serve as our playground.

Creating the cluster and deploying services

All hands-on parts of the past chapters started with the execution of a script that creates a cluster and deploys the services we'll need. This chapter is no exception. You know the drill so let's get to it.

All the commands from this chapter are available in the *11-instrumentation.sh* (https://gist.github.com/vfarcic/85bd6824032fb2a05d7fe624516548a7) Gist:

```
chmod +x scripts/dm-swarm-11.sh

./scripts/dm-swarm-11.sh

eval $(docker-machine env swarm-1)

docker stack ls
```

We executed the `dm-swarm-11.sh script` which, in turn, created a Swarm cluster composed of Docker Machines, created the networks, and deployed only one stack. The last command listed all the stacks in the cluster and showed that we are running only the proxy stack.

Let's move into the counter metric.

Instrumenting services using counter

There are many usages of the counter metric. We can measure the number of requests entering the system, the number of bytes sent through the network, the number of errors, and so on. Whenever we want to record an incremental value, a counter is a good choice.

We'll use counter to track errors produced by a service. With such a goal, a counter is usually put around code that handles errors.

The examples that follow are taken from *Docker Flow Swarm Listener* (http://swarmlistener.dockerflow.com/). The code is written in Go. Do not be afraid if that is not your language of choice. As you will see, examples are straightforward and can be easily extrapolated to any programming language.

Prometheus provides *client libraries* (`https://prometheus.io/docs/instrumenting/`
`clientlibs/`) for a myriad of languages. Even if your favorite language is not one of them,
it should be relatively easy to roll-out your own solution based on *exposition formats*
(`https://prometheus.io/docs/instrumenting/exposition_formats/`).

The reason for choosing Docker Flow Swarm Listener lies in its type. It is (mostly) an offline
service. Most of its objectives are to listen to Docker events through its socket and propagate
Swarm events to other services like Docker Flow Proxy and Docker Flow Monitor. It does
have an API but, since it is not its primary function, we'll ignore it. As such, it is not a good
candidate for more complex types of metrics thus making it suitable for a counter. That
does not mean that the counter is the only metric it implements. However, we need to start
from something simple, so we'll ignore the others.

There are a few essential things code needs to do to start producing metrics.

We must define a variable that determines the type of the metric. Since we want to count
errors, the code can be as follows:

```
var errorCounter = prometheus.NewCounterVec(
    prometheus.CounterOpts{
        Subsystem: "docker_flow",
        Name: "error",
        Help: "Error counter",
    },
    []string{"service", "operation"},
)
```

The snippet defines a variable `errorCounter` based on `CounterVec` structure provided
through the `NewCounterVec` function. The function requires two arguments. The first one
(`CounterOpts`) defines options of the counter. In our case, we set the `Subsytem` to
`docker_flow` and the name to `error`. The fully qualified metric name consists of the
namespace (we're not using it today), subsystem, and name. When combined, the metric we
are creating will be called `docker_flow_error`. Help is only for informative purposes and
should help users of our metrics understand better its purpose. As you can see, I was not
very descriptive with the help. Hopefully, it is clear what it does without a more detailed
explanation.

The second argument is the list of labels. They are critical since they allow us to filter
metrics. In our case, we want to know which service generated metrics. That way, we can
have the same instrumentation across many services and choose whether to explore them
all at once or filter by the service name.

Knowing which service produced errors is often not enough. We should be able to pinpoint a particular operation that caused a problem. The second label called `operation` provides that additional information.

It is important to specify all the labels we might need when filtering metrics, but not more. Each label requires extra resources. While that is in most cases negligible overhead, it could still have a negative impact when dealing with big systems. Just follow the rule of "everything you need, but not more" and you should be on the right track.

Please read the *Use labels* (`https://prometheus.io/docs/practices/instrumentation/#use-labels`)section of the instrumentation page for a discussion about dos and don'ts.

The `errorCounter` variable is, in Prometheus terms, called collector. Each collector needs to be registered. We'll do that inside `init` function that is executed automatically, thus saving us from worrying about it:

```
func init() {
    prometheus.MustRegister(errorCounter)
}
```

Now we are ready to start incrementing the `errorCounter`. Since I do not like repeated code, the code that increments the metric is wrapped into another function. It is as follows:

```
func recordError(operation string, err error) {
    metrics.errorCounter.With(prometheus.Labels{
        "service": metrics.serviceName,
        "operation": operation,
    }).Inc()
}
```

Whenever this function is called, `errorCounter` will be incremented by one (`Inc()`). Each time that happens, the name of the service and the operation that produced the error will be recorded as labels.

An example invocation of the `recordError` function is as follows:

```
...
err = n.ServicesCreate(
    newServices,
    args.Retry,
    args.RetryInterval,
)
if err != nil {
    metrics.RecordError("ServicesCreate")
}
...
```

The function `ServicesCreate` returns an `err` (short for error). If the `err` is not nil, the `recordError` is called passing `GetServices` as operation and thus incrementing the counter.

The last piece missing is to enable `/metrics` as the endpoint Prometheus can use to scrape metrics from out service:

```
func (m *Serve) Run() error {
    mux := http.NewServeMux()
    ...
    mux.Handle("/metrics", prometheus.Handler())
    ...
}
```

That code snippet should be self-explanatory. We registered `/metrics` as the address that is handled by Prometheus handler provided with the `GoLang` client library we're using.

I hope that those few snippets of Go code were not scary. Even if you never worked with Go, you probably managed to understand the gist of it and will be able to create something similar in your favorite language. Remember to visit *Client Libraries* (`https://prometheus.io/docs/instrumenting/clientlibs/`) page, choose the preferred language, and follow the instructions.

If you're interested in the full source code behind the snippets, please visit *vfarcic/docker-flow-swarm-listener* (`https://github.com/vfarcic/docker-flow-swarm-listener`) GitHub repository.

Let's see those metrics in action.

Since swarm-listener deployed through the proxy stack does not publish port `8080`, we'll create a new service attached to the proxy network. It will be global so that it is guaranteed to run on each node. That way it'll be easier to find the container, enter into it, and send requests to swarm-listener.

```
docker service create --name util \
    --mode global \
    --network proxy \
    alpine sleep 1000000
```

We created the `util` service based on the alpine image and made it sleep for a very long time. Please confirm that it is up-and-running by executing `docker service ps util`.

Let's find the ID of the container running on the node our Docker client points to and enter inside it by executing the following commands:

```
ID=$(docker container ls -q \
    -f "label=com.docker.swarm.service.name=util")

docker container exec -it $ID sh
```

The only thing missing is to install `curl`:

```
apk add --update curl
```

Now we can send a request to swarm-listener and retrieve metrics.

```
curl "http://swarm-listener:8080/metrics"
```

You'll see a lot of metrics that come out of the box when using Prometheus clients. In this case, most of the metrics are very particular to Go, so we'll skip them. What you won't be able to see is `docker_flow_error`. Since the service did not produce any errors, that metric does not show.

Let's get out of the container we're in:

```
exit
```

My guess is that you would not be delighted reaching this far without seeing the metric we discussed so let us generate a situation in which swarm-listener will produce errors.

Docker Flow Swarm Listener discovers services by communicating with Docker Engine through its socket. Typically, the service mounts the socket to the host and, in that way, Docker client inside the container communicates with Docker Engine running on the node. If we remove that mount, the communication will be broken, and Docker Flow Swarm Listener will start reporting errors.

Let's test it out:

```
docker service update \
    --mount-rm /var/run/docker.sock \
    proxy_swarm-listener
```

We removed the `/var/run/docker.sock mount` and the communication between Docker client inside the container and Docker engine on the host was cut. We should wait a few moments until Docker reschedules a new replica. If you want to confirm that the update was finished, please execute `docker stack ps proxy`.

Let's check the logs and confirm that the service is indeed generating errors:

```
docker service logs proxy_swarm-listener
```

One of the output entries should be similar to the one that follows:

```
. . .
```

Cannot connect to the Docker daemon at `unix:///var/run/docker.sock`. Is the `docker daemon` running?

Now that the service is generating errors, we can take another look at the metrics and confirm that `docker_flow_error` is indeed added to the list of metrics:

```
docker container exec -it $ID sh
curl "http://swarm-listener:8080/metrics"
```

We entered the `util` replica and sent a request to swarm-listener endpoint /metrics. The output, limited to the relevant parts, should be as follows:

```
. . .
# HELP docker_flow_error Error counter
# TYPE docker_flow_error counter
docker_flow_error{operation="GetServices",service="swarm_listener"} 10
. . .
```

Please note that metrics are ordered alphabetically, so `docker_flow_error` should be somewhere around the top.

As you can see, `docker_flow_error` generated 10 errors. By inspecting labels, we can see that the operation that causes errors is `GetServices` and that the service is `swarm_listener`. If this would be a production system, we'd know not only that there is a problem with the service but also which part of it caused the issue. That is very important since the actions the system should take are rarely the same for the whole service. Knowing that the problem is related to a particular operation or a function, lets us fine tune the actions the system should take when certain thresholds are reached.

Before we continue, let us exit the container we're in and restore the swarm-listener to its original state:

```
exit

docker stack deploy \
    -c stacks/docker-flow-proxy-mem.yml \
    proxy
```

We redeployed the stack and thus restored the mount we removed.

Let's try to generate the same metric with a different value. We can, for example, remove proxy service and deploy `go-demo` stack. Docker Flow Swarm Listener will detect a new service and try to send the information to the proxy. If it fails to do so, Prometheus client will increase `docker_flow_error` by one.

```
docker service rm proxy_proxy

docker stack deploy \
    -c stacks/go-demo-scale.yml \
    go-demo
```

We removed the proxy and deployed `go-demo` stack. Docker Flow Swarm Listener will try to send service information to the proxy and, since we removed it, fail to do so. By default, if `swarm-listener` fails to deliver information, it retries for fifty times with five seconds delay in between. That means that we need to wait a bit over 4 minutes for swarm-listener to give up and throw an error.

After a while, we can check the logs:

```
docker service logs proxy_swarm-listener
```

After fifty retries, you should see log entries similar to the ones shown in the following code block:

```
...
Retrying service created notification to ...
ERROR: Get ...: dial tcp: lookup proxy on 127.0.0.11:53: no such host
```

Now we can go back to the `util` container and take another look at the metrics:

```
docker container exec -it $ID sh
curl "http://swarm-listener:8080/metrics"
```

This time, `docker_flow_error` metric is slightly different:

```
# HELP docker_flow_error Error counter
# TYPE docker_flow_error counter
docker_flow_error{operation="notificationSendCreateServiceRequest",service=
"swarm_listener"} 1
...
```

The `operation` label has the value `notificationSendCreateServiceRequest` clearly indicating that it comes from a different place than the previous error.

The two errors we explored are of quite a different nature and should be treated differently. The one associated with the label `GetServices` means that there is no communication with the Docker socket. That could be caused by a faulty manager and the action that should remedy that could be to reschedule the service to a different node or maybe even to remove that node altogether. The code of the service will retry establishing socket connection so we should probably not react on the first occupancy of the metric but wait until, for example, it reaches twenty failed attempts over the `timespan` of five minutes or less.

The error related to the `notificationSendCreateServiceRequest` means that there is no communication with the services that should receive notifications. In this case, that destination is the proxy. The problem might be related to networking, or the proxy is not running. Our action might be to check whether the proxy is running and, if it isn't, deploy it again. Or maybe there should be no action at all. The proxy itself should have its own alerts that will remedy the situation. Moreover, the service does not throw an error when the connection with the proxy fails. Instead, it retries it for a while and errors only if all attempts failed. That means that we should react on the first occurrence of the error.

As you can see, even though those two errors come from the same service, the causes and the actions associated with them are entirely different. For that reason, we are using the `operation` label to distinguish them. Later on, it should be relatively easy to filter them in Prometheus and define different alerts.

Instrumenting our service with counters was easy. Let's see whether gauge is any different.

Since we removed the proxy service, we should exit the `util` container and restore the stack to its original state before we proceed further.

```
exit

docker stack deploy \
    -c stacks/docker-flow-proxy-mem.yml \
    proxy
```

Instrumenting services using gauges

Gauges are very similar to counters. The only significant difference is that we can not only increment, but also decrease their values. We'll continue exploring `vfarcic/docker-flow-swarm-listener` GitHub repository for an example of a gauge.

Since gauge is almost identical to counter, we won't go into many details but only briefly explore a few snippets.

Just as with a counter, we need to declare a variable that defines the type of the metric. A simple example is as follows:

```
var serviceGauge = prometheus.NewGaugeVec(
    prometheus.GaugeOpts{
        Subsystem: "docker_flow",
        Name: "service_count",
        Help: "Service gauge",
    },
    []string{"service"},
)
```

Next, we need to register it with Prometheus. We'll reuse the code from the `init` function where we defined the `errorCounter` and add `serviceGauge`.

```
func init() {
    prometheus.MustRegister(errorCounter, serviceGauge)
}
```

There's also a function that simplifies the usage of the metric:

```
func RecordService(count int) {
    serviceGauge.With(prometheus.Labels{
    "service": serviceName,
    }).Set(float64(count))
}
```

We're setting the value of the gauge using the `Set` function. Alternatively, we could have used `Add` or `Sub` functions to add or subtract the value. `Inc` or `Dec` can be used to increase of decrease the value by one.

Finally, on every iteration of the swarm-listener, we are setting the gauge to the number of services retrieved by swarm-listener.

```
metrics.RecordService(len(service.Services))
```

Let's take another look at the `/metrics` endpoint.

```
docker container exec -it $ID sh
curl "http://swarm-listener:8080/metrics"
```

One of the metric entries is as follows.

```
# HELP docker_flow_service_count Service gauge
# TYPE docker_flow_service_count gauge
docker_flow_service_count{service="swarm_listener"} 1
```

It might look confusing that the value of the metric is one since we are running a few other services. Docker Flow Swarm Listener fetches only services with the `com.df.notify` label. Among the services we're currently running, only `go-demo_main` has that label, hence being the only one included in the metric.

Let's see what happens if we remove `go-demo_main` service:

```
exit

    docker service rm go-demo_main
    docker container exec -it $ID sh
    curl "http://swarm-listener:8080/metrics"
```

The output of the `/metrics` API is as follows (limited to the relevant parts):

```
# HELP docker_flow_service_count Service gauge
# TYPE docker_flow_service_count gauge
docker_flow_service_count{service="swarm_listener"} 0
. . .
```

As you can see, the `docker_flow_service_count` metric is now set to zero thus accurately representing the number of services discovered by swarm-listener. If, in your case, the number is still one, please wait a few moments and try again. Docker Swarm Listener has five seconds iterations, and you might have requested metrics too soon.

Let us exit the `util` container and restore the `go-demo` stack before we proceed into histograms:

```
exit

docker stack deploy \
 -c stacks/go-demo-scale.yml \
 go-demo
```

Instrumenting services using histograms and summaries

When compared with counters and gauges, histograms are much more complex. That does not mean that they are harder to implement but that the data they provide is less simple when compared with the other metric types we explored. We'll comment on them by studying a sample code and the output it provides.

We'll switch from the *vfarcic/docker-flow-swarm-listener* (`https://github.com/vfarcic/docker-flow-swarm-listener`) repository to *vfarcic/go-demo* (`https://github.com/vfarcic/go-demo`) since it provides a simple example of a histogram.

Just as with the other types of metrics, histogram also needs to be declared as a variable of the particular type:

```
var (
    histogram = prometheus.NewHistogramVec(prometheus.HistogramOpts{
        Subsystem: "http_server",
        Name: "resp_time",
        Help: "Request response time",
    }, []string{
    "service",
    "code",
    "method",
    "path",
    })
)
```

The objective of the metric is to record information about response times. Its labels provide additional information like the name of the service (`service`), the response code (`code`), the method of the request (`method`), and the path (`path`). All those labels together should give us a fairly accurate picture of the response times of the service, and we'll be able to filter the results using any combination of the labels.

Next is a helper function that will allow us to record metrics easily:

```
func recordMetrics(start time.Time, req *http.Request, code int) {
    duration := time.Since(start)
    histogram.With(
        prometheus.Labels{
            "service": serviceName,
            "code": fmt.Sprintf("%d", code),
            "method": req.Method,
            "path": req.URL.Path,
        },
    ).Observe(duration.Seconds())
}
```

The `recordMetrics` function accepts argument that defines the time when a request started (`start`), the request itself (`req`), and the response code (`code`). We're calling histogram's' `Observe` function with the duration of the request expressed in seconds. The duration is obtained by calculating the time passed since the value of the start variable.

Let's take a look at one of the functions that invokes `recordMetrics`:

```
func HelloServer(w http.ResponseWriter, req *http.Request) {
    start := time.Now()
    defer func() { recordMetrics(start, req, http.StatusOK) }()

    // The rest of the code that processes the request.
}
```

Whenever a request is made to a particular path, the web server invokes the `HelloServer` function. That function starts by recording the current time and storing it in the `start` variable. Go has a special statement that defers execution of a function. In this case, we defined that the invocation of the `recordMetrics` should be deferred. As a result, it will be executed before the `HelloServer` function exists, thus giving us an (almost) exact duration of the requests.

A similar logic is applied to all endpoints of the service thus providing us with the response times of the whole service.

If you're interested in the full source code behind the snippets, please visit *vfarcic/go-demo* (`https://github.com/vfarcic/go-demo`) GitHub repository.

Let us send some traffic to the `go-demo` service before we explore the histogram metrics:

```
for i in {1..100}; do
    curl "http://$(docker-machine ip swarm-1)/demo/hello"
done
```

We'll repeat the already familiar process of entering the `util` container and retrieving the metrics. The only difference is that this time we'll explore `go-demo_main` metrics instead of those from the swarm-listener:

```
docker container exec -it $ID sh
```

```
curl "http://go-demo_main:8080/metrics"
```

The output, limited to relevant parts, is as follows:

```
...
# HELP resp_time Request response time
# TYPE resp_time histogram
resp_time_bucket{code="200",method="GET",path="/demo/hello",\
service="go-demo",le="0.005"} 69
resp_time_bucket{code="200",method="GET",path="/demo/hello",\
service="go-demo",le="0.01"} 69
resp_time_bucket{code="200",method="GET",path="/demo/hello",\
```

```
service="go-demo",le="0.025"} 69
resp_time_bucket{code="200",method="GET",path="/demo/hello",\
service="go-demo",le="0.05"} 69
resp_time_bucket{code="200",method="GET",path="/demo/hello",\
service="go-demo",le="0.1"} 69
resp_time_bucket{code="200",method="GET",path="/demo/hello",\
service="go-demo",le="0.25"} 69
resp_time_bucket{code="200",method="GET",path="/demo/hello",\
service="go-demo",le="0.5"} 69
resp_time_bucket{code="200",method="GET",path="/demo/hello",\
service="go-demo",le="1"} 69
resp_time_bucket{code="200",method="GET",path="/demo/hello",\
service="go-demo",le="2.5"} 69
resp_time_bucket{code="200",method="GET",path="/demo/hello",\
service="go-demo",le="5"} 69
resp_time_bucket{code="200",method="GET",path="/demo/hello",\
service="go-demo",le="10"} 69
resp_time_bucket{code="200",method="GET",path="/demo/hello",\
service="go-demo",le="+Inf"} 69
resp_time_sum{code="200",method="GET",path="/demo/hello",\
service="go-demo"} 0.003403602
resp_time_count{code="200",method="GET",path="/demo/hello",\
service="go-demo"} 69
...
```

Unlike counters and gauges, each histogram produces quite a few metrics. The major one is resp_time_sum that provides a summary of all the recorded responses. Below it is resp_time_counter with the number of responses. Based on those two, we can see that 69 responses took 0.0034 seconds. If we'd like to get the average time of the responses, we'd need to divide sum with count.

In addition to sum and count, we can observe the number of responses grouped into different buckets called quantiles. At the moment, all sixty-nine requests fall into all of the quantiles, so we'll postpone discussion about them until we reach the examples with more differencing response times.

One thing worth noting is that the metrics come from only one of the three replicas, so our current examples do not paint the full picture. Later on, when we start scraping the metrics with Prometheus, we'll see that they are aggregated from all the replicas.

Finally, you might have expected around thirty-three responses since we sent a hundred requests that were distributed across three replicas. However, the service continuously pings itself, so the final number was quite higher.

Let's get out of the `util` container and try to generate some requests that will end with errored responses.

```
exit
for i in {1..100}; do
    curl "http://$(docker-machine ip swarm-1)/demo/random-error"
done
```

The `/demo/random-error` endpoint produces response code `500` in approximately ten percent of cases. The rest should be "normal" responses with status code `200`.

The output should be similar to the one that follows:

```
. . .
Everything is still OK
Everything is still OK
Everything is still OK
Everything is still OK
ERROR: Something, somewhere, went wrong!
. . .
```

Let's see how `go-demo` metrics look like now:

```
docker container exec -it $ID sh
curl "http://go-demo_main:8080/metrics"
```

The output limited to the relevant parts is as follows:

```
. . .
# HELP http_server_resp_time Request response time
# TYPE http_server_resp_time histogram
. . .
http_server_resp_time_sum{code="200",method="GET",path="/demo\
/random-error",service="go-demo"} 0.001033751
http_server_resp_time_count{code="200",method="GET",path="/demo\
/random-error",service="go-demo"} 32
. . .
http_server_resp_time_sum{code="500",method="GET",path="/demo\
/random-error",service="go-demo"} 7.033700000000001e-05
http_server_resp_time_count{code="500",method="GET",path="/demo\
/random-error",service="go-demo"} 2
. . .
```

Since the response code is one of the labels, we got two metrics; one for the code 200, and the other for 500. Since those hundred requests were load balanced across three replicas, the one that produced this output got approximately one-third of them (32+2). We can see that the requests that produce errors take considerably longer time with the total of seven seconds for only two requests.

You might have been "unlucky" and did not get a single response with the code 500. If that was the case, feel free to send another hundred requests.

Now that we confirmed that our response metrics are separated by different labels, we should explore quantiles. For that, we need to simulate queries with varying response times. Fortunately, go-demo has such an endpoint.

```
exit
for i in {1..30}; do
    DELAY=$[ $RANDOM % 6000 ]
    curl "http://$(docker-machine ip swarm-1)/demo/hello?delay=$DELAY"
done
```

When delay query parameter is set, go-demo goes to sleep for the specified number of milliseconds. We made thirty iterations. Each generated a random number between 0 and 6000 and sent that number as the delay parameter. As a result, the service should have received requests with a wide range of response times.

Let's take another look at the metrics.

```
docker container exec -it $ID sh
curl "http://go-demo_main:8080/metrics"
```

The output, limited to relevant parts, is as follows:

```
...
# HELP http_server_resp_time Request response time
# TYPE http_server_resp_time histogram
http_server_resp_time_bucket{code="200",method="GET",path="/demo\
/hello",service="go-demo",le="0.005"} 78
http_server_resp_time_bucket{code="200",method="GET",path="/demo\
/hello",service="go-demo",le="0.01"} 78
http_server_resp_time_bucket{code="200",method="GET",path="/demo\
/hello",service="go-demo",le="0.025"} 78
http_server_resp_time_bucket{code="200",method="GET",path="/demo\
/hello",service="go-demo",le="0.05"} 78
http_server_resp_time_bucket{code="200",method="GET",path="/demo\
/hello",service="go-demo",le="0.1"} 78
http_server_resp_time_bucket{code="200",method="GET",path="/demo\
/hello",service="go-demo",le="0.25"} 78
```

```
http_server_resp_time_bucket{code="200",method="GET",path="/demo\
/hello",service="go-demo",le="0.5"} 79
http_server_resp_time_bucket{code="200",method="GET",path="/demo\
/hello",service="go-demo",le="1"} 80
http_server_resp_time_bucket{code="200",method="GET",path="/demo\
/hello",service="go-demo",le="2.5"} 83
http_server_resp_time_bucket{code="200",method="GET",path="/demo\
/hello",service="go-demo",le="5"} 87
http_server_resp_time_bucket{code="200",method="GET",path="/demo\
/hello",service="go-demo",le="10"} 88
http_server_resp_time_bucket{code="200",method="GET",path="/demo\
/hello",service="go-demo",le="+Inf"} 88
http_server_resp_time_sum{code="200",method="GET",path="/demo\
/hello",service="go-demo"} 29.430902277
http_server_resp_time_count{code="200",method="GET",path="/demo\
/hello",service="go-demo"} 88
...
```

Now we have the combination of the fast responses from before combined with those with a delay of up to six seconds. If we focus only on the last two lines, we can see that there are 88 responses in total with the summed time of `29.43` seconds. The average time of responses is around `0.33` seconds. That, in itself, does not give us enough information. Maybe two requests lasted for 10 seconds each, and all of the rest were lightning fast. Or, perhaps, all of the requests were below `0.5` seconds. We cannot know that by just looking at the sum of all response times and dividing them with the count. We need quantiles.

The histogram used in go-demo did not specify buckets, so the quantiles are those defined by default. They range from as low as `0.005` to as high as `10` seconds. If you pay closer attention to the numbers beside each of those buckets, you'll see that `78` requests were below `0.25` seconds, `79` below `0.5`, and so on all the way until all of the 88 requests being below `10` seconds. All the requests from a smaller bucket belong to the larger one. That might be confusing the first time we look at the metrics, but it makes perfect sense. A request that lasted less than, for example, `0.5` seconds, definitely lasted less than, `1` seconds, and so on.

Using quantiles (or buckets) will be essential when we start defining Prometheus alerts based on those metrics, so we'll postpone further discussion until we reach that part.

As you can see, unlike counters and gauges, histograms go beyond simple additions and subtractions. They provide observations over a period. They track the number of observations and their summaries thus allowing us to calculate average values. The number of observations behaves like a counter. It can only be increased. The sum, on the other hand, is similar to a gauge. It can be both increased and decreased depending on the values we observe. If it is negative, the sum will decrease. We did not explore such an example since response times are always positive.

The most common usage of histograms is to record request durations and response times. We explored one of those two through our examples.

How about summaries? They are the only metric type we did not explore.

Summary is similar to histogram metric type. Both sample observations. The major difference is that summary calculates quantiles based on a sliding time frame. We won't go deeper into summaries. Instead, please read the *Histograms And Summaries* (`https://prometheus.io/docs/practices/histograms/`) page that explains both in more detail and provides a comparison of the two.

What now?

We explored, through a few examples, how to instrument our services and provide more detailed metrics than what we would be able to do through exporters. Early in the book, I said that we should use exporters instead instrumentation unless they do not provide enough information. It turned out that they do not. If, for example, we used an exporter, we would get metrics based on requests coming through the proxy. We would not be aware of internal communication between services nor would we be able to obtain response times of certain parts of the services we're deploying. Actually, *HAProxy Exporter* (`https://github.com/prometheus/haproxy_exporter`) does not even provide response times since the internal metrics it exposes is not entirely compatible with Prometheus and cannot be exported without sacrificing accuracy. That does not mean that HAProxy metrics are not accurate but that they use a different logic. Instead of having a counter, HAProxy exposes response as exponentially decaying value. It cannot be transformed into a histogram.

If you're interested in the discussion about HAProxy Exporter response time, please visit *issue 37* (`https://github.com/prometheus/haproxy_exporter/issues/37`).

Without accurate response times, we cannot instruct our system to scale and de-scale them effectively. We need to obtain more information if we want to get closer to building a truly self-adapting system.

While instrumentation we explored through examples is by no means all the instrumentation we should add, it does provide a step forward. Even though response times are not the only metric we're missing, it is probably the most important one. Counting errors is useful as well but does not provide clear guidance. Some errors will need a different set of actions, and many cannot even be hooked into the system that auto-corrects itself. Generally speaking, errors often (but not always) require human intervention. Response times, on the other hand, are easy to grasp. They do provide clear guidance for the system. If it goes over a certain threshold within a predefined period, scale up. If it goes down, scale down.

The next chapter will continue exploring response times. We'll see what we can do with them in Prometheus and how we can improve our current alerts by incorporating this new data.

And now we need a break. Take a rest, go to sleep, recharge your batteries. Before you do any of that, remember that your computer needs a rest too. Get out of the `util` container and remove the machines we created.

```
exit

docker-machine rm -f swarm-1 swarm-2 swarm-3
```

12
Self-Adaptation Applied to Instrumented Services

An instrumented service (`https://prometheus.io/docs/practices/instrumentation/`) provides more detailed metrics then what we can scrape from exporters (`https://prometheus.io/docs/instrumenting/exporters/`). The ability to add all the metrics we might need, opens the doors that are often closed by exporters. That does not mean that they are any less useful but that we need to think of the nature of the resource we are observing.

Hardware metrics should be scraped from exporters. After all, we cannot instrument CPU. Third-party services are another good example of a use-case where exporters are often a better option. If we use a database, we should look for an exporter that fetches metrics from it and transforms them into the Prometheus-friendly format. The same goes for proxies, gateways, and just about almost any other service that we did not develop.

We might choose to write an exporter (`https://prometheus.io/docs/instrumenting/writing_exporters/`) even for services we are in control of if we already invested a lot of time implementing metrics that are not in Prometheus format.

Exporters can get us only half-way through. We can instruct the system to scale based on, for example, memory utilization. cAdvisor (`https://github.com/google/cadvisor`) provides information about the containers running inside the cluster, but the metrics it provides are too generic. We cannot get service-specific data. Inability to fine-tune metrics on per-service basis leaves us with insufficient information that can be used only for basic alerts. Instrumentation provides the missing piece of the puzzle.

In cases we are willing to invest time to instrument our services, the results are impressive. We can get everything we need without compromises. We can accomplish almost any level of details and instrument services in a way that we can write reliable alerts that will notify the system with all the information it needs. The result is a step closer towards self-healing and, more importantly, self-adaptation. The reason I'm putting self-adaptation into the "more important" group lies in the fact that self-healing is already mostly solved by other tools. Schedulers (for example, Docker Swarm) already do a decent job at self-healing services. If we exclude hardware from the scope, we are left with self-adaptation of services as the major obstacle left to solve.

Setting up the objectives

We need to define the scope of what we want to accomplish through instrumentation. We'll keep it small by limiting ourselves to a single goal. We'll scale services if their response times are over an upper limit and de-scale them if they're below a lower limit. Any other alert will lead to a notification to Slack. That does not mean that Slack notifications should exist forever. Instead, they should be treated as a temporary solution until we find a way to translate manual corrective actions into automated responses performed by the system.

A good example of alerts that are often treated manually are responses with errors (status codes 500 and above). We'll send alerts whenever they reach a threshold over a specified period. They will result in Slack notifications that will become pending tasks for humans. An internal rule should be to fix the problem first, evaluate why it happened, and write a script that will repeat the same set of steps. With such a script, we'll be able to instruct the system to do the same if the same alert is fired again. With such an approach, we (humans) can spend our time solving unexpected problems and leave machines to remedy those that are reoccurring.

The summary of the objectives we'll try to accomplish is as follows.

- Define maximum response time of a service and create the flow that will scale it
- Define minimum response time of a service and create the flow that will de-scale it
- Define thresholds based on responses with status codes 500 and above and send Slack notifications

Please note that response time thresholds cannot rely only on milliseconds. We must define quantiles, rates, and a few other things. Also, we need to set the minimum and the maximum number of replicas of a service. Otherwise, we risk scaling to infinity or de-scaling to zero replicas. Once we start implementing the system, we'll see whether those additional requirements are enough or we'll need to extend the scope further.

That was more than enough talk. Let's move to the practical exploration of the subject.

As always, the first step is to create a cluster and deploy a few services.

Creating the cluster and deploying services

You know the drill. We'll create a Swarm cluster and deploy a few stacks we are already familiar with. Once we're done, we'll have the base required for the exploration of the tasks at hand.

 All the commands from this chapter are available in the `12-alert-instrumentation.sh` Gist at (`https://gist.github.com/vfarcic/8bafbe912f277491eb2ce6f9d29039f9`).

```
chmod +x scripts/dm-swarm-12.sh

./scripts/dm-swarm-12.sh

eval $(docker-machine env swarm-1)

docker stack ls
```

We created the cluster and deployed three stacks. The output of the last command gives us the list of those stacks.

```
1  NAME        SERVICES
2  monitor     3
3  proxy       2
4  jenkins     2
```

Now we're ready to explore how to scrape metrics from instrumented services.

Scraping metrics from instrumented services

The `go-demo` (`https://github.com/vfarcic/go-demo`) service is already instrumented with a few metrics. However, they do not mean much by themselves. Their usage starts only once Prometheus scrapes them. Even then, they provide only a visual representation and the ability to query them after we find a problem. The major role of graphs and the capacity to query metrics comes after we detect an issue and we want to drill deeper into it. But, before we get there, we need to set up alerts that will notify us that there is a problem.

We cannot think about metrics before we have some data those metrics will evaluate. So, we'll start from the beginning and explore how to let Prometheus know that metrics are coming from services we instrumented. That should be a relatively easy thing to accomplish since we already have all the tools and processes we need.

Let's start by deploying the `go-demo` stack. The `main` service inside it is already instrumented and provides the `/metrics` endpoint Prometheus can query.

```
docker stack deploy \
    -c stacks/go-demo-instrument.yml \
    go-demo
```

We can use the time Swarm needs to initialize the replicas of the stack and explore the YAML file. The definition of the `go-demo-instrument.yml` (`https://github.com/vfarcic/docker-flow-monitor/blob/master/stacks/go-demo-instrument.yml`) stack is as follows (limited to relevant parts).

```
...
  main:
    ...
    networks:
      ...
      - monitor
    deploy:
      ...
      labels:
        - com.df.notify=true
        ...
        - com.df.scrapePort=8080
      ...
```

We used `com.df.notify=true` label to let *Docker Flow Swarm Listener* know that it should notify *Docker Flow Monitor*. The `com.df.scrapePort` is set to `8080` thus letting Prometheus know the port it should use to scrape metrics. The monitor network is added to the stack. Since *Docker Flow Monitor* is attached to the same network, they will be able to communicate internally by using service names.

Let's confirm that *Docker Flow Monitor* configured Prometheus correctly:

```
open "http://$(docker-machine ip swarm-1)/monitor/config"
```

As you can see, `job_name` is set to the name of the service (`go-demo_main`). The names argument is set to `tasks.go-demo_main`. When service DNS is prefixed with `tasks.`, Overlay network returns IPs of all the replicas. That way, Prometheus will be able to scrape metrics from all those that form the `go-demo_main` service.

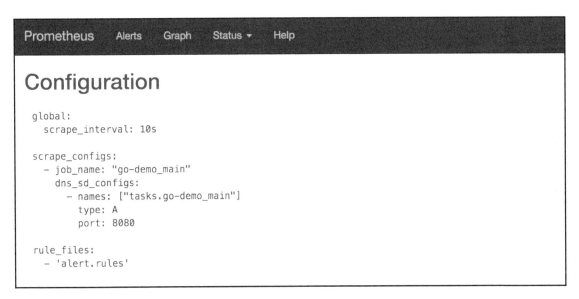

Figure 12-1: Prometheus configuration with the go-demo_main job

Before we proceed, please confirm that all the replicas of the services that form the `go-demo` stack are up-and-running.

```
docker stack ps \
    -f desired-state=Running go-demo
```

The output should show three replicas of `go-demo_main` and one replica of `go-demo_db` services with the current state `running`. If that's not the case, please wait a while longer.

The output should be similar to the one that follows (IDs are removed for brevity).

```
 1   NAME            IMAGE                   NODE     DESIRED STATE CURRENT STATE       \
 2         ERROR PORTS
 3   go-demo_main.1 vfarcic/go-demo:latest swarm-2 Running      Running about a minu\
 4   te ago
 5   go-demo_db.1    mongo:latest            swarm-1 Running      Running about a minu\
 6   te ago
 7   go-demo_main.2 vfarcic/go-demo:latest swarm-2 Running      Running about a minu\
 8   te ago
 9   go-demo_main.3 vfarcic/go-demo:latest swarm-3 Running      Running about a minu\
10   te ago
```

Now we can verify that all the targets (replicas) are indeed registered.

```
open "http://$(docker-machine ip swarm-1)/monitor/targets"
```

As you can see, Prometheus registered three targets that correspond to three replicas of the service. Now we know that it scrapes metrics from all of them and can explore different ways to query data.

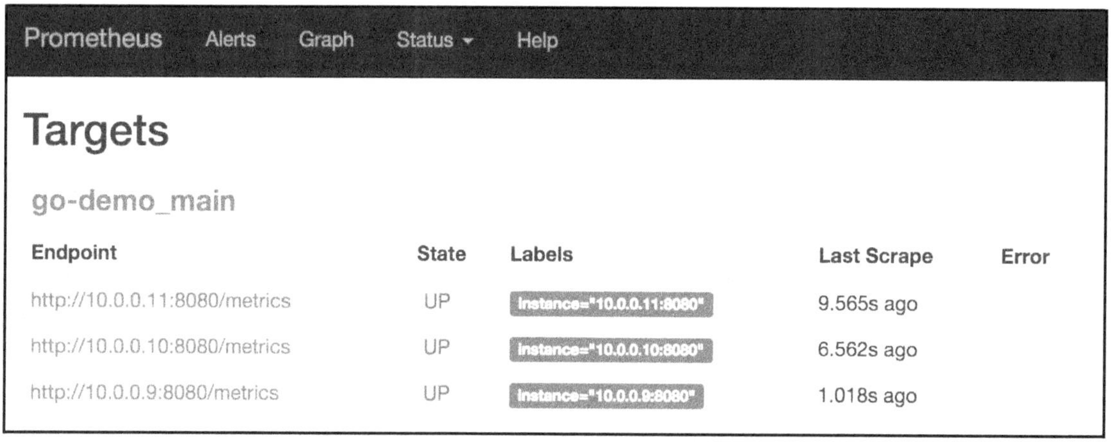

Figure 12-2: Prometheus targets that correspond with the replicas of the go-demo_main service

If we focus only on scraping instrumented services, the process can be described with a simple diagram from the following figure.

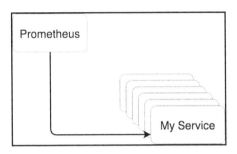

Figure 12-3: Prometheus scrapes metrics from services

Querying metrics from instrumented services

Let's open the Prometheus *graph* screen and explore different ways to query metrics scraped from the go-demo_main service.

```
open "http://$(docker-machine ip swarm-1)/monitor/graph"
```

Please click the **Graph** tab, enter the query that follows, and click the **Execute** button

```
http_server_resp_time_sum / http_server_resp_time_count
```

We divided the summary of response times with the count of the requests. You'll notice that the output graph shows that the average value is close to zero. Feel free to hover over one of the lines and observe that the values are only a few milliseconds. The go-demo_main service pings itself periodically and the responses are very fast.

We should generate some slower responses since the current result does not show metrics in their true glory.

The /demo/hello endpoint of the service can be supplemented with the delay parameter. When set to a value in milliseconds, the service will wait for the given period before responding to the request. Since we want to demonstrate a variety of response times, we should send a few requests with different delay values.

The commands that will send thirty requests with random delays are as follows.

```
for i in {1..30}; do
    DELAY=$[ $RANDOM % 6000 ]
    curl "http://$(docker-machine ip swarm-
  1)/demo/hello?delay=$DELAY"
done
```

The delay of each of the thirty requests was set to a random value between zero and six thousand milliseconds. Now we should have more variable metrics we can explore.

Please write the query that follows in the **Expression** field and click the **Execute** button.

```
http_server_resp_time_sum / http_server_resp_time_count
```

This time you should see a graph with more differentiating response times. You should note that the response times you're seeing are a combination of those we sent (with up to six seconds delay) and fast pings that the service executes periodically.

The previous query is not enough, and we should add a few functions into the mix.

We'll add `rate`. It calculates per-second average rate of increase of the time series in the range vector.

We'll also limit the metrics to the last five minutes. While that does not make much of a difference when presenting data in a graph, it is crucial for defining alerts. Since they are our ultimate goal while we're working with Prometheus, we should get used to such limits from the start.

Please write the query that follows in the **Expression** field and click the **Execute** button.

```
rate(http_server_resp_time_sum[5m]) / rate(http_server_resp\
_time_count[5m])
```

Since we are trying to define queries we'll use in alerts, we might want to limit the results only to a single service.

The expression limited to `go-demo_main` service is as follows.

```
rate(http_server_resp_time_sum{service="go-demo"}[5m]) / rate(http_
server_resp_time_count{service="go-demo"}[5m])
```

The graph output of the last query should show a spike in response times of each of the three replicas. That spike corresponds to the thirty requests we created with the delay parameter.

Figure 12-4: Prometheus graph with response duration spike

The `service` label comes from instrumentation. It is hard-coded to `go-demo` and, therefore, not very reliable. If we would be confident that there will be only one instance of that service, we could continue using that label as one of the filters. However, that might not be the case. Even though it is likely we'll use only one instance of the `go-demo` service in production, we might still run the same service as part of testing or some other processes. That would produce incorrect query results since we would be combining different instances of the service and potentially get unreliable data. Instead, it might be a better idea to use the `job` label.

The `job` label comes out-of-the-box with all metrics scraped by Prometheus. It corresponds to the `job_name` specified in the `scrape` section of the configuration. Since `Docker Flow Monitor` uses the "real" name of the service to register scraping target, it is always unique. That fixes one of our problems since we cannot have two services with the same name inside a single cluster. In our case, the full name of the service is the combination of the name of the stack and the name of the service defined in that YAML file. Since we deployed `go-demo` stack with the service `main`, the full name of the service is `go-demo_main`.

If we'd like to see metrics of all the services that provide instrumentation with the metric name `http_server_resp_time`, the query would be as follows.

```
sum(rate(http_server_resp_time_sum[5m])) by (job)   / sum(rate(\
http_server_resp_time_count[5m])) by (job)
```

Since we used `sum` to summarize data **by job**, each line represents a different service. That is not so obvious from the current graph since we are scraping metrics from only one service, so you'll need to trust me on this one. If we'd have metrics from multiple services, each would get its line in the graph.

That must be it. Doesn't it? We have an average response time for each job (service) as measured over last five minutes. Unfortunately, even though such expressions might be useful when watching graphs, they have little value when used for alerts. It might be even dangerous to instruct the system to do some corrective actions based on such an alert.

Let's say that we create an alert defined as follows.

```
sum(rate(http_server_resp_time_sum[5m])) by (job) / sum(rate(http_\
server_resp_time_count[5m])) by (job) > 0.1
```

It will fire if average response time is over one hundred milliseconds (0.1 seconds). Now let us imagine that nine out of ten responses are around ten milliseconds while one out of ten lasts for five hundred milliseconds (half a second). The preceding alert would not fire in such a scenario since the average is 59 milliseconds, which is still way below the 100 milliseconds alert threshold. As a result, we would never know that there is a problem experienced by ten percent of those who invoke this service.

Rejection of the preceding alert definition might lead you to write something simpler. The new alert could be as follows.

```
http_server_resp_time_sum > 0.25
```

If there is a request that lasted longer than the threshold, fire an alert. We even increased the threshold from 0.1 to 0.25 seconds. While I do like the simplicity of that alert, it is even worse than the one with average response time. It would be enough to have one request that passed the threshold to fire an alert and, potentially, initiate the process that would scale the number of replicas of that service. What if there were a million other responses that were way below that threshold. The alert would still fire and probably produce undesirable consequences. Do we really care that one out of million responses is slow?

The problem is that we were focused on averages. While there is value in them, they derailed us from creating a query that we could use to create a useful alert. Instead, we should focus on percentages. A better goal would be to construct an expression that would give us the percentage of requests that are above the certain threshold.

The new query is as follows.

```
sum(rate(http_server_resp_time_bucket{le="0.1"}[5m])) by
  (job) / sum(rate(http_server_resp_time_count[5m])) by (job)
```

The first part of the expression returns summary of the number of requests that are in the `0.1` bucket. In other words, it retrieves all the requests that are equal to or faster than `0.1` second. Further on, we are dividing that result with the summary of all the requests. The result is the percentage of requests that are below the `0.1` seconds threshold.

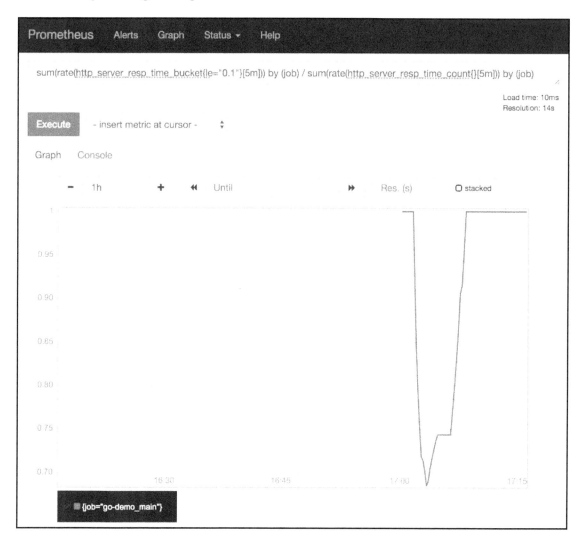

Figure 12-5: Prometheus graph with percentage of response times below `0.1` second threshold

If you do not see a drop in the percentage of requests, the likely cause is that more than one hour passed since you executed thirty requests with the delay. If that's the case, please rerun the commands that follow and, after that, re-execute the expression.

```
for i in {1..30}; do
    DELAY=$[ $RANDOM % 6000 ]
    curl "http://$(docker-machine ip swarm-1)/demo/hello?delay=$DELAY"
done
```

That was an expression worthy of an alert. We could use it to create something similar to a *service license agreement*. The alert would fire if, for example, less than 0.999 (99.9%) responses are below the defined time-based threshold. The only thing missing is to limit the output of the expression to the go-demo_main service.

```
sum(rate(http_server_resp_time_bucket{job="go-demo_main",
le="0.1"}[5m])) / sum(rate(http_server_resp_time_count{job=\
"go-demo_main"}[5m]))
```

Let's try to explore at least one more example.

Among others, the http_server_resp_time metric has the code label that contains status codes of the responses. We can use that information to define an expression that will retrieve the number of requests that produced an error. Since we are returning standard HTTP response codes (https://en.wikipedia.org/wiki/List_of_HTTP_status_codes), we can filter metrics so that only those with the label that starts with 5 are retrieved.

Before we start filtering metrics in search for errors, we should generate some requests that do result in error responses.

```
for i in {1..100}; do
    curl "http://$(docker-machine ip swarm-1)/demo/random-error"
done
```

We sent a hundred requests to the /demo/random-error endpoint. Approximately one out of ten requests resulted in error responses.

The expression that follows will retrieve the rate of error responses over the period of five minutes.

```
sum(rate(http_server_resp_time_count{code=~"^5..$"}[5m])) by (job)
```

The total number does not mean much unless you plan on sending an alert every time an error occurs. Such an action would likely result in too many alerts, and you'd run a risk of developing high-tolerance and start ignoring them. That's not the way to go. Instead, we should use a similar approach as with response times. We'll calculate the rate by dividing the number of errors with the total number of responses.

```
sum(rate(http_server_resp_time_count{code=~"^5..$"}[5m])) by \
  (job) / sum(rate(http_server_resp_time_count[5m])) by (job)
```

That would be an useful alert that could be fired if the number is higher than some threshold.

Figure 12-6: Prometheus graph with error rate percentage

Now that we defined two sets of expressions, we can take a step further and convert them into alerts.

Firing alerts based on instrumented metrics

Now that we have a solid understanding of some of the expressions based on instrumented metrics, we can proceed and apply that knowledge to create a few alerts.

Let us deploy updated version of the `go-demo` stack.

```
docker stack deploy \
    -c stacks/go-demo-instrument-alert.yml \
    go-demo
```

We'll take a couple of moments to discuss the changes to the updated stack while waiting for the services to become operational. The stack definition, limited to relevant parts, is as follows:

```
...
  main:
    ...
    deploy:
      ...
      labels:
        ...
        - com.df.alertName.1=mem_limit
        - com.df.alertIf.1=@service_mem_limit:0.8
        - com.df.alertFor.1=5m
        - com.df.alertName.2=resp_time
        - com.df.alertIf.2=sum(rate(http_server_resp_time_bucket{\
job="go-demo_main", le="0.1"}[5m])) / sum(rate(http_server_resp\
_time_count{job="go-demo_main"}[5m])) < 0.99
        - com.df.alertLabels.2=scale=up,service=go-demo_main
        - com.df.scrapePort=8080
        - com.df.scaleMin=2
        - com.df.scaleMax=4
      ...
```

The `com.df.alertName` label was present in the previous stack. However, since specifying memory limit is not enough anymore, we added an index suffix (`.1`) that allows us to specify multiple alerts. The same `.1` suffix was added to the rest of labels that form that alert.

The second alert will fire if the number of the responses in the `0.1` bucket (equal to or below 100 milliseconds) is smaller than 99% of all the requests. The rate is measured over the period of five minutes and the results are restricted to the job `go-demo_main`. The `if` statement we used is as follows:

```
sum(rate(http_server_resp_time_bucket{job="go-demo_main", \
  le="0.1"}[5m])) / sum(rate(http_server_resp_time_count{job=\
"go-demo_main"}[5m])) < 0.99
```

Since we are measuring the percentage of requests, there's no real need to set `for` statement. As soon as more than one percent of requests result in response times over 100 milliseconds, the alert will be fired. Later on we'll discuss what should be done with such an alert. For the moment, we'll limit the scope and let Alertmanager forward all alerts to Slack.

We also added `scale=up` and `service=go-demo_main` alert labels. Later on, the `scale` label will help the system know whether it should scale up or down.

Finally, we used `com.df.scaleMin` and `com.df.scaleMax` labels to specify the minimum and the maximum number of replicas allowed for this service. We won't use those labels just yet. Just remember that they are defined.

Next, we'll repeat the commands that will create slow responses and verify that the alerts are indeed fired. But, before we do that, we'll open the Prometheus' alert screen and confirm that the new alert is indeed registered.

```
open "http://$(docker-machine ip swarm-1)/monitor/alerts"
```

The `godemo_main_resp_time` row should be green meaning that the alert is registered but that the condition is not met. In other words, at least 99% of responses were generated in 100 milliseconds or less.

Now we can truly test the alert. Let's generate some slow responses.

```
for i in {1..30}; do
    DELAY=$[ $RANDOM % 6000 ]
    curl "http://$(docker-machine ip swarm-
1)/demo/hello?delay=$DELAY"
done
```

You already executed those commands at least once so there should be no reason to explain what happened. Instead, we'll go back to the alerts screen and confirm that the alert is indeed firing.

```
open "http://$(docker-machine ip swarm-1)/monitor/alerts"
```

The `godemo_main_resp_time` should be red. If it isn't, please wait a few moments and refresh the screen. Feel free to click it if you'd like to see the definition of the alert.

Figure 12-7: Prometheus alert in firing state

Please visit the *#df-monitor-tests* channel inside devops20.slack.com (`https://devops20.slack.com/`). You should see the `[FIRING] go-demo_main service is in danger!` message.

The process, so far, can be described through the diagram in the following figure:

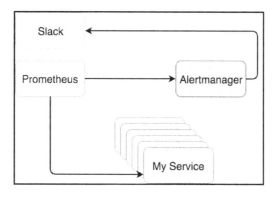

Figure 12-8: Alerts that result in Slack notifications

That worked out quite well. When slow responses start piling up, we'll get a Slack notification letting us know that we should enter the cluster and scale the service. The only problem is that we should not waste our time with such operations. We should let the system scale up automatically.

Scaling services automatically

With the alerts firing from Prometheus into Alertmanager, the only thing left to do is to send requests to Jenkins to scale the service. We already created a similar Alertmanager config in one of the previous chapters, so we'll comment only on a few minor differences. The configuration is injected into the `alert-manager` service as a Docker secret.

Since secrets are immutable, we cannot update the one that is currently used. Instead, we'll have to remove the stack and the secret and create them again.

```
docker stack rm monitor

docker secret rm alert_manager_config
```

Now we can create a new secret with the updated Alertmanager configuration.

```
echo "route:
  group_by: [service,scale]
  repeat_interval: 5m
  group_interval: 5m
  receiver: 'slack'
  routes:
  - match:
      service: 'go-demo_main'
      scale: 'up'
    receiver: 'jenkins-go-demo_main-up'

receivers:
  - name: 'slack'
    slack_configs:
      - send_resolved: true
        title: '[{{ .Status | toUpper }}] {{\
.GroupLabels.service }} service is in danger!'
        title_link: 'http://$(docker-machine ip\
swarm-1)/monitor/alerts'
        text: '{{ .CommonAnnotations.summary}}'
        api_url: 'https://hooks.slack.com/services\
/T308SC7HD/B59ER97SS/S0KvvyStVnIt3ZWpIaLnqLC u'
  - name: 'jenkins-go-demo_main-up'
```

```
      webhook_configs:
        - send_resolved: false
          url: 'http://$(docker-machine ip swarm-1)/jenkins/job\
  /service- scale/buildWithParameters?token=DevOps22&service=\
  go-demo_main&scale=1'
      " | docker secret create alert_manager_config -
```

Remember that the gist with all the commands from this chapter is available from `12-alert-instrumentation.sh` (`https://gist.github.com/vfarcic/8bafbe912f277491eb2ce6f9d29039f9`). Use it to copy and paste the command if you got tired of typing.

The difference, when compared with the similar configuration we used before, is the `scale` label and a subtle change in the Jenkins receiver name. This time we are not grouping routes based only on `service` but with the combination of the labels `service` and `scale`. Even though we are, at the moment, focused only on scaling up, soon we'll try to add another alert that will de-scale the number of replicas. While we would accomplish the current objective without the `scale` label, it might be a good idea to be prepared for what's coming next.

This time, the `match` section uses a combination of both `service` and `scale` labels. If they are set to `go-demo_main` and `up`, the alert will be forwarded to the `jenkins-go-demo_main-up` receiver. Any other combination will be sent to Slack. The `jenkins-go-demo_main-up` receiver is triggering a build of the Jenkins job `service-scale` with a few parameters. It contains the authentication token, the name of the service that should be scaled, and the increment in the number of replicas.

The `repeat_interval` is set to five minutes. Alertmanager will send a new notification every five minutes (plus the `group_interval`) unless the problem is fixed and Prometheus stops firing alerts. That is almost certainly not the value you should use in production. One hour (`1h`) is a much more reasonable period. However, I'd like to avoid making you wait for too long so, in this case, it's set to five minutes (`5m`).

Let us deploy the stack with the new secret.

```
  DOMAIN=$(docker-machine ip swarm-1) \
      docker stack deploy \
      -c stacks/docker-flow-monitor-slack.yml \
      monitor
```

There's only one thing missing before we see the alert in its full glory. We need to run the Jenkins job manually. The first build will fail due to a bug we already experienced in one of the previous chapters.

Please open the `service-scale` activity screen.

```
open "http://$(docker-machine ip swarm-\
 1)/jenkins/blue/organizations/jenkins/service-scale/activity"
```

You'll have to login with admin as both username and password. Afterward, click the **Run** button and observe the failure. The issue is that Jenkins was not aware that the job uses a few parameters. After the first run, it'll get that information, and the job should not fail again. If it does, it'll be for a different reason.

The `go-demo_main` service should have three replicas. Let's double-check that.

```
docker stack ps \
    -f desired-state=Running go-demo
```

The output should be similar to the one that follows (ID are removed for brevity).

```
 1  NAME            IMAGE                  NODE     DESIRED STATE CURRENT STATE        \
 2    ERROR PORTS
 3  go-demo_main.1 vfarcic/go-demo:latest swarm-1 Running       Running 42 minutes a\
 4  go
 5  go-demo_db.1   mongo:latest           swarm-3 Running       Running 42 minutes a\
 6  go
 7  go-demo_main.2 vfarcic/go-demo:latest swarm-3 Running       Running 42 minutes a\
 8  go
 9  go-demo_main.3 vfarcic/go-demo:latest swarm-1 Running       Running 42 minutes a\
10  go
```

Before we proceed, please make sure that all replicas of the `monitor` stack are up and running. You can use `docker stack ps monitor` command to check the status.

Now we can send requests that will produce delayed responses and open the Prometheus *alerts* screen.

```
for i in {1..30}; do
    DELAY=$[ $RANDOM % 6000 ]
    curl "http://$(docker-machine ip swarm-1)/demo/hello?delay=$DELAY"
done

open "http://$(docker-machine ip swarm-1)/monitor/alerts"
```

The `godemo_main_resp_time` alert should be red. If it is not, please wait a few moments and refresh the screen.

Prometheus fired the alert to Alertmanager which, in turn, notified Jenkins. As a result, we should see a new build of the `service-scale` job.

```
open "http://$(docker-machine ip \
swarm-1)/jenkins/blue/organizations/jenkins/service-\
 scale/activity"
```

Please click on the latest build. It should be green with the output of the last task set to `go-demo_main` was scaled from 3 to 4 replicas:

Figure 12-9: A build of a Jenkins job that scales Docker services

We should confirm that Jenkins indeed did the work it was supposed to do. The number of replicas of the `go-demo_main` service should be four.

```
docker stack ps \
    -f desired-state=Running go-demo
```

The output of the `stack ps` command is as follows (IDs are removed for brevity).

```
 1    NAME            IMAGE                    NODE     DESIRED STATE CURRENT STATE         \
 2        ERROR PORTS
 3    go-demo_main.1 vfarcic/go-demo:latest swarm-1 Running       Running about an hou\
 4    r ago
 5    go-demo_db.1    mongo:latest             swarm-2 Running       Running about an hou\
 6    r ago
 7    go-demo_main.2 vfarcic/go-demo:latest swarm-2 Running       Running about an hou\
 8    r ago
 9    go-demo_main.3 vfarcic/go-demo:latest swarm-3 Running       Running about an hou\
10    r ago
11    go-demo_main.4 vfarcic/go-demo:latest swarm-3 Running       Running 2 minutes ago
```

Since we stopped simulating slow responses, the alert in Prometheus should turn into green. Otherwise, if Prometheus would continue firing the alert, Alertmanager would send another notification to Jenkins ten minutes later. Since the service has the `com.df.scaleMax` label set to four, Jenkins job would not scale the service. Instead, it would send a notification to Slack so that we (humans) can deal with the problem.

Let's remove the stack and the secret and work on Alertmanager configuration that will also de-scale services.

```
docker stack rm monitor
```

```
docker secret rm alert_manager_config
```

The command that creates a new secret is as follows.

```
echo "route:
  group_by: [service,scale]
  repeat_interval: 5m
  group_interval: 5m
  receiver: 'slack'
  routes:
  - match:
      service: 'go-demo_main'
      scale: 'up'
    receiver: 'jenkins-go-demo_main-up'
  - match:
      service: 'go-demo_main'
      scale: 'down'
    receiver: 'jenkins-go-demo_main-down'
```

```
receivers:
  - name: 'slack'
    slack_configs:
      - send_resolved: true
        title: '[{{ .Status | toUpper }}] {{\
.GroupLabels.service }} service is in danger!'
        title_link: 'http://$(docker-machine ip\
 swarm-1)/monitor/alerts'
        text: '{{ .CommonAnnotations.summary}}'
        api_url: 'https://hooks.slack.com/services\
/T308SC7HD/B59ER97SS/S0KvvyStVnIt3ZWpIaLnqLCu'
  - name: 'jenkins-go-demo_main-up'
    webhook_configs:
      - send_resolved: false
        url: 'http://$(docker-machine ip swarm-\
 1)/jenkins/job/service-scale\
/buildWithParameters?token=DevOps22&service=go-demo_main&scale=1'
  - name: 'jenkins-go-demo_main-down'
    webhook_configs:
      - send_resolved: false
        url: 'http://$(docker-machine ip swarm-1)\
/jenkins/job/service-scale\
/buildWithParameters?token=DevOps22&service=go-demo_main&scale=-1'
" | docker secret create alert_manager_config -
```

We added an additional route and a receiver. Both are very similar to their counterparts in charge of scaling up. The only substantial difference is that the route match now looks for scale label with the value down and that a Jenkins build is invoked with scale parameter set to -1. As I mentioned earlier in one of the previous chapters, it is unfortunate that we need to produce so much duplication. But, since Webhook url cannot be parametrized, we need to hard-code each combination. I would encourage you, dear reader, to contribute to Alertmanager project by adding Jenkins receiver. Until then, repetition of similar configuration entries is unavoidable.

Let us deploy the monitor stack with the new configuration injected as a Docker secret:

```
DOMAIN=$(docker-machine ip swarm-1) \
    docker stack deploy \
    -c stacks/docker-flow-monitor-slack.yml \
    monitor
```

Please wait until the monitor stack is up-and-running. You can check the status of its services with docker stack ps monitor command.

While we're into creating services, we'll deploy a new definition of the go-demo stack as well.

```
docker stack deploy \
    -c stacks/go-demo-instrument-alert-2.yml \
    go-demo
```

The new definition of the stack, limited to relevant parts, is as follows.

```
...
  main:
    ...
    deploy:
      ...
      labels:
        ...
        - com.df.alertName.3=resp_time_below
        - com.df.alertIf.3=sum(rate(http_server_resp_\
time_bucket{job="my-service", le="0.025"}[5m]))\
/ sum(rate(http_server_resp_time_count{job="my-service"}[5m])) > 0.75
        - com.df.alertLabels.3=scale=down,service=go-demo_main
        ...
```

We added a new set of labels that define the alert that will send a notification that the service should be scaled down. The expression of the alert uses a similar logic as the one we're using to scale up. It calculates the percentage of responses that were created in twenty-five milliseconds or less. If the result is over 75 percent, the system has more replicas than it needs so it should be scaled down.

Since go-demo produces internal pings that are very fast, there's no need to create fake responses. The alert will fire soon.

If you doubt the new alert, we can visit the Prometheus *alerts* screen.

```
open "http://$(docker-machine ip swarm-1)/monitor/alerts"
```

The godemo_main_resp_time_below alert should be red.

Similarly, we can visit Jenkins *service-scale* job and confirm that a new build was executed.

```
open "http://$(docker-machine ip swarm-\
 1)/jenkins/blue/organizations/jenkins/service-scale/activity"
```

The output of the last step says that *go-demo_main was scaled from 3 to 2 replicas*. That might sound confusing since the previous build scaled it to four replicas. However, we re-deployed the `go-demo` stack which, among other things, specifies that the number of replicas should be three.

That leads us to an important note.

Once you adopt auto-scaling of services, you will not be able to use `docker stack deploy` commands to update services with new releases. Such actions would undo scaling and de-scaling performed by the system. Instead, you should use `docker service update --image` command to deploy new releases. Unlike `stack deploy`, `service update` changes only the specified aspect of a service, not the whole service definition.

Figure 12-10: A build of a Jenkins job that scales Docker services

Prometheus will continue firing alerts because the service is still responding faster than the defined lower limit. Since Alertmanager has both the `repeat_interval` and the `group_interval` set to five minutes, it will ignore the alerts until ten minutes expire. For more information about `repeat_interval` and `group_interval` options, please visit route (`https://prometheus.io/docs/alerting/configuration/#route`) section of Alertmanager configuration.

Once more than ten minutes pass, it will send a build request to Jenkins. This time, since the service is already using the minimum number of replicas, Jenkins will decide not to continue de-scaling and will send a notification message to Slack.

Please visit the *#df-monitor-tests* channel inside `devops20.slack.com` (`https://devops20.slack.com/`). Wait for a few minutes, and you should see a Slack notification stating that *go-demo_main could not be scaled*.

Specifying long `alertIf` labels can be daunting and error prone. Fortunately, *Docker Flow Monitor* provides shortcuts for the expressions we used.

Let's deploy the `go-demo` stack one last time.

```
docker stack deploy \
    -c stacks/go-demo-instrument-alert-short.yml \
    go-demo
```

The definition of the stack, limited to relevant parts, is as follows:

```
...
  main:
    ...
    deploy:
      ...
      labels:
        ...
        - com.df.alertIf.1=@service_mem_limit:0.8
        ...
        - com.df.alertIf.2=@resp_time_above:0.1,5m,0.99
        ...
        - com.df.alertIf.3=@resp_time_below:0.025,5m,0.75
        ...
```

This time we used shortcuts for all three alerts. `@resp_time_above:0.1,5m,0.99` was expanded into the expression that follows:

```
sum(rate(http_server_resp_time_bucket{job="my-service",
 le="0.1"}[5m])) / sum(rate(http_server_resp_time_count{job="my-\
 service"}[5m])) < 0.99'''
```

Similarly, `@resp_time_below:0.025,5m,0.75` became the following expression.

```
sum(rate(http_server_resp_time_bucket{job="my-service", \
 le="0.025"}[5m])) / sum(rate(http_server_resp_time_count{\
job="my-service"}[5m])) > 0.75 '''
```

> For more info, please visit **AlertIf Parameter Shortcuts**
> (`http://monitor.dockerflow.com/usage/#alertif-parameter-shortcut`
> `s`) section of the Docker Flow Monitor documentation.

Feel free to confirm that the alerts were correctly configured in Prometheus. They should be the same as they were before since the shortcuts expand to the same full expressions we deployed previously.

We managed to create a system that scales services depending on thresholds based on response times. It is entirely automated except if the service is already running the minimum or the maximum number of replicas. In those cases scaling probably does not help and humans need to find out what is the unexpected circumstance that generated the alerts.

We started with expected and created a fallback when unexpected happens. Next, we'll explore the situation when we start from unexpected.

Sending error notifications to slack

Errors inside our code usually fall into two groups.

There are those we are throwing to the caller function because we do not yet know how to handle it properly, or we are too lazy to implement proper recuperation from such a failure. For example, we might implement a function that reads files from a directory and returns an error if that fails. In such a case we might want to get a notification when the error occurs and do some actions to fix it.

After evaluating the problem, we might find out that the directory we're reading does not exist. Apart from the obvious fix to create the missing directory (immediate response), we should probably modify our code so that the directory is created as a result of receiving such an error. Even better, we should probably extend our code to check whether the directory exists before reading the files from it. Errors such as those fall into "I did not expect it the first time it happened, but it will not happen again" type of situations. There's nothing we would need to do outside the service. The solution depends entirely on code modifications.

Another common type of errors is related to problems with communication with other services. For example, we might get a notification that there was an error establishing communication with a database. The first action should be to fix the problem (restore DB connection). After that, we should create another set of alerts that will monitor the database itself and execute some corrective steps to fix the issue. Those metrics should not be inside the service that communicates with the database but probably coming from an exporter that is specialized with that particular database. If such an exporter does not exist, database probably has some metrics that could be transformed into Prometheus format. The alternative approach would be to ping the database periodically. We might be able to use Blackbox exporter (`https://github.com/prometheus/blackbox_exporter`) for that. If none of those options is applicable to your database, you might need to evaluate whether it is worth using something that does not have exporter, not it has metrics, nor it can be pinged.

The examples we explored do not warrant the effort of making anything more complicated than a simple notification to Slack. Self-adaptation does not apply, and self-healing depends on your code more than anything else.

Let us take a look at a few examples.

We'll continue using metrics coming from instrumentation added to the `go-demo` service. In the previous chapter you already saw the metrics with errors based on response codes, so let's deploy the updated stack with the labels that will add a new alert to *Docker Flow Monitor*.

```
docker stack deploy \
    -c stacks/go-demo-instrument-alert-error.yml \
    go-demo
```

The definition of the stack, limited to relevant parts, is as follows:

```
...
  main:
    ...
    deploy:
      ...
      labels:
        ...
#         - com.df.alertName.3=resp_time_below
#         - com.df.alertIf.3=@resp_time_below:0.025,5m,0.75
        - com.df.alertName.3=erro_rrate
        - com.df.alertIf.3=sum(rate\
(http_server_resp_time_count{job="go-demo_main",\
 code=~"^5..$$"}[5m])) / sum(rate(http_server_resp_time_count{job=\
 "go-demo_main"}[5m])) > 0.001
          - com.df.alertLabels.3=service=go-demo_main,type=errors
          - com.df.alertAnnotations.3=summary=Error rate is too\
 high,description=Do something or start panicking
        ...
```

We commented the `resp_time_below` alert because it would only create noise. Without "real" traffic, responses are too fast, and Prometheus would continuously fire alerts that would only derail us from the task at hand.

The new alert is as follows.

```
sum(rate(http_server_resp_time_count{job="go-demo_main", \
 code=~"^5..$$"}[5m])) \
/ sum(rate(http_server_resp_time_count{job="go-demo_main"}[5m]))\
 > 0.001
```

It takes the summary of all response time counts filtered by response codes that start with 5. That envelops all service side errors. That number is divided with the count of all responses thus giving us the percentage of requests that failed due to server errors. The alert will fire if the result is greater than `0.001` (0.1%). In other words, Prometheus will fire the alert if more than 0.1% of responses result in server side errors.

If you tried to write a similar alert, your first thought might have been to send an alert whenever there is an error. Don't do that! It would probably result in spam since errors are an unavoidable part of what we do. The real goal is not to be notified the system produces an error but when the rate of errors surpasses some threshold. Those thresholds will differ from one service to another. In our case, it is set to 0.1%. That does not mean that alerts should never fire after a single error. In some cases, they should. But this is not one of those. The service will produce errors, and we want to know when there are too many of them and thus discard a temporary problem or something that happened only once, but it will not repeat.

One thing you should note is that inside stack YML definition, dollar signs ($) need to be escaped with another dollar. For that reason, the part of the regular expression that should be `^5..$` is defined as `^5..$$`.

Let us open the Prometheus' alert screen and confirm that the new alert is indeed registered.

```
open "http://$(docker-machine ip swarm-1)/monitor/alerts"
```

Among others, there should be the `godemo_main_error_rate` alert marked as green thus indicating that the percentage of server error rate is below 0.1%.

We do not need to change Alertmanager configuration. It is already configured to send all alerts to Slack unless they match one of the routes.

Let us generate a few responses with fake errors and see whether the system works.

```
for i in {1..100}; do
    curl "http://$(docker-machine ip swarm-1)/demo/random-error"
done
```

Around ten out of those hundred requests should result in errored responses. That's just enough to confirm that the alerts work as expected.

Let's go back to the alerts screen.

```
open "http://$(docker-machine ip swarm-1)/monitor/alerts"
```

This time *godemo_main_error_rate* should be red indicating that Prometheus fired it to Alertmanager which, in turn, sent a Slack notification. Please visit the #df-monitor-tests channel inside `devops20.slack.com` (`https://devops20.slack.com/`) and confirm that the notification was indeed sent. The message should say *[FIRING] go-demo_main service is in danger!*.

If this would not be a simulation, your immediate action should be to go back to Prometheus and query metrics in search of the cause of the problem. The expression could be as follows.

```
sum(rate(http_server_resp_time_count{job="go-demo_main",\
  code=~"^5..$$"}[5m])) by (path)
```

By grouping data by path, we can discover which one generated those errors and relate it to the code that is in charge of that path. That would get us a step closer to the discovery of the cause of the problem. The rest would greatly differ from one case to another. Maybe we'd need to consult logs, make more queries in Prometheus, find out which node is causing the problem, correlate data with network information, and so on and so forth. No one can give you exact set of steps that should be followed in all cases. The most important part is that you know that there is an error, which service generated it, and what is the path of the requests behind it. You're on your own for the rest.

All the metrics we used so far have their shortcuts that let us write a more concise stack definition. The error rate is no exception. An example can be found in the stack `stacks/go-demo-instrument-alert-short-2.yml`. The definition, limited to relevant parts, is as follows:

```
...
  main:
    ...
    deploy:
      ...
      labels:
        ...
        - com.df.alertName.3=errorate
        - com.df.alertIf.3=@resp_time_server_error:5m,0.001
        ...
```

The system we built in this chapter can be described through the diagram in the following figure:

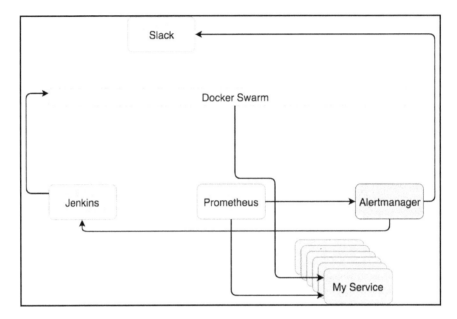

Figure 12-11: Alerts fired to Jenkins and Slack

What now?

Did we finish with self-adaptation applied to services? We're not even close. The exercises we passed through should give you only the base you'll need to extend and adapt to your specific use-cases. I hope that now you know what to do. What you need now, more than anything else, is time. Instrument your services, start scraping metrics, create alerts based both on exporters and instrumentation, start receiving notifications, and observe the patterns. The system should start small and grow organically.

Do not create a project out of the lessons you learned but adopt continuous improvement. Every alert is not only a potential problem but also an opportunity to make the system better and more robust.

The following figure provides a high-level overview of the system we built so far. Use it as a way to refresh your memory with everything we learned by now:

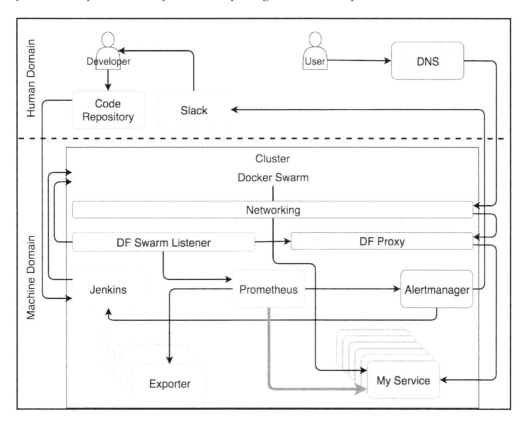

Figure 12-12: Self-healing and self-adapting system (so far)

The time has come to take another rest. Destroy the cluster and recharge your batteries. There's still a lot left to do.

```
docker-machine rm \
    -f swarm-1 swarm-2 swarm-3
```

13
Setting Up a Production Cluster

We explored quite a few techniques, processes, and tools that can help us build a self-sufficient system applied to services. Docker Swarm provides self-healing, and we created our own system for self-adaptation. By now, we should be fairly confident with our services and the time has come to explore how to accomplish similar goals applied to infrastructure.

The system should be capable of recreating failed nodes, of upgrading without downtime, and to scale servers depending on the fluctuating needs. We cannot explore those topics using clusters based on Docker machine nodes running locally. The capacity of our laptops is somewhat limited so we cannot scale nodes to a greater number. Even if we could, the infrastructure we'll use for production clusters is quite different. We'll need an API that will allow our system to communicate with infrastructure. Moreover, we did not have an opportunity to explore persistent storage of the services we used thus far. Those few examples are only a fraction of what we'll need, and we won't enter into details just yet. For now, we'll try to create a production-ready cluster that will allow us to continue on our path towards a self-sufficient system.

The immediate goal is to transition from locally running Swarm cluster based on Docker machines into something more reliable. We'll have to move into the cloud.

There are too many hosting vendors we could choose from, and it would be impossible to explain the process for each one of them. Even if we would focus only on those that are very popular, we would still have at least 10 vendors to go through. That would increase the scope of the book beyond manageable size so we'll pick one hosting provider that we'll use to demonstrate a setup of a production cluster. It had to be one and AWS is the most commonly used hosting vendor.

Depending on your current choice of a vendor, you might be very happy or extremely displeased with that. If you prefer using Microsoft Azure (https://azure.microsoft.com/en-us/?v=18.02), you'll see that you'll be able to follow the same steps as those we'll explore for AWS. The chances are that you prefer **Google Compute Engine** (**GCE**) (https://cloud.google.com/compute/), Digital Ocean (https://www.digitalocean.com/), OpenStack (https://www.openstack.org/) running on-premise, or any other among thousands of solutions and vendors. I'll do my best to explain the logic behind the setup we'll do in AWS. Hopefully, you should be able to apply the same logic to your infrastructure. I'll try to make it clear what you should do, and I'll expect you to roll-up your sleeves and do it on your own. I'll provide a blueprint, and you'll do the work.

You might be tempted to start translating the exercises that follow to your hosting solution. Don't! If you do not have it already, please create an account on **Amazon Web Services** (**AWS**) (https://aws.amazon.com/) and follow the instructions as they are. By doing that, you should have a clear idea of what can be done and what is the path to take. Only after that, once you're finished reading this book, you should try to translate the experience into your infrastructure. From my side, I'll do my best to explain everything we'll do in AWS in a way that the same principles can be translated to any other choice. Moreover, I'll do my best to keep AWS costs to a minimum.

I strongly advise against using corporate AWS accounts. They are often enhanced with security restrictions that might prevent you from having a smooth experience. Use your private AWS account instead or create one if you don't have it already. Later on, once you're comfortable with the solution, you should not have much of a problem to adapt it to your corporate environment.

That was more than enough talk. We'll move into a hands-on part of this chapter and create a Docker Swarm cluster. Once it's up-and-running, we'll proceed with deployment of all the services we used so far. Finally, we'll discuss which services might be missing and which modifications we should do to our stacks to make them production-ready. Let's go!

Creating a Docker for AWS cluster

In the book, *The DevOps 2.1 Toolkit: Docker Swarm*
(`https://www.amazon.com/dp/1542468914`), I argued that the best way to create a Swarm cluster in AWS is with a combination of Packer (`https://www.packer.io/`) and Terraform (`https://www.terraform.io/`). One of the alternatives was to use Docker CE for AWS (`https://store.docker.com/editions/community/docker-ce-aws`). At that time *Docker for AWS* was too immature. Today, the situation is different. *Docker for AWS* provides a robust Docker Swarm cluster with most, if not all the services we would expect from it.

We'll create a *Docker for AWS* cluster and, while in progress, discuss some of its aspects.

Before we start creating a cluster, we should choose a region. The only thing that truly matters is whether a region of your choice supports at least three **Availability Zones** (**AZ**). If there's only one availability zone, we'll risk downtime if it would become unavailable. With two availability zones, we'd lose Docker manager's quorum if one zone would go down. Just as we should always run an odd number of Docker managers, we should spread our cluster into an odd number of availability zones. Three is a good number. It fits most of the scenarios.

In case you're new to AWS, an availability zone is an isolated location inside a region. Each region is made up of one or more availability zones. Each AZ is isolated, but AZs in a region are connected through low-latency links. Isolation between AZs provides high-availability. A cluster spread across multiple AZs would continue operating even if a whole AZ goes down. When using AZs inside the same region, latency is low thus not affecting the performance. All in all, we should always run a cluster across multiple AZs within the same region.

Let's check whether your favorite AWS region has at least three availability zones. Please open EC2 screen (`https://console.aws.amazon.com/ec2/v2/home`) from the *AWS console*. You'll see one of the availability zones selected in the top-right corner of the screen. If that's not the location you'd like to use for your cluster, click on it to change it.

Scroll down to the *Service Health* section. You'll find *Availability Zone Status* inside it. If there are at least three zones listed, the region you selected is OK. Otherwise, please change the region and check one more time whether there are at least three availability zones.

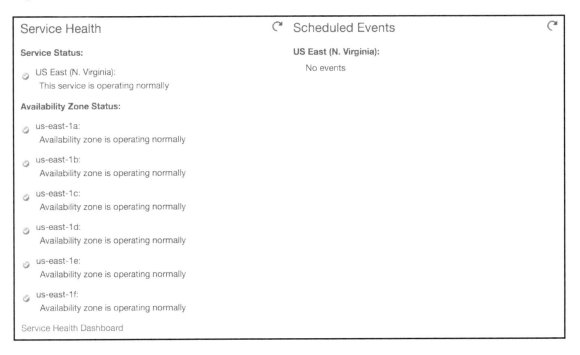

Figure 13-1: The list of availability zones supported by the US East region

There's one more prerequisite we need to fulfill before we create a cluster. We need to create an SSH key. Without it, we would not be able to access any of the nodes that form the cluster.

Please go back to the *AWS console* and click the **Key Pairs** link from the left-hand menu. Click the **Create Key Pair** button, type `devops22` as the *Key pair name*, and, finally, click the **Create** button. The newly created SSH key will be downloaded to your system. Please copy it to the `docker-flow-monitor` directory. The project already has `/*.pem` entry in the `.gitignore` file so your key will not be accidentally committed to GitHub. Still, as an additional precaution, we should make sure that only you can read the contents of the file.

All the commands from this chapter are available in the `13-production-cluster.sh` Gist at `https://gist.github.com/vfarcic/5f87855e2a31b23af01eca9e3f8c2efe`.

```
chmod 400 devops22.pem
```

Now we are ready to create the cluster. Please open `https://store.docker.com/editions/community/docker-ce-aws` in your favorite browser and click the **Get Docker** button.

You might be asked to log in to *AWS console*. The region should be set to the one you chose previously. If it isn't, please change it by clicking the name of the current region (For example, *N. Virginia*) button located in the top-right section of the screen.

We can proceed once you're logged in, and the desired region is selected. Please click the **Next** button located at the bottom of the screen. You will be presented with the **Specify Details** screen.

Please type `devops22` as the *Stack name*.

We'll leave the number of managers set to three, but we'll change the number of workers to `0`. For now, we will not need more nodes. We can always increase the number of workers later on if such a need arises. For now, we'll go with a minimal setup.

Please select **devops22** as the answer to **Which SSH key to use?**.

We'll do the opposite from the default values for the rest of the fields in the **Swarm Properties** section.

We do want to *enable daily resource cleanup* so we'll change it to **yes**. That way, our cluster will be nice and clean most of the time since Docker will prune it periodically.

We will select **no** as the value of the **Use CloudWatch for container logging?** drop-box. CloudWatch is very limiting. There are much better and cheaper solutions for storing logs, and we'll explore them soon.

Finally, please select **yes** as the value of the **Create EFS prerequisites for CloudStor** drop-box. The setup process will make sure that all the requirements for the usage of EFS are created and thus speed up the process of mounting network drives.

We should select the type of instances. One option could be to use *t2.micro* which is one of the free tiers. However, in my experience, *t2.micro* is just too small. *1 GB* memory and *1***virtual CPU* (**vCPU**) is not enough for some of the services we'll run. We'll use *t2.small* instead. With *2 GB* of memory and *1* vCPU, it is still very small and would not be suitable for "real" production usage. However, it should be enough for the exercises we'll run throughout the rest of this chapter.

Please select *t2.small* as both the *Swarm manager instance type* and *Agent worker instance type* values. Even though we're not creating any workers, we might choose to add some later on so having the proper size set in advance might be a good idea. We might discover that we need bigger nodes later on. Still, any aspect of the cluster is easy to modify, so there's no reason to aim for perfection from the start.

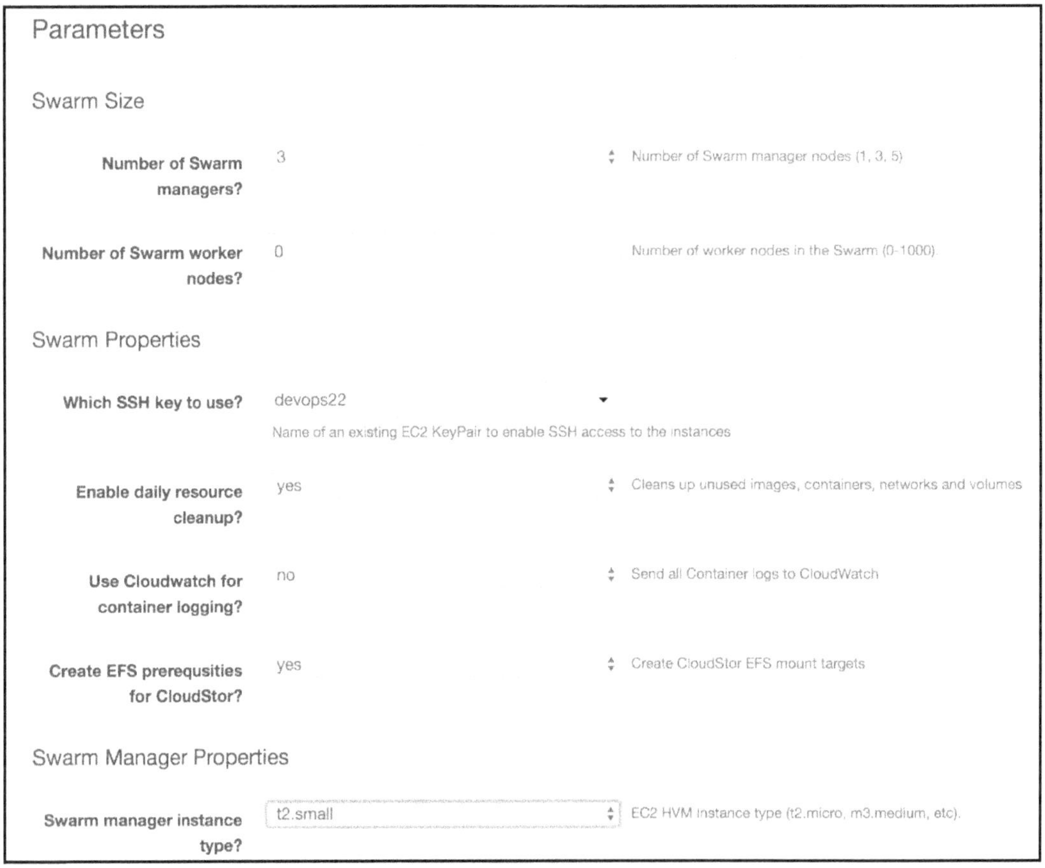

Parameters

Swarm Size

| Number of Swarm managers? | 3 | Number of Swarm manager nodes (1, 3, 5) |
| Number of Swarm worker nodes? | 0 | Number of worker nodes in the Swarm (0-1000). |

Swarm Properties

Which SSH key to use?	devops22	Name of an existing EC2 KeyPair to enable SSH access to the instances
Enable daily resource cleanup?	yes	Cleans up unused images, containers, networks and volumes
Use Cloudwatch for container logging?	no	Send all Container logs to CloudWatch
Create EFS prerequsities for CloudStor?	yes	Create CloudStor EFS mount targets

Swarm Manager Properties

| Swarm manager instance type? | t2.small | EC2 HVM Instance type (t2.micro, m3.medium, etc). |

Figure 13-2: Docker For AWS Parameters screen

Please click the **Next** button. You'll be presented with the **Options** screen. We won't modify any of the available options so please click the **Next** button on this screen as well.

We reached the last screen of the setup. It shows the summary of all the options we chose. Please go through the information and confirm that everything is set to the correct values. Once you're done, click the **I acknowledge that AWS CloudFormation might create IAM resources** checkbox followed by the **Create** button.

It'll take around ten to fifteen minutes for the CloudFormation to finish creating all the resources. We can use that time to comment on a few of them. If you plan to transfer this knowledge to a different hosting solution, you'll probably need to replicate the same types of resources and the processes behind them. The list of all the resources created by the template can be found by selecting the **devops22** stack and clicking the **Resources** tab. Please click the **Restore** icon from the bottom-right part of the page if you don't see the tabs located at the bottom of the screen.

We won't comment on all the resources *Docker for AWS* template creates but only on the few that are crucial if you'd like to replicate a similar setup with a different vendor.

VPC (**Virtual Private Cloud**) makes the system secured by closing all but a few externally accessible ports. The only port open by default is 22 required for SSH access. All others are locked down. Even the port 22 is not open directly but through a load balancer.

ELB (**Elastic Load Balancer**) is sitting on top of the cluster. In the beginning, it forwards only SSH traffic. However, it is configured in a way that forwarding will be added to the ELB every time we create a service that publishes a port. As a result, any service with a published port will be accessible through *ELB* only. The load balancer itself cannot (in its current setting) forward requests based on their paths, domains, and other information from their headers. It does (a kind of) layer 4 load balancing that uses only port as the forwarding criteria. It does a similar job as the ingress network. That, in itself, is not very useful if all your services are routed through a layer 7 proxy like Docker Flow Proxy (http://proxy.dockerflow.com/), and since it lacks proper routing, it cannot replace it. However, the more important feature ELB provides is load balancing across healthy nodes. It provides a DNS that we can use to setup our domain's *C Name* entries. No matter whether a node fails or is replaced during upgrades, ELB will always forward requests to one of the healthy nodes.

EFS (**Elastic File System**) will provide network drives we'll use to persist stateful services that do not have replication capabilities. It can be replaced with **EBS** (**Elastic Block Storage**). Each has advantages and disadvantages. EFS volumes can be used across multiple availability zones thus allowing us to move services from one to another without any additional steps. However, EFS is slower than EBS so, if IO speed is of the essence, it might not be the best choice. EBS, on the other hand, is opposite. It is faster than EFS, but it cannot be used across multiple AZs. If a replica needs to be moved from one to another, a data snapshot needs to be created first and restored on the EBS volume created in a different AZ.

ASGs (**Auto-Scaling Groups**) provide an effortless way to scale (or de-scale) nodes. It will be essential in our quest for self-healing system applied to infrastructure.

Overlay Network, even though it is not unique to AWS, envelops all the nodes of the cluster and provides communication between services.

Dynamo DB is used to store information about the primary manager. That information is changed if the node hosting the primary manager goes down and a different one is promoted. When a new node is added to the cluster, it uses information from Dynamo DB to find out the location of the primary manager and join itself to the cluster.

The cluster, limited to the most significant resources, can be described through the following figure:

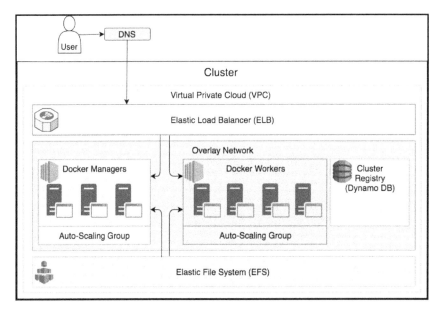

Figure 13-3: Simplified diagram with the key services created through the Docker For AWS template

By this time, the cluster should be up and running and waiting for us to deploy the first stack. We can confirm that it is finished by checking the **Status** column of the *devops22* CloudFormation stack. We're all set if the value is CREATE_COMPLETE. If it isn't, please wait a few more minutes until the last round of resources is created.

We'll need to retrieve a few pieces of information before we proceed. We'll need to know the DNS of the newly created cluster as well as the IP of one of the manager nodes.

All the information we need is in the **Outputs** tab. Please go there and copy the value of the **DefaultDNSTarget** key. We'll paste it into an environment variable. That will allow us to avoid coming back to this screen every time we need to use the DNS.

```
CLUSTER_DNS=[...]
```

Please change [...] with the actual DNS of your cluster.

You should map your domain to that DNS in a "real" world situation. But, for the sake of simplicity, we'll skip that part and use the DNS provided by AWS.

The only thing left before we enter the cluster is to get the IP of one of the managers. Please click the link next to the *Managers* key. You will be presented with the **EC2 Instances** screen that lists all the manager nodes of the cluster. Select any of them and copy the value of the **IPv4 Public IP** key.

Just as with DNS, we'll set that value as an environment variable.

```
CLUSTER_IP=[...]
```

Please change [...] with the actual public IP of one of the manager nodes.

The moment of truth has come. Does our cluster indeed work? Let's check it out.

```
ssh -i devops22.pem docker@$CLUSTER_IP

docker node ls
```

We entered into one of the manager nodes and executed docker node ls. The output of the latter command is as follows (IDs are removed for brevity).

```
HOSTNAME                      STATUS AVAILABILITY MANAGER STATUS
ip-172-31-2-46.ec2.internal   Ready  Active       Reachable
ip-172-31-35-26.ec2.internal  Ready  Active       Leader
ip-172-31-19-176.ec2.internal Ready  Active       Reachable
```

As you can see, all three nodes are up and running and joined into a single Docker Swarm cluster. Even though this looks like a simple cluster, many things are going on in the background, and we'll explore many of the cluster features later on. For now, we'll concentrate on only a few observations.

The nodes we're running has an OS created by Docker and designed with only one goal. It runs containers, and nothing else. We cannot install packages directly. The benefits such an OS brings are related mainly to stability and performance. An OS designed with a specific goal is often more effective than general distributions capable of fulfilling all needs. Those often end up being fine at many things but not excellent with any. Docker's OS is optimized for containers, and that makes it more stable. When there are no things we don't use, there are fewer things that can cause trouble. In this case, the only thing we need is Docker Server (or Engine). Whatever else we might need must be deployed as a container. The truth is that we do not need much with Docker. A few things that we do need are already available.

Let's take a quick look at the containers running on this node.

```
docker container ls -a
```

The output is as follows (IDs are removed for brevity):

```
 1   IMAGE                                     COMMAND                CREATED        \
 2   STATUS          PORTS                     NAMES
 3   docker4x/l4controller-aws:17.06.0-ce-aws2 "loadbalancer run ..." 10 minutes ago \
 4   Up 10 minutes                             l4controller-aws
 5   docker4x/meta-aws:17.06.0-ce-aws2         "metaserver -iaas_..." 10 minutes ago \
 6   Up 10 minutes 172.31.19.205:9024->8080/tcp meta-aws
 7   docker4x/guide-aws:17.06.0-ce-aws2        "/entry.sh"            10 minutes ago \
 8   Up 10 minutes                             guide-aws
 9   docker4x/shell-aws:17.06.0-ce-aws2        "/entry.sh /usr/sb..." 10 minutes ago \
10   Up 10 minutes 0.0.0.0:22->22/tcp          shell-aws
11   docker4x/init-aws:17.06.1-ce-aws1         "/entry.sh"            10 minutes ago \
12   Exited (0) 10 minutes ago                 lucid_leakey
```

We'll explore those containers only briefly so that we understand their high level purposes.

The *l4controller-aws* container is in charge of ELB. It monitors services and updates load balancer whenever a service that publishes a port is created, updated, or removed. You'll see the ELB integration in action soon. For now, the important part to note is that we do not need to worry what happens when a node goes down nor we need to update security groups when a new port needs to be opened. ELB and *l4controller-aws* containers are making sure those things are always up-to-date.

The *meta-aws* container provides general server metadata to the rest of the swarm cluster. Its main purpose is to provide tokens for members to join a Swarm cluster.

The *guide-aws* container is in charge of house keeping. It removes unused images, stopped containers, volumes, and so on. On top of those responsibilities, it updates Dynamo DB with information about managers and a few other things.

The *shell-aws* container provides Shell, FPT, SSH, and a few other essential tools. When we entered the node we're in right now, we actually entered this container. We're not running commands (that is, `docker container ls`) from the OS but from inside this container. The OS is so specialized that it does not even have SSH.

The *lucid_leakey* (your name might be different) is based on *docker4x/init-aws* might be the most interesting system container. It was run, did its job, and exited. It has only one purpose. It discovered the IP and the token of the primary manager and joined the node to the cluster. With that process in place, we can add more nodes whenever we need them knowing that they will join the cluster automatically. If a node fails, the auto-scaling group will create a new one which will, through this container, join the cluster.

We did not explore all of the features of the cluster. We'll postpone the discussion for the next chapter when we explore self-healing capabilities of the cluster and, later on, self-adaptation. Instead, we'll proceed by deploying the services we used in the previous chapters. The immediate goal is to reach the same state as the one we left in the previous chapter. The only real difference, for now, will be that the services will run on a production-ready cluster.

Deploying services

We'll start by deploying the stacks we used so far. We will not modify them in any form or way but deploy them as they are. Further on, we'll explore what modifications we should add to those stacks to make them more production-ready.

We'll execute `scripts/aws-services.sh` (`https://github.com/vfarcic/docker-flow-monitor/blob/master/scripts/aws-services.sh`) script that contains all the commands we used thus far.

Please replace [...] with the DNS of your cluster.

```
export CLUSTER_DNS=[...]

curl -o aws-services.sh \
    https://raw.githubusercontent.com/vfarcic/docker-\
flow-monitor/master/scripts/aws-services.sh

chmod +x aws-services.sh
```

The commands we executed created the environment variable CLUSTER_DNS, downloaded the script, and assigned it execute permissions.

We won't go into details of the script since it deploys the same stacks we used before. Feel free to explore it yourself.

Now we can execute the script which will deploy the familiar stacks and services.

```
./aws-services.sh

docker stack ls
```

We executed the script and listed all the stacks we deployed with it. The output of the docker stack ls command is as follows.

```
NAME              SERVICES
exporter          3
go-demo           2
jenkins           2
monitor           3
proxy             2
```

You should be familiar with all those stacks. At this moment, the services in our AWS cluster behave in the same way as when we deployed them to Docker machine clusters. As you might have guessed, there are a few things we're still missing before those services can be considered production-ready.

The first problem we'll tackle is security.

Securing services

There's not much reason to secure internal services that do not publish any ports. Such services are usually intended to be accessed by other services that are attached to the same internal network. For example, the `go-demo` stack deploys two services. One of them is the `db` service that can be accessed only by the other service from the stack (`main`). We accomplished that by having both services attached to the same network and by not publishing any ports.

The main objective should be to secure communication between clients outside your cluster and services residing inside. We usually accomplish that by adding SSL certificates to a proxy and, potentially, disabling HTTP communication. *Docker Flow Proxy* makes that an easy task. If you haven't set up your SSL, you might want to explore Configuring SSL Certificates (`http://proxy.dockerflow.com/certs/`) tutorial.

There are quite a few ways to get certificates, but the one that sticks above the crowd is Let's Encrypt (`https://letsencrypt.org/`). It's free and commonly used by a massive community. Two projects integrate *Let's Encrypt* with *Docker Flow Proxy*. You can find them in GitHub repositories `n1b0r/docker-flow-proxy-letsencrypt` (`https://github.com/n1b0r/docker-flow-proxy-letsencrypt`) and `hamburml/docker-flow-letsencrypt` (`https://github.com/hamburml/docker-flow-letsencrypt`) They use different approaches to obtain certificates and pass them to the proxy. I urge not to explore both before making a decision which one to use (if any).

Unfortunately, we won't be able to set up certificates since we do not have a valid domain. Let's Encrypt would not allow us to use DNS name AWS gave us and I could not know in advance whether you have a domain name you could use for this exercise. So, we'll skip the examples of how to set up it on your own. Feel free to reach me on DevOps20 (`http://slack.devops20toolkit.com/`) Slack channel if you have a question or you run into a problem.

Encryption is only a part of what we need to do to secure our services. One of the obvious things we're missing is authentication.

Let us review the publicly available services we're currently running inside our cluster and discuss the authentication strategies we might apply.

We'll start with Jenkins.

```
exit

open "http://$CLUSTER_DNS/jenkins"
```

Jenkins service was created from a custom built image that already has an admin user set through Docker secrets. That was a great first step that allowed us to skip the manual setup and, at the same time, have a relatively secure initial experience. However, we need more. Potentially, every member of our organization should be able to access Jenkins. We could add them all as users of Jenkins' internal registry, but that would prove to be too much work for anything but small teams.

Fortunately, Jenkins allows authentication through almost any provider. All you have to do is install and configure one of the authentication plugins. GitHub Authentication (`https://plugins.jenkins.io/github-oauth`), Google Login (`https://plugins.jenkins.io/google-login`), LDAP (`https://plugins.jenkins.io/ldap`), and Gitlab Authentication (`https://plugins.jenkins.io/gitlab-oauth`) are only a few among many other available solutions.

We won't go into details how to setup a "proper" authentication since there are too many of them and I cannot predict which one would suit your needs. In most cases, following the instructions on the plugin page should be more than enough to get you up and running in no time. For now, it is important that the image we're running is secured by default with the user we defined through Docker secrets and that you can easily replace it with authentication through one of the plugins. The current setup allows any user to see the jobs, but only the administrator to create new ones, to build them, or to update them.

Let's move to Prometheus and explore how to secure it with authentication.

While Jenkins that has both its internal credentials storage as well as the ability to connect to many third-party credential providers, Prometheus has neither. There is no internal authentication, nor it has a built-in ability to integrate with an external authentication service. All that does not mean that everything is lost. Prometheus holds metrics of your cluster and the services inside it. Metrics have labels, and they might keep confidential information. It needs to be protected, and the only option is to deny external access to the service or to authenticate requests before they reach it. The first option would entail VPN and black-listing Prometheus domain or some other method that would deny access to anyone but those inside the VPN. The alternative is to use authentication gateway or instruct the proxy to request authentication. We won't go into a discussion of pros and cons of each method since it often depends on personal preferences, the company culture, and the existing infrastructure. Instead, we'll roll with the simplest solution. We'll instruct the proxy to authenticate requests to Prometheus.

```
ssh -i devops22.pem docker@$CLUSTER_IP

curl -o proxy.yml \
    https://raw.githubusercontent.com/vfarcic/docker-flow-\
```

```
monitor/master/stacks/docker-flow-proxy-aws.yml

cat proxy.yml
```

We entered the cluster, downloaded a new proxy stack and displayed its content. The output of the `cat` command, limited to relevant parts, is as follows.

```
...
  proxy:
    ...
    secrets:
      - dfp_users_admin
    ...

secrets:
  dfp_users_admin:
    external: true
```

We added Docker secret `dfp_users_admin`. We'll use it to store username and password we'll use later one with services that require authentication through the proxy.

Now that we know that the stack requires a secret, we can create it and redeploy the services.

```
echo "admin:admin" | docker secret \
    create dfp_users_admin -

docker stack deploy -c proxy.yml \
    proxy
```

We piped the value `admin:admin` to the command that created the `dfp_users_admin` secret and deployed the new definition of the stack. All that's left now is to update the *monitor* service by adding a few labels that will tell the proxy that the service requires authentication using the credentials from the secret we created.

```
curl -o monitor.yml \
    https://raw.githubusercontent.com/vfarcic/docker-\
flow-monitor/master/stacks/docker-flow-monitor-user.yml

cat monitor.yml
```

We downloaded a new monitor stack and displayed its content. The output, limited to relevant parts, is as follows.

```
    . . .
      monitor:
        . . .
        deploy:
          labels:
            - com.df.usersPassEncrypted=false
            - com.df.usersSecret=admin
          . . .
```

Docker Flow Proxy uses a naming convention to resolve names of Docker secrets that contain users and passwords. The value of the `userSecret` parameter will be prepended with `dfp_users_` thus matching the name of the secret we created a moment ago. We used the `usersPassEncrypted` parameter to tell the proxy that the credentials are not encrypted. Please check HTTP Mode Query Parameters (`http://proxy.dockerflow.com/usage/#http-mode-query-parameters`) section of the documentation for more details and additional options.

The monitor stack requires the DNS of our cluster so we'll define it as environment variable `CLUSTER_DNS`. Please replace `[...]` with the `CLUSTER_DNS` value obtained from the variable defined locally.

```
exit

echo $CLUSTER_DNS

ssh -i devops22.pem docker@$CLUSTER_IP

CLUSTER_DNS=[...]
```

We exited the cluster so that we can output the value of the `CLUSTER_DNS` variable we created locally, entered back, and defined the same variable inside one of the nodes of the cluster. Those commands might seem like overkill but, in my case, they are easier than opening CloudFormation UI and looking for the outputs. You probably guessed by now that I prefer doing as much as possible from the command line.

Now we can deploy the updated stack.

```
DOMAIN=$CLUSTER_DNS docker stack \
    deploy -c monitor.yml monitor
```

Before we check whether authentication is indeed applied, we should wait for a moment or two until all the services of the stack are up-and-running. You can check the status by executing `docker stack ps monitor` command.

All that's left now is to open Prometheus and authenticate.

```
exit
```

```
open "http://$CLUSTER_DNS/monitor"
```

We exited the cluster and opened Prometheus in our default browser. This time we were asked to enter username and password before being redirected to the UI. Authentication works! While it might not be a perfect solution (nothing is), it is more secure than it was a moment ago when anyone could enter Prometheus.

Now we can try to solve one more problem. Our cluster runs a few stateful services that might need to be persisted somewhere.

Persisting state

What shall we do with the stateful services inside our cluster? If any of them fails and Swarm reschedules it, the state will be lost. Even if impossible happens and none of the replicas of the service ever fail, sooner or later we'll have to upgrade the cluster. That means that existing nodes will be replaced with new images and Swarm will have to reschedule your services to the new nodes. In other words, services will fail or be rescheduled, and we might need to persist state when they are stateful.

Let us go through each of the stateful services we're currently running inside our cluster.

The obvious case of stateful services is databases. We are running MongoDB. Should we persist its state? Many would answer positively to that question. I'll argue against persisting data on disk. Instead, we should create a replica set with at least three MongoDBs. That way, data would be replicated across multiple instances, and a failure of one or even two of them would not mean a loss of data.

Unfortunately, MongoDB is not a container-friendly database (almost none of the DBs are) so scaling Mongo service to a few replicas will not do the trick. We'd need to create three services and do some custom plumbing. It's nothing too complicated, and yet it's not what we're used to with Docker Swarm services. We won't go into details how to setup Mongo replica-set inside Docker services. I'll leave that up to your Google-ing skills. The important note I tried to convey is that we do not always need to persist state. If stateful service can replicate state across different instances, there might not be a need to store that state on a network drive as well.

Moving on...

Docker Flow Proxy is also a stateful service. It uses HAProxy which uses file system for its configuration. Since we are changing that configuration whenever a service is created, updated, or removed, we can consider that configuration as its state. If it gets lost, *Docker Flow Proxy* would not be able to forward requests to all our public facing services.

Fortunately, there's no need to persist proxy state either. *Docker Flow Swarm Listener* sends service notifications to all proxy replicas. On the other hand, when a new replica of the proxy is created, the first thing it does is to request all the info it needs from the listener. All in all, if we ignore possible bugs, all the replicas of the proxy should always be up-to-date and with identical configuration. In other words, there's one less stateful service to worry.

Moving on...

Prometheus is also a stateful service. However, it cannot be scaled so its state cannot be replicated among its instances. It is a good example of a service that needs to persist its data on disk.

Let's open Prometheus flags screen and see the checkpoint interval.

```
open "http://$CLUSTER_DNS/monitor/flags"
```

You'll see a property called `storage.local.checkpoint-interval` set to `5m0s`. Prometheus will flush its state to a file every five minutes.

By now, you should have a decent amount of data stored in Prometheus. We can confirm that by opening the graph screen.

```
open "http://$CLUSTER_DNS/monitor/graph"
```

Please type the query that follows into the **Expression** field.

```
container_memory_usage_bytes{container_label_com_docker_swarm_service_n
ame!=""}
```

Click the **Execute** button followed with a switch to the **Graph** tab. You should see the memory usage of each container in the cluster. However, the reason we got here is not to admire metrics but to demonstrate state persistence.

Let's see what happens when we simulate a failure of the service.

```
ssh -i devops22.pem docker@$CLUSTER_IP

docker service scale monitor_monitor=0

docker service scale monitor_monitor=1

exit
```

We entered the cluster, scaled the service to zero replicas, scaled it back to one, and exited. That was probably the fastest way to simulate a failure.

Let's go back to the graph screen.

```
open "http://$CLUSTER_DNS/monitor/graph"
```

If Prometheus does not load, you might need to wait for a few moments and refresh the screen.

Repeat the execution of the same query like the one we used a short while ago.

```
container_memory_usage_bytes{container_label_com_docker_swarm_service_n
ame!=""}
```

You should notice that metrics are gone. You might have a minute or two of data. Those from before the failure simulation are gone.

Let's download a new version of the monitor stack and see how it solves our persistence problem.

```
ssh -i devops22.pem docker@$CLUSTER_IP
curl -o monitor.yml \
    https://raw.githubusercontent.com/vfarcic/docker-flow-\
    monitor/master/stacks/docker-flow-monitor-aws.yml
cat monitor.yml
```

We entered into the cluster and downloaded an updated version of the `monitor` stack. The output of the `cat` command, limited to relevant parts, is as follows.

```
...
  monitor:
    image: vfarcic/docker-flow-monitor
    environment:
      - ARG_STORAGE_LOCAL_PATH=/data
      ...
    volumes:
      - prom:/data
      ...

volumes:
  prom:
    driver: cloudstor:aws
    external: false
```

We specified the storage path using the environment variable `ARG_STORAGE_LOCAL_PATH`, mapped `prom` volume to the directory `/data`, and defined the volume with the driver `cloudstor:aws`.

The `cloudstor` driver was developed by Docker specifically for usage in AWS and Azure. It will create a network drive (in this case EFS) and attach it to the service. Since the `prom` volume has `external` set to `false`, the volume will be created automatically when we deploy the stack. Otherwise, we'd need to execute `docker volume create` command first.

Let's deploy the new stack. Please make sure to replace `[...]` with the value of the `CLUSTER_DNS` variable defined locally (the second command):

```
exit
echo $CLUSTER_DNS
ssh -i devops22.pem docker@$CLUSTER_IP
CLUSTER_DNS=[...]
DOMAIN=$CLUSTER_DNS docker stack \
    deploy -c monitor.yml monitor
```

We exited the cluster only to output the DNS, went back, created `CLUSTER_DNS` variable, and deployed the new stack.

Now we should wait for a while so that Prometheus can accumulate some metrics. If we repeat the failure simulation right away, we would not be able to confirm whether data is persisted or not. Instead, you should grab a coffee and come back in ten minutes or more. That should be enough for a checkpoint or two to flush data to disk.

Now, after a while, we can repeat the failure simulation steps and verify whether data is indeed persisted across failures.

```
docker service scale monitor_monitor=0

docker service scale monitor_monitor=1
```

We changed the number of replicas to zero only to increase them to one a few moments later. As a result, Swarm created a new instance of the service.

Let's go back to the graph screen and confirm that the data survived the failure.

```
exit

open "http://$CLUSTER_DNS/monitor/graph"
```

Please type the query that follows in the **Expression** field, click the **Execute** button, and switch to the **Graph** tab.

```
container_memory_usage_bytes{container_label_com_docker_swarm_service_n
ame!=""}
```

You should see that metrics go back in time longer then the duration of the newly scheduled replica. Data persistence works! Partly... Prometheus is an in-memory database. It keeps all the metrics in memory and periodically flushes them to disk. It is not designed to be transactional but fast. We might have lost some data that was scraped between the last checkpoint and the (simulated) failure of the service. However, that, in most cases, is not a real problem since metrics are supposed to show us tendencies, not every single transaction. If you compare the graphs from before and after the (simulated) crash, you'll notice that they are, more or less, the same even though some data might be lost.

We have one more service left to fix.

Jenkins is also a stateful service. It stores its state as files. They are, in a way, its database, and we need to persist them.

Let's download a new Jenkins stack.

```
ssh -i devops22.pem docker@$CLUSTER_IP

curl -o jenkins.yml \
    https://raw.githubusercontent.com/vfarcic/docker-\
flow-monitor/master/stacks/jenkins-aws.yml

cat jenkins.yml
```

The output of the `cat` command, limited to relevant parts, is as follows.

```
  ...
    master:
      ...
      volumes:
        - master:/var/jenkins_home
      ...

  volumes:
    master:
      driver: cloudstor:aws
      external: false
```

By now, all the additions should be familiar. We defined a volume called `master` and mapped it to Jenkins home directory. Further down, we defined the `master` volume to use `cloudstor:aws` driver and set `external` to `false` so that `docker stack deploy` command can take care of creating the volume.

We'll deploy the new stack before checking whether persistence works.

```
docker stack deploy -c jenkins.yml \
    Jenkins

docker stack ps jenkins
```

It will take a couple of minutes until the volume is created, the image is pulled, and Jenkins process inside the container is initialized. You'll know that Jenkins is initialized when you see the message `INFO: Jenkins is fully up and running` in its logs. Use `docker service logs jenkins_master` command to see the output.

Now that Jenkins is initialized and uses EFS to store its state, we should confirm that persistence indeed works. We'll do that by creating a new job, shutting down Jenkins, letting Swarm reschedule a new replica, and, finally, checking that the newly created job is present.

```
exit

open "http://$CLUSTER_DNS/jenkins/newJob"
```

We exited the cluster and opened **New Job** screen. Please use *admin* and *username* and *password* if you're asked to authenticate.

Next, type `test` as the *item name*, select **Pipeline** as *job type* and click the **OK** button.

Once inside the job configuration screen, please click the **Pipeline** tab. We are about to write a very complicated pipeline script. Are you ready?

Please type the script that follows inside the *Pipeline Script* field and press the **Save** button.

```
echo "This is a test"
```

Now that we created a mighty pipeline job, we can simulate Jenkins failure by sending it an `exit` command.

```
open "http://$CLUSTER_DNS/jenkins/exit"
```

We exited the cluster and opened the **exit** screen. You'll see a button saying **Try POSTing**. Click it. Jenkins will shut down, and Swarm will detect that as a failure and schedule a new replica of the service.

Wait a few moments until Jenkins inside a new replica is initialized and open the home screen.

```
open "http://$CLUSTER_DNS/jenkins"
```

As you can see, the newly created job is there. Persistence works!

If you visit Jenkins nodes screen, you'll notice that we are running only one agent labeled `prod`. That's the agent we should use only to deploy a new release to production and, potentially, run production tests. We still need to setup agents we'll use to run unit tests, build images, run integration tests, and so on. We'll postpone that part for one of the next chapters since efficient usage of agents is related to self-adaptation applied to infrastructure. We are yet to reach that section.

Alternatives to CloudStor volume driver

If you're not using *Docker for AWS* or *Azure*, using CloudStor might not be the best idea. Even though it can be made to work with AWS or Azure without the template we used to create the cluster, it is not well documented. For now, its goal is only to be used with AWS or Azure clusters made with Docker templates. For anything else, I'd recommend you choose one of the alternatives. My personal preference is REX-Ray (http://rexray.readthedocs.io/en/stable/).

All in all, stick with *CloudStor* if you choose to create your Swarm cluster using *Docker For AWS* or *Azure* templates. It is well integrated and provides great out-of-the-box experience. For anything else use *REX-Ray* if it supports your hosting vendor. Otherwise, look for some other alternative. There are plenty others, and more is yet to come. The most important part of the story is to know when to persist the state and when to let replication do the work. When persistence is paramount, use any of the volume drivers that support your hosting vendor and fit your requirements.

The only thing left before we can call this cluster production-ready is to set up centralized logging.

Setting up centralized logging

We choose not to integrate our cluster with CloudWatch. Actually, I chose not to use it, and you blindly followed my example. Therefore, I guess that an explanation is in order. It's going to be a short one. I don't like CloudWatch. I think it is a bad solution that is way behind the competition and, at the same time, it can become quite expensive when dealing with large quantities of data. More importantly, I believe that we should use services coming from hosting vendors only when they are essential or provide an actual benefit. Otherwise, we'd run a risk of entering the trap called *vendor locking*. Docker Swarm allows us to deploy services in the same way, no matter whether they are running in AWS or anywhere else. The only difference would be a volume driver we choose to plug in. Similarly, all the services we decided to deploy thus far can run anywhere. The only "lock-in" is with Docker Swarm but, unlike AWS, it is open source. If needed we can even fork it to our repository and build our own Docker Server. That is not to say that I would recommend forking Docker but rather that I am trying to make a clear distinction between being locked into an open source project and with a commercial product. Moreover, with relatively moderate changes, we could migrate our Swarm services to Kubernetes or even Mesos and Marathon. Again, that is not something I recommend but more of a statement that a choice to change the solution is not as time demanding as it might seem on the first look.

I think I run astray from the main subject so let me summarize it. CloudWatch is bad, and it costs money. Many of the free alternatives are much better. If you read my previous books, you probably know that my preference for a logging solution is the **ELK** (**ElasticSearch, LogStash, and Kibana**) stack. I used them for both logging and metrics but, since then, metrics solution was replaced with Prometheus. How about centralized logging? I think that ELK is still one of the best self-hosted solutions even though I'm not entirely convinced I like the new path Elastic is taking as a company. I'll leave the discussion about their direction for later and, instead, we'll dive right into setting up the ELK stack in our cluster.

```
ssh -i devops22.pem docker@$CLUSTER_IP

curl -o logging.yml \
    https://raw.githubusercontent.com/vfarcic/docker-\
flow-monitor/master/stacks/logging-aws.yml

cat logging.yml
```

We went back to the cluster, downloaded the logging stack, and displayed its contents. The YML file defines the **ELK** stack as well as LogSpout. ElasticSearch is an in-memory database that will store our logs. LogSpout will be sending logs from all containers running inside the cluster to LogStash, which, in turn, will process them and send the output to ElasticSearch. Kibana will be used as UI to explore logs. That was all the details of the stack you'll get. I'll assume that you are already familiar with the services we'll use. They were described in the book, *The DevOps 2.1 Toolkit: Docker Swarm* (https://www.amazon.com/dp/1542468914). If you did not read it, information could be easily found on the Internet. Google is your friend.

The first service in the stack is `elasticsearch`. It is an in-memory database we'll use to store logs. Its definition is as follows.

```
elasticsearch:
  image: docker.elastic.co/elasticsearch/elasticsearch:5.5.2
  environment:
    - xpack.security.enabled=false
  volumes:
    - es:/usr/share/elasticsearch/data
  networks:
    - default
  deploy:
    labels:
      - com.df.distribute=true
      - com.df.notify=true
      - com.df.port=80
      - com.df.alertName=mem_limit
      - com.df.alertIf=@service_mem_limit:0.8
```

```
        - com.df.alertFor=30s
      resources:
        reservations:
          memory: 3000M
        limits:
          memory: 3500M
      placement:
        constraints: [node.role == worker]
  ...
  volumes:
    es:
      driver: cloudstor:aws
      external: false
  ...
```

There's nothing special about the service. We used the environment variable `xpack.security.enabled` to disable X-Pack. It is a commercial product baked into ElasticSearch image. Since this book uses only open source services, we had to disable it. That does not mean that X-Pack is not useful. It is. Among other things, it provides authentication capabilities to ElasticSearch. I encourage you to explore it and make your own decision whether it's worth the money.

I could argue that there's not much reason to secure ElasticSearch since we are not exposing any ports. Only services that are attached to the same network will be able to access it. That means that only people you trust to deploy services would have direct access to it.

Usually, we'd run multiple ElasticSearch services and join them into a cluster (ElasticSearch calls replica set a cluster). Data would be replicated between multiple instances and would be thus preserved in case of a failure. However, we do not need multiple ElasticSearch services, nor do we have enough hardware to host them. Therefore, we'll run only one ElasticSearch service and, since there will be no replication, we'll store its state on a volume called `es`.

The only other noteworthy part of the service definition is the placement defined as `constraints: [node.role == worker]`. Since ElasticSearch is very resource demanding, it might not be a wise idea to place it on a manager. Therefore, we defined that it should always run on one of the workers and reserved 3 GB of memory. That should be enough to get us started. Later on, depending on a number of log entries you're storing and the cleanup strategy, you might need to increase the memory allocated to it and scale it to multiple services.

Let's move to the next service.

```
...
  logstash:
    image: docker.elastic.co/logstash/logstash:5.5.2
    networks:
      - default
    deploy:
      labels:
        - com.df.distribute=true
        - com.df.notify=true
        - com.df.port=80
        - com.df.alertName=mem_limit
        - com.df.alertIf=@service_mem_limit:0.8
        - com.df.alertFor=30s
      resources:
        reservations:
          memory: 600M
        limits:
          memory: 1000M
    configs:
      - logstash.conf
    environment:
      - LOGSPOUT=ignore
    command: logstash -f /logstash.conf
...
configs:
  logstash.conf:
    external: true
```

LogStash will accept logs using syslog format and protocol and forward them to ElasticSearch. You'll see the configuration soon.

The only interesting part about the service is that we're injecting a Docker config. It works in almost the same way as secrets except that it is not encrypted at rest. Since it will not contain anything compromising, there's no need to set it up as a secret. We did not specify config destination, so it will be available as file /logstash.conf. The command is set to reflect that.

We're halfway through. The next service in line is kibana.

```
  kibana:
    image: docker.elastic.co/kibana/kibana:5.5.2
    networks:
      - default
      - proxy
    environment:
```

```
        - xpack.security.enabled=false
        - ELASTICSEARCH_URL=http://elasticsearch:9200
      deploy:
        labels:
          - com.df.notify=true
          - com.df.distribute=true
          - com.df.usersPassEncrypted=false
          - com.df.usersSecret=admin
          -
com.df.servicePath=/app,/elasticsearch,/api,/ui,/bundles,/plugins,\
/status,/es_admin
          - com.df.port=5601
          - com.df.alertName=mem_limit
          - com.df.alertIf=@service_mem_limit:0.8
          - com.df.alertFor=30s
        resources:
          reservations:
            memory: 600M
          limits:
            memory: 1000M
```

Kibana will provide a UI that will allow us to filter and display logs. It can do many other things but logs are all we need for now. Unfortunately, Kibana is not proxy-friendly. Even though there are a few environment variables that can configure the base path, they do not truly work as expected. We had to specify multiple paths through the com.df.servicePath. They reflect all the combinations of requests Kibana makes. I'd recommend that you replace com.df.servicePath with com.df.serviceDomain. The value could be a subdomain (for example, kibana.acme.com).

The rest of the definition is pretty uneventful, so we'll move on.

We, finally, reached the last service of the stack.

```
logspout:
  image: gliderlabs/logspout:v3.2.2
  networks:
    - default
  environment:
    - SYSLOG_FORMAT=rfc3164
  volumes:
    - /var/run/docker.sock:/var/run/docker.sock
  command: syslog://logstash:51415
  deploy:
    mode: global
    labels:
      - com.df.notify=true
      - com.df.distribute=true
```

```
      - com.df.alertName=mem_limit
      - com.df.alertIf=@service_mem_limit:0.8
      - com.df.alertFor=30s
    resources:
      reservations:
        memory: 20M
      limits:
        memory: 30M
```

LogSpout will monitor Docker events and send all logs to ElasticSearch. We're exposing Docker socket as a volume so that the service can communicate with Docker server. The command specifies `syslog` as protocol and `logstash` running on `51415` as the destination address. Since all the services of the stack are connected through the same `default` network, the name of the service (`logstash`) is all we need as address.

The service will run in the `global` mode so that a replica is present on each node of the cluster.

We need to create the `logstash.conf` config before we deploy the stack. The command is as follows:

```
echo '
input {
  syslog { port => 51415 }
}

output {
  elasticsearch {
    hosts => ["elasticsearch:9200"]
  }
}
' | docker config create logstash.conf -
```

We echoed a configuration and piped the output to the `docker config create` command. The configuration specifies `syslog` running on port `51415` as `input`. The output is ElasticSearch running on port `9200`. The address of the output is the name of the destination service (`elasticsearch`).

Now we can deploy the stack:

```
docker stack deploy -c logging.yml \
    logging
```

A few of the images are big, and it will take a moment or two until all services are up-and-running. We'll confirm the state of the stack by executing the command that follows.

```
docker stack ps \
    -f desired-state=running logging
```

The output is as follows (IDs are removed for brevity):

```
 1   NAME                    IMAGE                                            NODE \
 2                                       DESIRED STATE CURRENT STATE          ERR \
 3   OR PORTS
 4   logging_logspout...     gliderlabs/logspout:v3.2.2                       ip-1 \
 5   72-31-46-204.us-east-2.compute.internal Running      Running 3 minutes ago
 6   logging_logspout...     gliderlabs/logspout:v3.2.2                       ip-1 \
 7   72-31-12-85.us-east-2.compute.internal  Running      Running 2 minutes ago
 8   logging_logspout...     gliderlabs/logspout:v3.2.2                       ip-1 \
 9   72-31-31-76.us-east-2.compute.internal  Running      Running 3 minutes ago
10   logging_kibana.1        docker.elastic.co/kibana/kibana:5.5.2            ip-1 \
11   72-31-46-204.us-east-2.compute.internal Running      Running 15 seconds ago
12   logging_logstash.1      docker.elastic.co/logstash/logstash:5.5.2        ip-1 \
13   72-31-31-76.us-east-2.compute.internal  Running      Running 3 minutes ago
14   logging_elasticsearch.1 docker.elastic.co/elasticsearch/elasticsearch:5.5.2   \
15                                           Running      Pending 3 minutes a
```

You'll notice that `elasticsearch` is in `pending` state. Swarm cannot deploy it because none of the servers meet the requirements we set. We need at least 3 GB of memory and a worker node. We should either change the constraint and reservations to fit out current cluster setup or add a worker as a new node. We'll go with latter.

As a side note, Kibana might fail after a while. It will try to connect to ElasticSearch for a few times and stop the process. Soon after, it will be rescheduled by Swarm, only to stop again. That will continue until we manage to run ElasticSearch.

Please exit the cluster before we proceed.

```
exit
```

Extending the capacity of the cluster

Among other resources, *Docker For AWS* template created two auto-scaling groups. One is used for masters and the other for workers. Those security groups have multiple purposes.

If we choose to update the stack to, for example, change the size of the nodes or upgrade Docker server to a newer version, the template will temporarily increase the number of nodes by one and shut down one of the old ones. The replicas that were running on the old server will be moved to the new one. Once the new server is created, it will move to the next, and the next after that, all the way until all the nodes are replaced. The process is very similar to rolling updates we performed by Swarm when updating services. The same process is done whenever we decide to update any aspect of the *Docker For AWS* stack.

Similarly, if one of the nodes fail health checks, the template will increase auto-scaling group by one so that a new node is created in its place and, once everything goes back to "normal" update the ASG back to its initial value.

In all those cases, not only that new nodes will be created through auto-scaling groups, but they will also join the cluster as a manager or a worker depending on the type of the server that is being replaced.

We will explore failure recovery in the chapter dedicated to self-healing applied to infrastructure. For now, we'll limit the scope to an example how to update the CloudFormation stack that created our cluster. We even have a perfect use-case. Our ElasticSearch service needs a worker node, and it needs it to be bigger than those we use as managers. Let's create it.

We'll start by opening CloudFormation home screen.

```
open "https://us-east-2.console.aws.amazon.com/cloudformation/home"
```

Please select the **devops22** stack. Click the **Actions** drop-down list and select the **Update Stack** item. Click the **Next** button

You will be presented with the same initial screen you saw while we were creating the *Docker For AWS* stack. The only difference is that the values are now populated with choices we made previously.

We can change anything we want. Not only that the changes will be applied accordingly, but the process will use rolling updates to avoid downtime. Whether you will have downtime or not depends on the capabilities of your services. If needed, the process will change one node at the time. If you're running multiple replicas of a service, the worst case scenario is that you will experience degraded performance for a short period. However, services that are not scalable like, for example, Prometheus, will experience downtime.

When a node is destroyed, Swarm will move it to a newly created server. If the state of that service is on a network drive like EFS, it will continue working as if nothing happened. However, we must count the time between the service failure due to the destruction of the node and until it is up and running again. In most cases that should be only a couple of seconds. No matter how short the downtime is, it is still a period during which our non-scalable services are not operational. Be it as it may, not all services are scalable, and the process is the best we can do. If there is downtime, let it be as short as possible.

In this case, we won't make an update that will force the system to recreate nodes. Instead, we'll only add a new worker node.

Please scroll to the **Number of Swarm worker nodes?** field and change the value from **0** to **1**.

Since we defined that ElasticSearch should reserve 3 GB of memory, we should change worker instance type. Our managers are using *t2.small* that comes with 2 GB. The smallest instance that fulfills our requirements is `t2.medium` that comes 4 GB of allocated memory.

Please change the value of the **Agent worker instance type?** drop-down list to **t2.medium**.

We will not change any other aspect of the cluster, so all that's left is to click the **Next** button twice, and select the **I acknowledge that AWS CloudFormation might create IAM resources**. checkbox.

After a few moments, the *Preview your changes* section of the screen will be populated with the list of changes that will be applied to the cluster. Since this is a simple and non-destructive update, only a few resources related to auto-scaling groups will be updated.

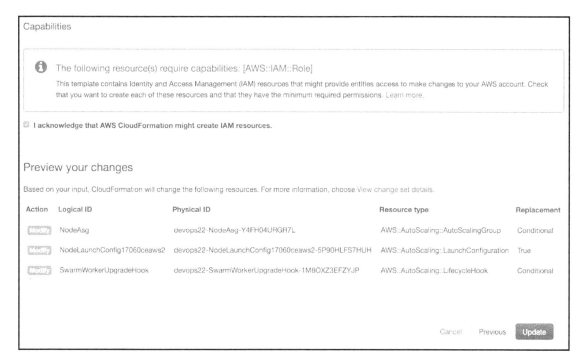

Figure 13-4: Preview your changes screen from the Docker For AWS template

Click the **Update** button and relax. It'll take a minute or two until the new server is created and it joins the cluster.

While waiting, we should explore a different method to accomplish the same result.

Please open the *Auto-Scaling Groups Details* screen.

```
open "https://console.aws.amazon.com/ec2/autoscaling\
/home?#AutoScalingGroups:view=details"
```

You'll be presented with the *Welcome to Auto Scaling* screen. Click the **Auto Scaling Groups: 2** link.

Select the item with the name starting with **devops22-NodeAsg**, click the **Actions** drop-down list, and select the **Edit** item. We're looking for the **Desired** field located in the **details** tab. It can be changed to any value, and the number of workers would increase (or decrease) accordingly. We could do the same with the auto-scaling group associated with manager nodes. Do not make any change. We're almost finished with this chapter, and we already have more than enough nodes for the services we're running.

The knowledge that we can change the number of manager or worker nodes by changing the values in auto-scaling groups is essential. Later on, we'll combine that with AWS API and Prometheus alerts to automate the process when certain conditions are met.

The new worker node should be up-and-running by now unless you are a very fast reader. If that's the case, go and grab a coffee.

Let's go back to the cluster and list the available nodes.

```
ssh -i devops22.pem docker@$CLUSTER_IP

docker node ls
```

The output is as follows (IDs are removed for brevity):

```
1   HOSTNAME                                     STATUS AVAILABILITY MANAGER STATUS
2   ip-172-31-2-119.us-east-2.compute.internal   Ready  Active
3   ip-172-31-32-225.us-east-2.compute.internal  Ready  Active       Leader
4   ip-172-31-10-207.us-east-2.compute.internal  Ready  Active       Reachable
5   ip-172-31-30-18.us-east-2.compute.internal   Ready  Active       Reachable
```

As you can see, a new node is added to the mix. Since its a worker, manager status is empty.

Your first thought might be that it is a simple process. After all, all that AWS did was create a new VM. That is right from AWS point of view, but there are a few other things that happened in the background.

During VM initialization, it contacted Dynamo DB to find out the address of the primary manager and the access token. Equipped with that info, it sent a request to that manager to join the cluster. From there on, the new node (in this case worked) is available as part of the Swarm cluster:

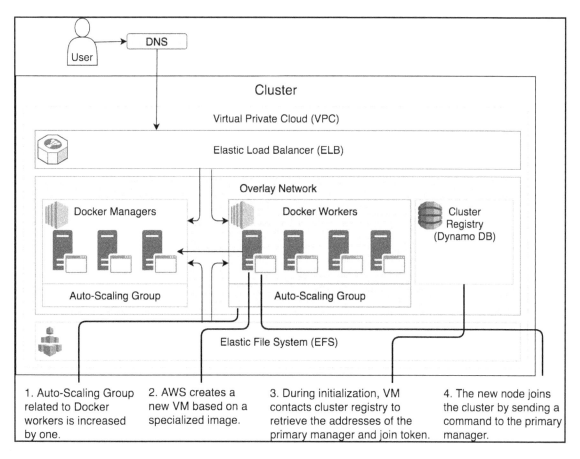

Figure 13-5: The process of increasing the number of worker nodes

Let's take a look at the `logging` stack and confirm that adding a new worker node accomplished the mission.

```
docker stack ps \
    -f desired-state=running logging
```

The output is as follows (IDs are removed for brevity):

```
 1   NAME                    IMAGE                                                NODE\
 2                                     DESIRED STATE  CURRENT STATE                E\
 3   RROR               PORTS
 4   logging_logspout...     gliderlabs/logspout:v3.2.2                           ip-1\
 5   72-31-30-18.us-east-2.compute.internal  Running       Running 4 minutes ago
 6   logging_logspout...     gliderlabs/logspout:v3.2.2                           ip-1\
 7   72-31-10-207.us-east-2.compute.internal Running       Running 4 minutes ago
 8   logging_logspout...     gliderlabs/logspout:v3.2.2                           ip-1\
 9   72-31-32-225.us-east-2.compute.internal Running       Running 4 minutes ago
10   logging_logspout...     gliderlabs/logspout:v3.2.2                           ip-1\
11   72-31-2-119.us-east-2.compute.internal  Running       Running 4 minutes ago
12   logging_elasticsearch.1 docker.elastic.co/elasticsearch/elasticsearch:5.5.2 ip-1\
13   72-31-2-119.us-east-2.compute.internal  Running       Running 3 seconds ago
14   logging_kibana.1        docker.elastic.co/kibana/kibana:5.5.2                ip-1\
15   72-31-30-18.us-east-2.compute.internal  Running       Running 28 seconds ago
16   logging_logstash.1      docker.elastic.co/logstash/logstash:5.5.2            ip-1\
17   72-31-10-207.us-east-2.compute.internal Running       Running 52 seconds
```

Since `logspout` is a global service, a new replica was created in the new node. More importantly, `elasticsearch` changed its current state from pending to running. Swarm detected that a worker was added to the cluster and deployed a replica of the `elasticsearch` service.

Our whole production setup is up and running. The only thing left to do is to confirm that Kibana is indeed working as expected and that logs are shipped to ElasticSearch.

```
exit
open "http://$CLUSTER_DNS/app/kibana"
```

We exited the cluster and opened Kibana in a browser. Since we defined the `com.df.usersSecret` label, *Docker Flow Proxy* will not allow access to it without authentication. Please use `admin` as both username and password.

The first time you open Kibana, you'll be presented with the *Configure an index pattern* screen. Select `@timestamp` as *Time Filter field name* and click the **Create** button. Kibana and the rest of the ELK stack are ready for use.

What now?

Our production cluster is up and running, and it already has most of the vertical services we'll need. The next steps will build on top of that. We'll explore *Docker For AWS* features that make it self-heal and, later on, discuss how we can make it self-adapt as well.

We explored how to update our cluster through UI. That is useful as a way to learn what's going on but not that much if we're planning to automate the processes. Fortunately, everything that can be done through UI can be accomplished through AWS API. We'll use it soon.

Docker folks did a great job with *Docker For AWS* and *Azure*. The result is fantastic. It is a very simple, yet very powerful tool in our belt.

I hope you're hosting your Swarm cluster in AWS or Azure (both behave almost the same). If you're not, it will be very useful to use *Docker For AWS* for a while. That, together with this chapter and those that follow, should give you inspiration how to create a cluster with your vendor of choice. Even though the resources will be different, the logic should be the same. The major difference is that you will have to roll your sleeves and replicate many of the features you already saw. More is yet to come so be prepared.

I still recommend using Terraform for anything but a cluster running in AWS or Azure. It is the best tool for creating infrastructure resources. I wish Docker chose it as well instead of relying on the tools that are native to AWS and Azure. That would simplify the process of extending them to other vendors and foster contributions that would enable the same features elsewhere. On the other hand, providing a "native" experience like the one you saw in this chapter has its benefits.

There's nothing else left to say (until the next chapter).

There's no reason to pay for things you don't use. We'll destroy the cluster and take a break.

```
open "https://console.aws.amazon.com/cloudformation"
```

Select the **devops22** stack, click the **Actions** drop-down list, select the **Delete Stack** item, and click the **Yes, Delete** button. The cluster will be gone in a few minutes. Don't worry. We'll create a new one soon. Until then, you won't be able to complain that I'm forcing you to make unnecessary expense.

14
Self-Healing Applied to Infrastructure

We already saw how Docker Swarm provides self-healing applied to services. If a replica of a service goes down, it will be rescheduled on one of the healthy nodes. Soon after, the desired number of replicas will be running inside the cluster. We combined that feature with volumes attached to network drives so that the state of the stateful services is persisted.

The time has come to explore how to accomplish the same self-healing features applied to infrastructure. We already know how to create a cluster based on the *Docker For AWS* template or its equivalent in *Azure*. If you are not using one of those hosting vendors, we explored the essential features you should implement yourself.

Before we move into infrastructure self-healing, we need to create the cluster we destroyed at the end of the previous chapter. We'll use this opportunity to explore how to accomplish the same result without the usage of AWS UI.

Automating cluster setup

The first thing we should do is get the AWS credentials.

Please open the Amazon EC2 console (`https://console.aws.amazon.com/ec2/v2/home`), click on your name from the top-right menu, and select **My Security Credentials**. You will see the screen with different types of credentials. Expand the **Access Keys (Access Key ID and Secret Access Key)** section and click the **Create New Access Key** button. Expand the **Show Access Key** section to see the keys.

You will not be able to view the keys later on, so this is the only chance you'll have to *Download Key File*.

We'll put the keys as environment variables that will be used by the **AWS Command Line Interface** (**AWS CLI**) (`https://aws.amazon.com/cli/`).

Please replace `[...]` with your keys before executing the commands that follow.

 All the commands from this chapter are available in the `14-self-healing-infra.sh` Gist at (`https://gist.github.com/vfarcic/b27e0d4dcfa3af5eb2b58316aae13c53`).

```
export AWS_ACCESS_KEY_ID=[...]

export AWS_SECRET_ACCESS_KEY=[...]

export AWS_DEFAULT_REGION=us-east-1
```

You're free to change the region to any that suits you as long as it has at least three availability zones.

Before we proceed, please make sure that AWS CLI (`https://aws.amazon.com/cli/`) and `jq` (`https://stedolan.github.io/jq/download/`) are installed. We'll use the *CLI* to communicate with AWS and `jq` to format and filter JSON output returned by the *CLI*.

AWS Command Line Interface

The AWS Command Line Interface (CLI) is a unified tool to manage your AWS services. With just one tool to download and configure, you can control multiple AWS services from the command line and automate them through scripts.

The AWS CLI introduces a new set of simple file commands for efficient file transfers to and from Amazon S3.

Windows

Download and run the 64-bit or 32-bit Windows installer.

Mac and Linux

Requires Python 2.6.5 or higher. Install using pip.

```
pip install awscli
```

Amazon Linux

The AWS CLI comes pre-installed on Amazon Linux AMI.

Release Notes

Check out the Release Notes for more information on the latest version.

Getting Started » | CLI Reference » | GitHub Project » | Community Forum »

Figure 14-1: AWS Command Line Interface screen

Let's take a look at the *Docker For AWS* template.

```
curl https://editions-us-east-\
  1.s3.amazonaws.com/aws/stable/Docker.tmpl
    | jq "."
```

The output is vast, and we won't have time to go through the details of all the services it defines. Instead, we'll focus on the parameters since they have to be specified during the execution of the template.

Let's take another look at the template but, this time, limited to the .Metadata section.

```
curl https://editions-us-east-\
  1.s3.amazonaws.com/aws/stable/Docker.tmpl
    | jq ".Metadata"
```

We output the template and used `jq` to filter the result. The output is as follows:

```
{
  "AWS::CloudFormation::Interface": {
    "ParameterGroups": [
      {
        "Label": {
          "default": "Swarm Size"
        },
        "Parameters": [
          "ManagerSize",
          "ClusterSize"
        ]
      },
      {
        "Label": {
          "default": "Swarm Properties"
        },
        "Parameters": [
          "KeyName",
          "EnableSystemPrune",
          "EnableCloudWatchLogs",
          "EnableCloudStorEfs"
        ]
      },
      {
        "Label": {
          "default": "Swarm Manager Properties"
        },
        "Parameters": [
          "ManagerInstanceType",
          "ManagerDiskSize",
          "ManagerDiskType"
        ]
      },
      {
        "Label": {
          "default": "Swarm Worker Properties"
        },
        "Parameters": [
          "InstanceType",
          "WorkerDiskSize",
          "WorkerDiskType"
        ]
      }
    ],
    "ParameterLabels": {
```

```
      "ClusterSize": {
        "default": "Number of Swarm worker nodes?"
      },
      "EnableCloudStorEfs": {
        "default": "Create EFS prerequsities for CloudStor?"
      },
      "EnableCloudWatchLogs": {
        "default": "Use Cloudwatch for container logging?"
      },
      "EnableSystemPrune": {
        "default": "Enable daily resource cleanup?"
      },
      "InstanceType": {
        "default": "Agent worker instance type?"
      },
      "KeyName": {
        "default": "Which SSH key to use?"
      },
      "ManagerDiskSize": {
        "default": "Manager ephemeral storage volume size?"
      },
      "ManagerDiskType": {
        "default": "Manager ephemeral storage volume type"
      },
      "ManagerInstanceType": {
        "default": "Swarm manager instance type?"
      },
      "ManagerSize": {
        "default": "Number of Swarm managers?"
      },
      "WorkerDiskSize": {
        "default": "Worker ephemeral storage volume size?"
      },
      "WorkerDiskType": {
        "default": "Worker ephemeral storage volume type"
      }
    }
  }
}
```

You should be familiar with those parameters. They are the same as those you saw when you created the cluster through AWS UI.

Now we are ready to create a cluster.

```
aws cloudformation create-stack \
    --template-url https://editions-us-east-\
  1.s3.amazonaws.com/aws/stable/Docker.tmpl \
```

```
--capabilities CAPABILITY_IAM \
--stack-name devops22 \
--parameters \
ParameterKey=ManagerSize,ParameterValue=3 \
ParameterKey=ClusterSize,ParameterValue=0 \
ParameterKey=KeyName,ParameterValue=devops22 \
ParameterKey=EnableSystemPrune,ParameterValue=yes \
ParameterKey=EnableCloudWatchLogs,ParameterValue=no \
ParameterKey=EnableCloudStorEfs,ParameterValue=yes \
ParameterKey=ManagerInstanceType,ParameterValue=t2.micro \
ParameterKey=InstanceType,ParameterValue=t2.micro
```

We named the stack `devops22` and used the parameters to set the number of managers (3) and workers (0) and SSH key (`devops22`). We enabled prune and EFS, and disabled *CloudWatch*. This time we used `t2.micro` instances. We won't deploy many services so 1 vCPU and 1 GB of memory should be more than enough. At the same time, `t2.micro` is *free tier eligible* making it a perfect instance type for the exercises in this chapter.

We can use `aws cloudformation` command to list the resources defined in the stack and see their current status.

```
aws cloudformation describe-stack-resources \
    --stack-name devops22 | jq "."
```

The output is too big to be listed here so we'll move on. Our immediate goal is to find out the status of the stack and confirm that it was created successfully before we SSH into it. We can describe a stack through the `aws cloudformation describe-stacks` command.

```
aws cloudformation describe-stacks \
    --stack-name devops22 | jq "."
```

We retrieved the description of the `devops22` stack. The output is as follows:

```
{
  "Stacks": [
    {
      "StackId": "arn:aws:cloudformation:us-east-
2:036548781187:stack/devops22/bf859420-99f1-11e7-92af-50a68a26e835",
      "Description": "Docker CE for AWS 17.06.1-ce (17.06.1-ce-aws1)",
      "Parameters": [
        {
          "ParameterValue": "yes",
          "ParameterKey": "EnableCloudStorEfs"
        },
        {
          "ParameterValue": "devops22",
```

```
          "ParameterKey": "KeyName"
      },
      {
          "ParameterValue": "t2.micro",
          "ParameterKey": "ManagerInstanceType"
      },
      {
          "ParameterValue": "0",
          "ParameterKey": "ClusterSize"
      },
      {
          "ParameterValue": "standard",
          "ParameterKey": "ManagerDiskType"

      },
      {
          "ParameterValue": "20",
          "ParameterKey": "WorkerDiskSize"
      },
      {
          "ParameterValue": "20",
          "ParameterKey": "ManagerDiskSize"
      },
      {
          "ParameterValue": "standard",
          "ParameterKey": "WorkerDiskType"
      },
      {
          "ParameterValue": "yes",
          "ParameterKey": "EnableSystemPrune"
      },
      {
          "ParameterValue": "no",
          "ParameterKey": "EnableCloudWatchLogs"
      },
      {
          "ParameterValue": "t2.small",
          "ParameterKey": "InstanceType"
      },
      {
          "ParameterValue": "3",
          "ParameterKey": "ManagerSize"
      }
  ],
  "Tags": [],
  "CreationTime": "2017-09-15T08:47:10.306Z",
  "Capabilities": [
      "CAPABILITY_IAM"
```

```
            ],
            "StackName": "devops22",
            "NotificationARNs": [],
            "StackStatus": "CREATE_IN_PROGRESS",
            "DisableRollback": false
        }
    ]
}
```

Most of the description reflects the parameters we used to create the stack. The value we're interested in is StackStatus. In my case, it is set to CREATE_IN_PROGRESS meaning that the cluster is still not ready. We should wait for a while and query the status again. This time, we'll use jq to limit the output only to the StackStatus field.

```
aws cloudformation describe-stacks \
    --stack-name devops22 | \
    jq -r ".Stacks[0].StackStatus"
```

If the output of the command is CREATE_COMPLETE, the cluster is created, and we can move on. Otherwise, please wait for a bit more and recheck the status. It should take around ten minutes to create the whole stack.

Now that the cluster is created, we need to get the DNS and the IP of one of the masters.

Cluster DNS is available through the Outputs section of the stack description.

```
aws cloudformation describe-stacks \
    --stack-name devops22 | \
    jq -r ".Stacks[0].Outputs"
```

The output is as follows.

```
[
    {
        "Description": "Use this name to update your DNS records",
        "OutputKey": "DefaultDNSTarget",
        "OutputValue": "devops22-ExternalL-EEU3J540N4S0-1231273358.\
us-east-2.elb.amazonaws.com"
    },
    {
        "Description": "Availabilty Zones Comment",
        "OutputKey": "ZoneAvailabilityComment",
        "OutputValue": "This region has at least 3 Availability Zones\
  (AZ). This is ideal to ensure a fully functional Swarm in case\
you lose an AZ."
    },
    {
```

```
    "Description": "You can see the manager nodes associated with\
  this cluster here.  Follow the instructions here:\
https://docs.docker.com/docker-for-aws/deploy/",
    "OutputKey": "Managers",
    "OutputValue": "https://us-east\
-2.console.aws.amazon.com/ec2/v2/home?region=us-\
 east-2#Instances:tag:aws:autoscaling:groupName=\
devops22-ManagerAsg-RA4ECZRYJ37C;sort=desc:dnsName"
  },
  {
    "Description": "Use this as the VPC for configuring \
 Private Hosted Zones",
    "OutputKey": "VPCID",
    "OutputValue": "vpc-99311ff0"
  },
  {
    "Description": "SecurityGroup ID of NodeVpcSG",
    "OutputKey": "NodeSecurityGroupID",
    "OutputValue": "sg-0d852c65"
  },
  {
    "Description": "Use this zone ID to update your DNS records",
    "OutputKey": "ELBDNSZoneID",
    "OutputValue": "Z3AADJGX6KTTL2"
  },
  {
    "Description": "SecurityGroup ID of ManagerVpcSG",
    "OutputKey": "ManagerSecurityGroupID",
    "OutputValue": "sg-4c832a24"
  },
  {
    "Description": "SecurityGroup ID of SwarmWideSG",
    "OutputKey": "SwarmWideSecurityGroupID",
    "OutputValue": "sg-aa852cc2"
  }
]
```

What we need is the `DefaultDNSTarget` value. We'll have to refine our `jq` filters a bit more.

```
aws cloudformation describe-stacks \
    --stack-name devops22 | \
    jq -r ".Stacks[0].Outputs[] | \
    select(.OutputKey=="DefaultDNSTarget")\
    .OutputValue"
```

We used `select` statement of `jq` to retrieve only the section with `OutputKey` set to `DefaultDNSTarget` and retrieved the `OutputValue`.

The output should be similar to the one that follows.

```
devops22-ExternalL-EEU3J540N4S0-1231273358.us-east-\
 2.elb.amazonaws.com
```

We should store the output of the previous command as an environment variable so that we can have it at hand if we need to open one of the services in a browser or, even better, to set it as the address of our domain.

```
CLUSTER_DNS=$(aws cloudformation \
    describe-stacks \
    --stack-name devops22 | \
    jq -r ".Stacks[0].Outputs[] | \
    select(.OutputKey=="DefaultDNSTarget")\
    .OutputValue")
```

Even though we will not need the DNS in this chapter, it's good to know how to retrieve it. We'll need it later on in the chapters that follow.

The only thing left is to get the public IP of one of the managers. We can use `aws ec2 describe-instances` command to list all the EC2 instances running in the region.

```
aws ec2 describe-instances | jq -r "."
```

The output is too big to be presented in a book.

You should see three instances if the cluster we just created is the only one running in your region. Otherwise, there might be others. Since we do not want to risk retrieving anything but managers that belong to the `devops22` stack, we'll refine the command to the one that follows.

```
aws ec2 describe-instances | \
    jq -r ".Reservations[].Instances[] \
    | select(.SecurityGroups[].GroupName \
    | contains("devops22-ManagerVpcSG")) \
    .PublicIpAddress"
```

We used `jq` to filter the output and limit the results only to the instances attached to the security group with the name that starts with `devops22-ManagerVpcSG`. Further on, we retrieved the `PublicIpAddress` values.

The output is as follows.

```
52.14.246.52
13.59.130.67
13.59.132.147
```

Those three IPs belong to the three managers that for the cluster.

We'll use the previous command to set the environment variable CLUSTER_IP.

```
CLUSTER_IP=$(aws ec2 describe-instances \
    | jq -r ".Reservations[] \
    .Instances[] \
    | select(.SecurityGroups[].GroupName \
    | contains("devops22-ManagerVpcSG")) \
    .PublicIpAddress" \
    | tail -n 1)
```

Since we needed only one of the IPs, we piped the result of the describe-instances command to tail which limited the output to a single line.

Now that we have both the DNS and the IP of one of the managers, we can enter the cluster and confirm that all the nodes joined it:

```
ssh -i devops22.pem docker@$CLUSTER_IP
docker node ls
```

The output of the node ls command is as follows (IDs are removed for brevity):

```
1   HOSTNAME                                    STATUS AVAILABILITY MANAGER STATUS
2   ip-172-31-21-57.us-east-2.compute.internal  Ready  Active       Reachable
3   ip-172-31-44-182.us-east-2.compute.internal Ready  Active       Reachable
4   ip-172-31-15-30.us-east-2.compute.internal  Ready  Active       Leader
```

As expected, all three nodes joined the cluster, and we can explore self-healing applied to infrastructure through AWS services created with the *Docker For AWS* template.

Exploring fault tolerance

Since we are exploring self-healing (not self-adaptation), there's no need to deploy all the stacks we used thus far. A single service will be enough to explore what happens when a node goes down. Our cluster, formed out of `t2.micro instances`, would not support much more anyways.

```
docker service create --name test \
    --replicas 10 alpine sleep 1000000
```

We created a service with ten replicas. Let's confirm that they are spread across the three nodes of the cluster:

```
docker service ps test
```

The output is as follows (IDs are removed for brevity):

```
 1  NAME     IMAGE         NODE                                               DESIRED STATE \
 2  CURRENT STATE          ERROR PORTS
 3  test.1   alpine:latest ip-172-31-44-182.us-east-2.compute.internal Running       \
 4  Running 12 seconds ago
 5  test.2   alpine:latest ip-172-31-15-30.us-east-2.compute.internal  Running       \
 6  Running 12 seconds ago
 7  test.3   alpine:latest ip-172-31-21-57.us-east-2.compute.internal  Running       \
 8  Running 12 seconds ago
 9  test.4   alpine:latest ip-172-31-44-182.us-east-2.compute.internal Running       \
10  Running 12 seconds ago
11  test.5   alpine:latest ip-172-31-15-30.us-east-2.compute.internal  Running       \
12  Running 12 seconds ago
13  test.6   alpine:latest ip-172-31-21-57.us-east-2.compute.internal  Running       \
14  Running 12 seconds ago
15  test.7   alpine:latest ip-172-31-15-30.us-east-2.compute.internal  Running       \
16  Running 12 seconds ago
17  test.8   alpine:latest ip-172-31-21-57.us-east-2.compute.internal  Running       \
18  Running 12 seconds ago
19  test.9   alpine:latest ip-172-31-15-30.us-east-2.compute.internal  Running       \
20  Running 12 seconds ago
21  test.10  alpine:latest ip-172-31-44-182.us-east-2.compute.internal Running       \
22  Running 12 seconds ago
```

Let's exit the cluster before we move onto a discussion how to simulate a failure of a node.

```
exit
```

We'll simulate failure of an instance by terminating it. We'll do that by executing `aws ec2 terminate-instances` command that requires `--instance-ids` argument. So, the first line of business is to figure out how to find ID of one of the nodes.

We already saw that we could use `aws ec2 describe-instances` command to get information about the instances of the cluster. This time we'll output `InstanceId` of all the nodes that belong to the security group used by managers.

```
aws ec2 describe-instances \
    | jq -r ".Reservations[] \
    .Instances[] \
    | select(.SecurityGroups[].GroupName \
    | contains(\"devops22-ManagerVpcSG\"))\
    .InstanceId"
```

The output is as follows.

```
i-091ad925d0243f7ab
i-0e850f3073ec25acd
i-05b25bc6fb6730ce1
```

We'll repeat the same command, limit the output to only one row, and store the result as an environment variable.

```
INSTANCE_ID=$(aws ec2 describe-instances \
    | jq -r ".Reservations[] \
    .Instances[] \
    | select(.SecurityGroups[].GroupName \
    | contains(\"devops22-ManagerVpcSG\"))\
    .InstanceId" \
    | tail -n 1)
```

Now that we have the ID, we can terminate the instance associated with it.

```
aws ec2 terminate-instances \
    --instance-ids $INSTANCE_ID
```

The output is as follows:

```
{
    "TerminatingInstances": [
        {
            "InstanceId": "i-0fa78489dca8125e8",
            "CurrentState": {
                "Code": 32,
                "Name": "shutting-down"
            },
```

```
            "PreviousState": {
                "Code": 16,
                "Name": "running"
            }
        }
    ]
}
```

We can see that the previous state is running and that it changed to shutting-down.

Let's see the state of the instances that form the cluster.

```
aws ec2 describe-instances \
    | jq -r ".Reservations[] \
    .Instances[] \
    | select(.SecurityGroups[].GroupName \
    | contains(\"devops22-ManagerVpcSG\"))\
    .State.Name"
```

We retrieved statuses of all the manager instances attached to the security group with a name starting with devops22-ManagerVpcSG. The output is as follows.

```
running
running
```

There are two manager instances in the cluster, and both are running. The node was indeed removed, and we are one server short from the desired setup. Let's wait for a moment or two and take another look at the manager instances.

```
aws ec2 describe-instances \
    | jq -r ".Reservations[] \
    .Instances[] \
    | select(.SecurityGroups[].GroupName \
    | contains(\"devops22-ManagerVpcSG\"))\
    .State.Name"
```

This time the output is different.

```
pending
running
running
```

Besides the two running managers, the third was added and is currently pending. The auto-scaling group associated with the managers detected that one node is missing and started creating a new VM that will restore the cluster to the desired state. The new node is still not ready, so we'll need to wait for a while longer.

```
aws ec2 describe-instances \
    | jq -r ".Reservations[] \
    .Instances[] \
    | select(.SecurityGroups[].GroupName \
    | contains(\"devops22-ManagerVpcSG\"))\
    .State.Name"
```

The output is as follows.

```
running
running
running
```

Auto-scaling group's desired state was restored, and the cluster is operating at its full capacity.

We cannot be certain whether the node we destroyed is different than the one we were entering before. Therefore, we should retrieve IP of one of the nodes one more time, and place it in the environment variable CLUSTER_IP.

```
CLUSTER_IP=$(aws ec2 describe-instances \
    | jq -r ".Reservations[] \
    .Instances[] \
    | select(.SecurityGroups[].GroupName \
    | contains(\"devops22-ManagerVpcSG\"))\
    .PublicIpAddress" \
    | tail -n 1)
```

Even though we know that the new node was created automatically, we should still confirm that it also joined the cluster as a Swarm manager.

```
ssh -i devops22.pem docker@$CLUSTER_IP
docker node ls
```

We entered into one of the managers and listed all the nodes. The output is as follows (IDs are removed for brevity):

```
1  HOSTNAME                                        STATUS AVAILABILITY MANAGER STATUS
2  ip-172-31-21-57.us-east-2.compute.internal  Down   Active       Unreachable
3  ip-172-31-44-182.us-east-2.compute.internal Ready  Active       Reachable
4  ip-172-31-15-30.us-east-2.compute.internal  Ready  Active       Leader
```

If the output of the `node ls` command is `Error response from daemon: This node is not a swarm manager...`, it means that you entered the node that was just created and it did not yet join the cluster. If that's the case, all you have to do is wait for a while longer and try it again. I'll assume that you entered to one of the "old" nodes.

The new node is not there. We can see only the three nodes that were initially created. One of them is `unreachable`.

Does that mean that the system does not work? Is self-healing working only partially and we need to join the new node manually? Should we create a script that will join new nodes to the cluster? The answer to all those questions is *no*. We were too impatient.

Even though AWS reported that the new node is running, it still requires a bit more time until it is fully initialized. Once that is finished, and the VM is fully operational, Docker's system containers will run and automatically join the node to the cluster.

Let's wait for a few moments and list the nodes one more time:

```
docker node ls
```

The output is as follows.

```
1  HOSTNAME                                         STATUS AVAILABILITY MANAGER STATUS
2  ip-172-31-26-141.us-east-2.compute.internal Ready  Active       Reachable
3  ip-172-31-21-57.us-east-2.compute.internal  Down   Active       Unreachable
4  ip-172-31-44-182.us-east-2.compute.internal Ready  Active       Reachable
5  ip-172-31-15-30.us-east-2.compute.internal  Ready  Active       Leader
```

The new node joined the cluster. Now we have four nodes, with one of them `unreachable`. Swarm cannot know that we destroyed the node. All it does know is that one manager is not reachable. That might be due to many reasons besides destruction.

The unreachable node will be removed from the list after a while.

Let's see what happened to the replicas of the test service:

```
docker service ps test
```

The output is as follows (IDs are removed for brevity):

```
NAME        IMAGE        NODE                                      DESIRED STA\
TE CURRENT STATE           ERROR PORTS
test.1      alpine:latest ip-172-31-44-182.us-east-2.compute.internal Running    \
    Running 10 minutes ago
test.2      alpine:latest ip-172-31-15-30.us-east-2.compute.internal  Running    \
    Running 10 minutes ago
test.3      alpine:latest ip-172-31-15-30.us-east-2.compute.internal  Running    \
    Running 4 minutes ago
 \_ test.3 alpine:latest ip-172-31-21-57.us-east-2.compute.internal   Shutdown   \
    Running 4 minutes ago
test.4      alpine:latest ip-172-31-44-182.us-east-2.compute.internal Running    \
    Running 10 minutes ago
test.5      alpine:latest ip-172-31-15-30.us-east-2.compute.internal  Running    \
    Running 10 minutes ago
test.6      alpine:latest ip-172-31-44-182.us-east-2.compute.internal Running    \
    Running 4 minutes ago
 \_ test.6 alpine:latest ip-172-31-21-57.us-east-2.compute.internal   Shutdown   \
    Running 4 minutes ago
test.7      alpine:latest ip-172-31-15-30.us-east-2.compute.internal  Running    \
    Running 10 minutes ago
test.8      alpine:latest ip-172-31-44-182.us-east-2.compute.internal Running    \
    Running 4 minutes ago
 \_ test.8 alpine:latest ip-172-31-21-57.us-east-2.compute.internal   Shutdown   \
    Running 4 minutes ago
test.9      alpine:latest ip-172-31-15-30.us-east-2.compute.internal  Running    \
    Running 10 minutes ago
test.10     alpine:latest ip-172-31-44-182.us-east-2.compute.internal Running    \
    Running 10 minutes ago
```

When Swarm detected that one of the nodes is unreachable, it rescheduled replicas that were running there to the nodes that were healthy at the time. It did not wait for the new node to join the cluster.

Swarm cannot know whether we (or auto-scaling groups, or any other process) will restore the infrastructure to the desired state. What if we removed the node purposefully and had no intention to add a new one in its place? Even if Swarm would be confident that a new node will be added to the cluster, it would still not make sense to wait for it. Creating a new node is a costly operation. It takes too much time. Therefore, as soon as Swarm detected that some of the replicas are not running (those from the failed node), it rescheduled them to the other two nodes. As a result, the third node is currently empty. It will start getting replicas the next time we deploy something or update one of the existing services. Let's try it out.

We'll update our `test` service:

```
docker service update \
    --env-add "FOO=BAR" test
```

Before we take a look at the service processes (or tasks), we should give Swarm a bit of time to perform rolling update to all the replicas. After a moment or two, we can execute `docker service ps` and discuss the result

```
docker service ps \
    -f desired-state=running test
```

The output is as follows (IDs are removed for brevity):

```
1   NAME     IMAGE         NODE                                      DESIRED STATE \
2   CURRENT STATE                  ERROR PORTS
3   test.1  alpine:latest ip-172-31-44-182.us-east-2.compute.internal Running      \
4   Running about a minute ago
5   test.2  alpine:latest ip-172-31-15-30.us-east-2.compute.internal  Running      \
6   Running 32 seconds ago
7   test.3  alpine:latest ip-172-31-15-30.us-east-2.compute.internal  Running      \
8   Running about a minute ago
9   test.4  alpine:latest ip-172-31-26-141.us-east-2.compute.internal Running      \
10  Running about a minute ago
11  test.5  alpine:latest ip-172-31-26-141.us-east-2.compute.internal Running      \
12  Running about a minute ago
13  test.6  alpine:latest ip-172-31-44-182.us-east-2.compute.internal Running      \
14  Running 55 seconds ago
15  test.7  alpine:latest ip-172-31-26-141.us-east-2.compute.internal Running      \
16  Running 20 seconds ago
17  test.8  alpine:latest ip-172-31-26-141.us-east-2.compute.internal Running      \
18  Running about a minute ago
19  test.9  alpine:latest ip-172-31-15-30.us-east-2.compute.internal  Running      \
20  Running 43 seconds ago
21  test.10 alpine:latest ip-172-31-44-182.us-east-2.compute.internal Running      \
22  Running 8 seconds ago
```

Since containers are immutable, any update of a service always results in a rolling update process that replaces all the replicas. You'll notice that, this time, they are spread across all the nodes of the cluster, including the new one.

```
exit
```

Self-healing applied to infrastructure works! We closed the circle. Swarm makes sure that our services are (almost) always in the desired state. With *Docker For AWS*, we accomplished a similar behavior with nodes.

> *Docker For AWS* will be able to recuperate from almost any failure as long as over 50% of managers are up-and-running. If we're running three managers and two of them fail at the same time, the cluster will not be able to re-establish the desired state.

The reason why over 50% of managers must be operational at any given moment lies in the Raft protocol that synchronizes data. Every piece of information is propagated to all the managers. An action is performed only if the majority agrees. That way we can guarantee data integrity. There is no majority if half or more members are absent.

You might be compelled to create clusters with five managers as a way to decrease chances of a complete cluster meltdown if two managers fail at the same time. In some cases that is a good strategy. However, the chances that two managers running in separate availability zones will go down at the same time are very slim. Don't take this advice as a commandment. You should experiment with both approaches and make your own decision. I tend to run all my clusters smaller than ten nodes with three managers. When they are bigger, five is a good number.

You might go even further and opt for seven managers. The more, the better. Right? Wrong! Data synchronization between managers is a costly operation. The more managers, the more time is required until a consensus is reached. Seven managers often produce more overhead than benefit.

What now?

We proved that self-healing works not only with services but also with infrastructure. We are getting close to having a self-sufficient system. The only thing missing is to find out a way to add self-adaptation applied to infrastructure. If we accomplish that, we'll be able to leave our system alone. We can go on vacation knowing that it will be operational without us. We could even go to one of those exotic places that still do not have the Internet. Wouldn't that be great?

Even though we are one step closer to our goal, we are still not there yet. We'll take another break before moving on.

We'll continue the practice from previous chapters. We'll destroy the cluster and save us from unnecessary cost.

```
aws cloudformation delete-stack \
    --stack-name devops22

aws cloudformation describe-stacks \
    --stack-name devops22 | \
    jq -r ".Stacks[0].StackStatus"
```

The output of the `describe-stacks` command is as follows.

```
DELETE_IN_PROGRESS
```

Cluster will be removed soon.

Feel free to repeat the command if you don't trust the system and want to see it through. You'll know that the cluster is fully removed when you see the error output that follows:

```
An error occurred (ValidationError) when calling the DescribeStacks
operation: Stack with id devops22 does not exist
```

15
Self-Adaptation Applied to Infrastructure

Our goal is within reach. We adopted schedulers (Docker Swarm in this case) that provide self-healing applied to services. We saw how *Docker For AWS* accomplishes a similar goal but on the infrastructure level. We used Prometheus, Alertmanager, and Jenkins to build a system that automatically adapts services to ever-changing conditions. The metrics we're storing in Prometheus are a combination of those gathered through exporters and those we added to our services through instrumentation. The only thing we're missing is self-adaptation applied to infrastructure. If we manage to build it, we'll close the circle and witness a self-sufficient system capable of running without (almost) any human intervention.

The logic behind self-adaptation applied to infrastructure is not much different from the one we used with services. We need metrics, alerts, and scripts that will adapt cluster capacity whenever conditions change.

We already have all the tools we need. Prometheus will continue gathering metrics and firing alerts. Alertmanager is still an excellent choice to receive those alerts and resend them to different system components. We'll keep using Jenkins as a tool that allows us to quickly write scripts that can interact with the system. Since we're using AWS to host our cluster, Jenkins will have to interact with its API.

We are so close to the final objective that I feel we should skip the theory and jump straight into practical hands-on parts of the chapter. So, without further ado, we'll create our cluster one more time.

Creating a cluster

In the previous chapter, we already explored how to create a cluster without UI. The commands that follow should be familiar and, hopefully, should not require much explanation.

 All the commands from this chapter are available in the `15-self-adaptation-infra.sh` Gist at `https://gist.github.com/vfarcic/7f49e5d1565b2234b84d8fe01e5c2356`.

Please replace `[...]` with your keys before executing the commands that follow.

```
export AWS_ACCESS_KEY_ID=[...]

export AWS_SECRET_ACCESS_KEY=[...]

export AWS_DEFAULT_REGION=us-east-1

export STACK_NAME=devops22

export KEY_NAME=devops22

aws cloudformation create-stack \
    --template-url https://editions-us-east-1.s3.amazonaws.com/aws\
/stable/Docker.tmpl
    --capabilities CAPABILITY_IAM \
    --stack-name $STACK_NAME \
    --parameters \
ParameterKey=ManagerSize,ParameterValue=3 \
ParameterKey=ClusterSize,ParameterValue=0 \
ParameterKey=KeyName,ParameterValue=$KEY_NAME \
ParameterKey=EnableSystemPrune,ParameterValue=yes \
ParameterKey=EnableCloudWatchLogs,ParameterValue=no \
ParameterKey=EnableCloudStorEfs,ParameterValue=yes \
ParameterKey=ManagerInstanceType,ParameterValue=t2.small \
ParameterKey=InstanceType,ParameterValue=t2.small
```

We defined a few environment variables and executed the `aws cloudformation create-stack` command that initiated creation of a cluster. It should take around five to ten minutes until it is finished.

```
aws cloudformation describe-stacks \
--stack-name $STACK_NAME | \
jq -r ".Stacks[0].StackStatus"
```

If the output of the `describe-stacks` command is CREATE_COMPLETE, our cluster is fully operational, and we can continue. Otherwise, please wait for a while longer and recheck the stack status.

Next, we'll retrieve cluster DNS and public IP of one of the manager nodes and store those values as environment variables CLUSTER_DNS and CLUSTER_IP.

```
CLUSTER_DNS=$(aws cloudformation \
    describe-stacks \
    --stack-name $STACK_NAME | \
    jq -r ".Stacks[0].Outputs[] | \
    select(.OutputKey==\"DefaultDNSTarget\")\
    .OutputValue")

CLUSTER_IP=$(aws ec2 describe-instances \
    | jq -r ".Reservations[] \
    .Instances[] \
    | select(.SecurityGroups[].GroupName \
    | contains("$STACK_NAME-ManagerVpcSG"))\
    .PublicIpAddress" \
    | tail -n 1)
```

Once we enter the cluster, we'll create a file that will hold the environment variables we'll need inside the cluster. Those are the same variables we already defined on our host. We'll output them so that we can easily copy and paste them when we enter one of the nodes.

```
echo "
export CLUSTER_DNS=$CLUSTER_DNS
export AWS_ACCESS_KEY_ID=$AWS_ACCESS_KEY_ID
export AWS_SECRET_ACCESS_KEY=$AWS_SECRET_ACCESS_KEY
export AWS_DEFAULT_REGION=$AWS_DEFAULT_REGION
"
```

Please copy the output of the `echo` command. We'll use it soon.

Now that we got all the cluster information we'll need, we can `ssh` into one of the manager nodes.

```
ssh -i $KEY_NAME.pem docker@$CLUSTER_IP
```

Next, we'll create a file that will hold all the information we'll need. That way we'll be able to get in and out of the cluster without losing the ability to retrieve that data quickly.

```
echo "
export CLUSTER_DNS=[...]
export AWS_ACCESS_KEY_ID=[...]
export AWS_SECRET_ACCESS_KEY=[...]
export AWS_DEFAULT_REGION=[...]
">creds
```

Instead of typing the preceding command, please type `echo "`, paste the output you copied a moment ago, and close it with `">creds`. The result should be four `export` commands inside the `creds` file.

Let's download a script that will deploy (almost) all the services we used in the previous chapter.

```
curl -o aws-services-15.sh \
    https://raw.githubusercontent.com/vfarcic\
/docker-flow-monitor/master/scripts/aws-services-15.sh

chmod +x aws-services-15.sh
```

We download the script and gave it execute permissions.

Now we are ready to deploy the services.

```
source creds
./aws-services-15.sh
docker stack ls
```

Since `aws-services-15.sh` needs environment variable `CLUSTER_DNS`, we exported it by executing `source`. Further on, we executed the script and listed all the stacks deployed to the cluster. The output is as follows:

```
1  NAME                SERVICES
2  exporter            3
3  go-demo             2
4  jenkins             2
5  monitor             3
6  proxy               2
```

You'll notice that the `logging` stack is missing. We did not deploy it since it is not relevant to the goals we're trying to accomplish in this chapter and, at the same time, it requires extra nodes. Since I am committed towards not making you spend more money than needed, it seemed like a sensible thing not to deploy that stack.

Finally, let's get out of the cluster and explore how we could scale it manually. That will give us an insight into the processes we'll want to automate.

```
exit
```

Scaling nodes manually

Let's explore how we can scale nodes manually and, later on, try to apply the same logic to our automated processes.

We're running the cluster in AWS which already has auto-scaling groups defined for both managers and workers. In such a setting, the most sensible way to scale the nodes is to change the desired capacity of those groups.

When new nodes are created by auto-scaling groups in *Docker For AWS* or *Azure*, they will join the cluster as managers or workers. If you choose not to use *Docker For AWS* or *Azure*, you'll have to do some additional work to replicate the same functionality as the one we're about to explore. You'll have to create init scripts that will find IP of one of the managers, retrieve join token, and, finally, execute `docker swarm join` command.

> If your hosting vendor does not provide functionality similar to auto-scaling groups, you might need to create new nodes using tools like Terraform (`https://www.terraform.io/`).

No matter which hosting vendor you're using, the logic should, more or less, be always the same. We need to change the number of running managers or workers and, in case that number increased, join new nodes to the cluster. I am confident that you'll be able to modify the logic that follows to your cluster setup.

The first thing we need to do is find out the name of the auto-scaling group created for our cluster. A good start is to list all the groups by executing `aws autoscaling describe-auto-scaling-groups` command.

```
aws autoscaling \
    describe-auto-scaling-groups \
    | jq "."
```

The output is too big to be presented in a book format, and we do not need it in its entirety. Therefore, we'll limit the output. Luckily, we know that the name of the auto-scaling group starts with `[STACK_NAME]-Node`. We can use that to filter the output.

A command that will retrieve only the auto-scaling group assigned to worker nodes and retrieve just the name of the group is as follows.

```
aws autoscaling \
    describe-auto-scaling-groups \
    | jq -r ".AutoScalingGroups[] \
    | select(.AutoScalingGroupName \
    | startswith(\"$STACK_NAME-NodeAsg-\"))\
    .AutoScalingGroupName"
```

We used `jq` to retrieve all data within the root node `AutoScalingGroups`. Further on, we used `select` command to retrieve only records with `AutoScalingGroupName` that starts with `[STACK_NAME]-Node`. Finally, we limited the output further so that only the name of the name of the group is retrieved.

The output will vary from one case to another. It should be similar to the one that follows:

```
devops22-NodeAsg-1J93DRR7VYUHU
```

We cannot change the auto-scaling group desired capacity without knowing what the current number of nodes is. Therefore, we need to construct another query that will provide that information. Fortunately, the command is very similar since all we need is to retrieve a different value based on the same filter.

```
aws autoscaling \
    describe-auto-scaling-groups \
    | jq -r ".AutoScalingGroups[] \
    | select(.AutoScalingGroupName \
    | startswith(\"$STACK_NAME-NodeAsg-\"))\
    .DesiredCapacity"
```

When compared with the previous command, the only change is that, this time, we retrieved `DesiredCapacity` instead `AutoScalingGroupName`. The output is 0. That should come as no surprise since we specified that we did not want any workers when we created the cluster.

We'll repeat the command we used to retrieve the name of the auto-scaling group and, this time, we'll put the result as a value of an environment variable. That way we'll be able to reuse it across the commands we'll execute later on.

```
ASG_NAME=$(aws autoscaling \
    describe-auto-scaling-groups \
    | jq -r ".AutoScalingGroups[] \
    | select(.AutoScalingGroupName \
    | startswith(\"$STACK_NAME-NodeAsg-"))\
    .AutoScalingGroupName")
```

Now that we have the name of the auto-scaling group, we can increase the desired capacity from 0 to 1.

```
aws autoscaling \
    update-auto-scaling-group \
    --auto-scaling-group-name $ASG_NAME \
    --desired-capacity 1
```

Let's confirm that the capacity is indeed increased.

```
aws autoscaling \
    describe-auto-scaling-groups \
    --auto-scaling-group-names $ASG_NAME \
    | jq ".AutoScalingGroups[0] \
    .DesiredCapacity"
```

We executed `describe-auto-scaling-groups` one more time. However, since now we know the name of the group, there was no need for `jq` filters.

As expected, the output is 1 confirming that the update indeed worked.

The fact that the desired capacity of the group was updated does not necessarily mean that a new node was created. We can check that easily by executing `ec2 describe-instances` combined with a bit of `jq` magic.

```
aws ec2 describe-instances | jq -r \
    ".Reservations[].Instances[] \
    | select(.SecurityGroups[].GroupName \
    | startswith(\"$STACK_NAME-NodeVpcSG\"))\
    .InstanceId"
```

We executed `ec2 describe-instances` and used `jq` to retrieve all instances, filter them by the security group which has a name that starts with a predictable string, and retrieved the ID of the only worker instance. The output should be similar to the one that follows.

```
i-06f7e78c063fedeb3
```

Creation of an EC2 instance is fast. What takes a bit of time is its initialization. We should check its status and confirm that it finished initializing.

```
INSTANCE_ID=$(aws ec2 \
    describe-instances | jq -r \
    ".Reservations[].Instances[] \
    | select(.SecurityGroups[].GroupName \
    | startswith(\"$STACK_NAME-NodeVpcSG\"))\
    .InstanceId")

aws ec2 describe-instance-status \
    --instance-ids $INSTANCE_ID \
    | jq -r ".InstanceStatuses[0]\
    .InstanceStatus.Status"
```

We repeated the previous command but, this time, stored the instance ID as the environment variable `INSTANCE_ID`. Later on, we used it with the `ec2 describe-instance-status` command to retrieve the status.

If the output is ok, the new node is created, is initialized, and (probably) joined the cluster. Otherwise, please wait for a minute or two and recheck the status.

Finally, let's confirm that the new node indeed joined the Swarm cluster.

```
ssh -i $KEY_NAME.pem docker@$CLUSTER_IP

docker node ls

exit
```

We entered one of the manager servers, listed all the nodes of the cluster, and returned to the host.

The output of the node `ls` command is as follows (IDs are removed for brevity):

```
1  HOSTNAME                                    STATUS AVAILABILITY MANAGER STATUS
2  ip-172-31-40-169.us-east-2.compute.internal Ready  Active
3  ip-172-31-24-32.us-east-2.compute.internal  Ready  Active       Reachable
4  ip-172-31-2-29.us-east-2.compute.internal   Ready  Active       Leader
5  ip-172-31-42-64.us-east-2.compute.internal  Ready  Active       Reachable
```

That's brilliant! The new worker joined the cluster, and our capacity increased. If, in your case, the new node did not yet join the cluster, please wait for a few moments and list the nodes again.

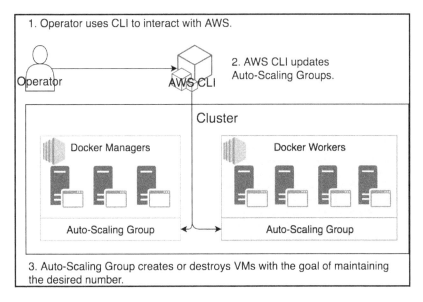

Figure 15-1: Manual updates of Auto-Scaling Groups

There are a few other manual actions we should explore before we move towards automation. But, before we proceed, we'll change the auto-scaling group one more time. We'll set the desired capacity back to 0. That way we'll not only confirm that the process works in both directions, but also save a bit of money by not running more nodes than we need.

```
aws autoscaling \
    update-auto-scaling-group \
    --auto-scaling-group-name $ASG_NAME \
    --desired-capacity 0
```

We updated the auto-scaling group back to the desired capacity of 0.

After a while, we can return to the cluster and confirm that the worker is removed from the cluster.

```
ssh -i $KEY_NAME.pem docker@$CLUSTER_IP
```

```
docker node ls
```

The output of the `node ls` command is as follows (IDs are removed for brevity):

```
1  HOSTNAME                                      STATUS AVAILABILITY MANAGER STATUS
2  ip-172-31-40-169.us-east-2.compute.internal Down   Active
3  ip-172-31-24-32.us-east-2.compute.internal  Ready  Active       Reachable
4  ip-172-31-2-29.us-east-2.compute.internal   Ready  Active       Leader
5  ip-172-31-42-64.us-east-2.compute.internal  Ready  Active       Reachable
```

We still have one more problem to solve. We cannot run aws commands from the cluster. Docker For AWS does not let us install any additional software. Even if we would find the way to install the CLI, we should not pollute our production servers. Instead, we should run any tool we need thorough a container.

Since there is no official AWS CLI Docker image, I created one for the exercises in this chapter. Let's take a look at the Dockerfile.

 curl "https://raw.githubusercontent.com/vfarcic/docker-aws-cli/master/Dockerfile"

```
FROM alpine

MAINTAINER Viktor Farcic <viktor@farcic.com>

RUN apk --update add python py-pip jq && \
    pip install awscli && \
    apk del py-pip && \
    rm -rf /var/cache/apk/*

ENV AWS_ACCESS_KEY_ID ""
ENV AWS_SECRET_ACCESS_KEY ""
ENV AWS_DEFAULT_REGION "us-east-1"
```

As you can see, it's pretty straightforward. The image is based on `alpine` and installs `python`, `py-pip`, and `jq`. We're installing Python since `pip` is the easiest way to install `awscli`. The rest of the image specification defines a few environment variables required by the AWS CLI. The image was built and pushed as `vfarcic/aws-cli`.

Let's do a test run of a container based on the image.

```
source creds

docker container run --rm \
    -e AWS_ACCESS_KEY_ID=$AWS_ACCESS_KEY_ID \
    -e AWS_SECRET_ACCESS_KEY=$AWS_SECRET_ACCESS_KEY \
    -e AWS_DEFAULT_REGION=$AWS_DEFAULT_REGION \
    vfarcic/aws-cli \
    aws ec2 describe-instances
```

We sourced the `creds` file that contains the environment variables we need. Further on we run a container based on the `vfarcic/aws-cli image`. We used aws ec2 describe-instances as the command only to demonstrate that any `aws` command could be executed through a container. The result should be information about all the EC2 nodes we have in that region.

We're using the `creds` file only as a convenience and for demo purposes since we cannot inject a secret into a container. It must be a Swarm service.

Do not keep credentials stored in files on servers. That is a huge security risk. Instead, store them as Docker secrets.

The docker container run command we executed is too long to remember. We can mitigate that by creating a Docker Compose YAML file with all the aws commands we need. An example of such a file can be found in the `vfarcic/docker-aws-cli` repository. It contains all the commands we'll use in this chapter.

Let's take a brief look at it.

```
curl "https://raw.githubusercontent.com/vfarcic/docker-\
aws-cli/master/docker-compose.yml"
```

The output is as follows:

```
version: '3.2'
services:
  asg-name:
    image: vfarcic/aws-cli
    environment:
      - AWS_ACCESS_KEY_ID=${AWS_ACCESS_KEY_ID}
      - AWS_SECRET_ACCESS_KEY=${AWS_SECRET_ACCESS_KEY}
      - AWS_DEFAULT_REGION=${AWS_DEFAULT_REGION}
    command: sh -c "aws autoscaling describe-auto-scaling-groups\
 | jq -r '.AutoScalingGroups[] | select(.AutoScalingGroupName |\
startswith(\"${STACK_NAME}--NodeAsg\")).AutoScalingGroupName'"

  asg-desired-capacity:
    image: vfarcic/aws-cli
    environment:
      - AWS_ACCESS_KEY_ID=${AWS_ACCESS_KEY_ID}
      - AWS_SECRET_ACCESS_KEY=${AWS_SECRET_ACCESS_KEY}
      - AWS_DEFAULT_REGION=${AWS_DEFAULT_REGION}
    command: sh -c "aws autoscaling describe-auto-scaling-groups\
 --auto-scaling-group-names $ASG_NAME | jq\
'.AutoScalingGroups[0].DesiredCapacity'"
```

```
asg-update-desired-capacity:
  image: vfarcic/aws-cli
  environment:
    - AWS_ACCESS_KEY_ID=${AWS_ACCESS_KEY_ID}
    - AWS_SECRET_ACCESS_KEY=${AWS_SECRET_ACCESS_KEY}
    - AWS_DEFAULT_REGION=${AWS_DEFAULT_REGION}
  command: sh -c "aws autoscaling update-auto-scaling-group\
  --auto-scaling-group-name $ASG_NAME --desired-capacity\
$ASG_DESIRED_CAPACITY"
```

We won't go into details of the services defined in that YAML file. It should be self explanatory what each of them does.

Please note that docker-compose is not installed on the nodes of the cluster. We will not need it since the plan is to use those Compose services through Jenkins agents which will have Docker Compose.

Let's move on and explore how to transform the commands we used so far into automated scaling solution.

Creating scaling job

Let's try to translate the commands we executed manually into a Jenkins job. If we manage to do that, we can go further and let Alertmanager trigger that job whenever certain thresholds are reached in Prometheus.

We'll start by downloading Jenkins stack from the `vfarcic/docker-flow-monitor` (https://github.com/vfarcic/docker-flow-monitor) repository.

```
curl -o jenkins.yml \
    https://raw.githubusercontent.com/vfarcic/docker-\
flow-monitor/master/stacks/jenkins-aws-secret.yml

cat jenkins.yml
```

The stack definition we just downloaded is almost identical to the one we used before so we'll comment only the differences.

```
version: "3.2"

services:

  ...

  agent:
    image: vfarcic/jenkins-swarm-agent
    ...
    secrets:
      - aws
      ...

secrets:
  aws:
    external: true
  ...
```

The only new addition to the Jenkins stack is the `aws` secret. It should contain AWS keys and the region we'll need for AWS CLI. So, let's start by creating the secret.

```
source creds

echo "
export AWS_ACCESS_KEY_ID=$AWS_ACCESS_KEY_ID
export AWS_SECRET_ACCESS_KEY=$AWS_SECRET_ACCESS_KEY
export AWS_DEFAULT_REGION=$AWS_DEFAULT_REGION
export STACK_NAME=devops22
" | docker secret create aws -
```

We sourced the `creds` file and used the environment variables to construct the `aws` secret.

Now we can deploy the `jenkins` stack.

```
docker stack deploy \
    -c jenkins.yml jenkins

exit
```

We deployed the stack and exited the cluster.

Jenkins has a small nuance with its URL. If we do not change anything, it will not know what its address is and, when we construct notification messages, it'll resolve itself to null. Fortunately, the fix is reasonably easy. All we have to do is open the configuration page and click the **Save** button.

```
open "http://$CLUSTER_DNS/jenkins/configure"
```

Please login using `admin` as both the **User** and the **Password**. Once you're authenticated, you'll see the configuration screen which, among other fields, contains Jenkins URL. Please confirm that it is correct and click the **Save** button:

Jenkins Location

Jenkins URL   http://devops22-externall-1kbk8bu01fk8z-1538396981.us-east-2.elb.amazonaws.

System Admin e-mail address   address not configured yet <nobody@nowhere>

Figure 15-2: Jenkins URL configuration

Now that we resolved Jenkins' identity crisis, we can create a new job capable of scaling nodes of the cluster.

```
open "http://$CLUSTER_DNS/jenkins/view/all/newJob"
```

Please type `aws-scale` as the job name, select **Pipeline** as the job type, and click the **OK** button. You'll see the job configuration screen.

Since we're planning to trigger builds remotely, we should create an authentication token. Please click the **Build Triggers** tab, select the **Trigger builds remotely** checkbox, and type `DevOps22` as the `Authentication Token`.

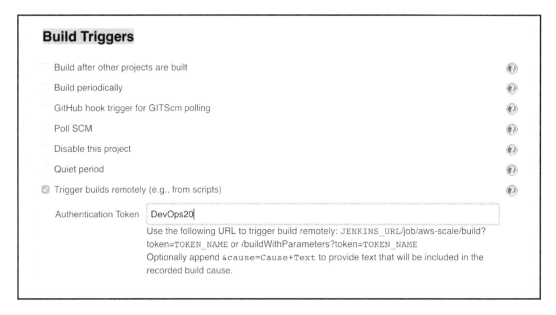

Figure 15-3: Jenkins job build triggers

Now we're ready to define a pipeline script.

Please click the `Pipeline` tab and type the script that follows in the **Pipeline Script** field.

If you're not thrilled with the prospect of typing, feel free to copy and paste the script from the `15-self-adaptation-infra-jenkins-pipeline-01.groovy` gist at `https://gist.github.com/vfarcic/03b302f7ce31cf3bafb0529da7601126`.

```
pipeline {
  agent {
    label "prod"
  }
  options {
    buildDiscarder(logRotator(numToKeepStr: '2'))
    disableConcurrentBuilds()
  }
  parameters {
    string(
      name: "scale",
      defaultValue: "1",
      description: "The number of worker nodes to add or remove"
    )
  }
```

```
  stages {
    stage("scale") {
      steps {
        git "https://github.com/vfarcic/docker-aws-cli.git"
        script {
          def asgName = sh(
            script: "source /run/secrets/aws && \
docker-compose run --rm asg-name",
            returnStdout: true
          ).trim()
          if (asgName == "") {
            error "Could not find auto-scaling group"
          }
          def asgDesiredCapacity = sh(
            script: "source /run/secrets/aws && ASG_NAME=\
${asgName} docker-compose run --rm asg-desired-capacity",
            returnStdout: true
          ).trim().toInteger()
          def asgNewCapacity = asgDesiredCapacity + scale.toInteger()
          if (asgNewCapacity < 1) {
            error "The number of worker nodes is already at the\
 minimum capacity of 1"
          } else if (asgNewCapacity > 3) {
            error "The number of worker nodes is already at the\
 maximum capacity of 3"
          } else {
            sh "source /run/secrets/aws && ASG_NAME=${asgName}\
ASG_DESIRED_CAPACITY=${asgNewCapacity} docker-compose run --rm\
 asg-update-desired-capacity"
            echo "Changed the number of worker nodes from\
 ${asgDesiredCapacity} to ${asgNewCapacity}"
          }
        }
      }
    }
  }
  post {
    success {
      slackSend(
        color: "good",
        message: """Worker nodes were scaled.
Please check Jenkins logs for the job ${env.JOB_NAME} #${env.BUILD_NUMBER}
 ${env.BUILD_URL}console"""
      )
    }
    failure {
      slackSend(
        color: "danger",
```

```
        message: """Worker nodes could not be scaled.
  Please check Jenkins logs for the job ${env.JOB_NAME} #${env.BUILD_NUMBER}
  ${env.BUILD_URL}console"""
        )
      }
    }
  }
```

You should be able to understand most of the Pipeline without any help so I'll limit the discussion on the steps of the `scale` stage.

We start by cloning the `vfarcic/docker-aws-cli` repository that contains `docker-compose.yml` file with AWS CLI services we'll need.

Next, we're executing Docker Compose service `asg-name` that retrieves the name of the auto-scaling group associated with worker nodes. The result is stored in the variable `asgName`. Since all the services defined in that Compose file require environment variables with AWS keys and the region where the cluster is running, we're executing `source /run/secrets/aws` before `docker-compose` commands. The file was injected as the Docker secret `aws`.

Further on, we're retrieving the current desired capacity. The new capacity is calculated by adding the value of the `scale` parameter to the current capacity. Finally, we have a simple `if...else` statement that throws an error if the future capacity would be lower than 1 or higher than 3 nodes. That way we are setting boundaries so that the system cannot expand or contract too much. You should change those limits to better match your current size of the cluster.

Finally, if the new capacity is within the boundaries, we are updating the auto-scaling group.

As you can see, the script is relatively simple and straightforward. Even though this might not be the final version that fits everyone's purposes, the general gist is there, and I'm confident that you'll have no problem adapting it to suit your needs.

Do not forget to click the Save button before moving forward.

Let's give the job a spin.

```
open "http://$CLUSTER_DNS/jenkins/blue/organizations/jenkins/aws-scale/activity"
```

You should see the `aws-scale` screen with the **Run** button in the middle. Please click it.

We already discussed the bug that makes the first build of a Pipeline job with properties fail. All subsequent builds should work properly, so we'll give it another try.

Please reload the page and click the **Run** button. You'll be presented with a screen with a single parameter that allows us to specify how many nodes we'd like to add or remove. Leave the default value of `1` and click the **Run** button. A new build will start.

Please click on the row that represents the new build and explore it. The second to last step should state that the number of workers changed from `0` to `1`.

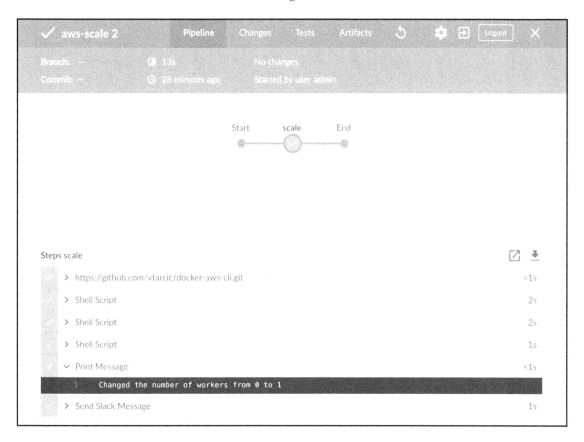

Figure 15-4: Jenkins build results

As you saw before, it takes a minute or two until a new node is created and initialized. Fetch a coffee. By the time you come back, the new node will be fully operational within the cluster.

Let's enter one of the manager nodes and confirm that the new node joined the Swarm cluster.

```
ssh -i $KEY_NAME.pem docker@$CLUSTER_IP

docker node ls
```

The output is as follows (IDs are removed for brevity):

```
1  HOSTNAME                                         STATUS AVAILABILITY MANAGER STATUS
2  ip-172-31-24-32.us-east-2.compute.internal Ready  Active       Reachable
3  ip-172-31-2-29.us-east-2.compute.internal  Ready  Active       Leader
4  ip-172-31-42-64.us-east-2.compute.internal Ready  Active       Reachable
5  ip-172-31-24-95.us-east-2.compute.internal Down   Active
6  ip-172-31-34-28.us-east-2.compute.internal Ready  Active
7  ip-172-31-4-136.us-east-2.compute.internal Down   Active
```

As you can see, the new worker indeed joined the cluster. In your cluster, the new node might not yet be initialized. If that's the case, please wait for a minute or two and re-execute `docker node ls` command.

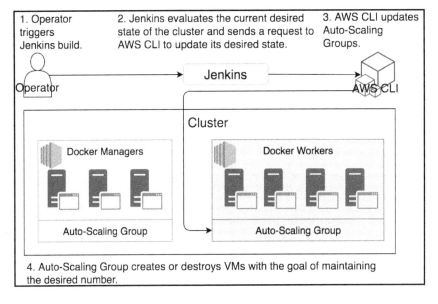

Figure 15-5: Infrastructure scaling orchestrated by Jenkins

UI is useful as a learning experience, but our goal is to trigger the job remotely. Let's check whether we can send a `POST` request.

```
exit

curl -XPOST -i \
 "http://$CLUSTER_DNS/jenkins/job/aws-scale\
/buildWithParameters?token=DevOps22&scale=2"
```

We exited the cluster and sent a post request with the token and the scale parameter set to 2. The response is as follows:

```
HTTP/1.1 201 Created
Connection: close
Date: Sat, 23 Sep 2017 20:07:21 GMT
X-Content-Type-Options: nosniff
Location: http://devops22-ExternalL-1OG8BA7IMZCT0-900324820.us-east-2.elb.amazon\
aws.com/jenkins/queue/item/5/
Server: Jetty(9.4.z-SNAPSHOT)
```

Let's confirm that Jenkins build was executed successfully.

```
open "http://$CLUSTER_DNS/jenkins/blue/organizations/jenkins\
/aws-scale/activity"
```

Please click the last build and observe that the number of nodes scaled. Similarly, you should see a new notification in *#df-monitor-tests* in the *DevOps20 Slack* channel.

Figure 15-6: Slack notification indicating that nodes scaled

Finally, we'll go back to the cluster and confirm not only that a new node was created but also that it joined the cluster.

```
ssh -i $KEY_NAME.pem docker@$CLUSTER_IP

docker node ls
```

The output is as follows (IDs are removed for brevity):

```
 1  HOSTNAME                                      STATUS AVAILABILITY MANAGER STATUS
 2  ip-172-31-24-32.us-east-2.compute.internal Ready  Active       Reachable
 3  ip-172-31-2-29.us-east-2.compute.internal  Ready  Active       Leader
 4  ip-172-31-42-64.us-east-2.compute.internal Ready  Active       Reachable
 5  ip-172-31-24-95.us-east-2.compute.internal Ready  Active
 6  ip-172-31-34-28.us-east-2.compute.internal Ready  Active
 7  ip-172-31-4-136.us-east-2.compute.internal Ready  Active
```

The number of worker nodes increased from one to three. If you do not yet see three worker nodes, please wait for a minute or two and re-run the `docker node ls` command.

Let's test whether the limits we set are respected. Remember, our Pipeline script should not allow less than one nor more than three worker nodes. Since we are already running three workers, we should be able to test it by attempting to add one more.

```
exit

curl -XPOST -i
    "http://$CLUSTER_DNS/jenkins/job/aws-scale\
/buildWithParameters?token=DevOps22&scale=1"
```

We exited the cluster and sent a `POST` request to build the `aws-scale` job with the `scale` parameter set to `1`.

Let's see the result in Jenkins UI.

```
open "http://$CLUSTER_DNS/jenkins/blue/organizations/jenkins/aws-
scale/activity"
```

You should see that the last build failed. We tried to add more workers than allowed and the build responded with an error. Similarly, we should see an error notification in *#df-monitor-tests* in the *DevOps20 Slack* channel.

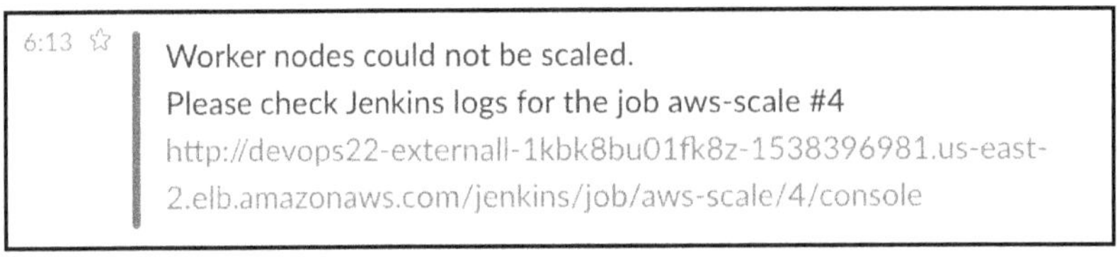

6:13 ☆ Worker nodes could not be scaled.
        Please check Jenkins logs for the job aws-scale #4
        http://devops22-externall-1kbk8bu01fk8z-1538396981.us-east-
        2.elb.amazonaws.com/jenkins/job/aws-scale/4/console

Figure 15-7: Slack notification indicating that node scaling failed

It won't hurt to check whether de-scaling nodes works as well.

```
curl -XPOST -i \
    "http://$CLUSTER_DNS/jenkins/job/aws-scale\
/buildWithParameters?token=DevOps22&scale=-2"
```

We sent a similar POST request like a few times before. The only notable difference is that the scale param is now set to -2. As a result, two worker nodes should be removed, leaving us with one.

At this point, there should be no need to check build results in Jenkins or notifications in Slack. The system proved to be working well. So, we'll skip through those and jump straight into the cluster and output the list of joined nodes.

```
ssh -i $KEY_NAME.pem docker@$CLUSTER_IP

docker node ls
```

We entered the cluster and listed all the nodes.

The output is as follows (IDs are removed for brevity):

```
HOSTNAME                                    STATUS  AVAILABILITY  MANAGER STATUS
ip-172-31-24-32.us-east-2.compute.internal  Ready   Active        Reachable
ip-172-31-2-29.us-east-2.compute.internal   Ready   Active        Leader
ip-172-31-42-64.us-east-2.compute.internal  Ready   Active        Reachable
ip-172-31-24-95.us-east-2.compute.internal  Down    Active
ip-172-31-34-28.us-east-2.compute.internal  Ready   Active
ip-172-31-4-136.us-east-2.compute.internal  Down    Active
```

You'll notice that status of two of the nodes is set to **Down**. If, in your case, all the nodes are still **Ready**, you might need to wait for a minute or two and re-execute the docker node ls command. On the other hand, if you were not fast enough, Swarm might have cleaned its registry, and the two nodes that were **Down** might have been removed altogether.

Finally, the last verification we should do is to check whether the lower limit is respected as well.

```
exit

curl -XPOST -i
    "http://$CLUSTER_DNS/jenkins/job/aws-scale\
/buildWithParameters?token=DevOps22&scale=-1"
```

You know what to do. Visit the last build in Jenkins, check Slack, list Swarm nodes, or trust me blindly. The number of worker nodes should be left intact since we are running only one and reducing them to zero would violate the lower limit we set in the pipeline job.

Now that we confirmed that triggering the `aws-scale` job (de)scales our worker nodes, we can turn our attention to Prometheus and Alertmanager and try to tie them all together into a system that will, for example, scale the number of workers depending on memory usage.

Scaling cluster nodes automatically

We created the last piece of the chain. Jenkins job will scale nodes of a cluster only if something triggers it. We did that manually by sending `POST` requests but, as you might have guessed, that is not our ultimate goal. We need to run those builds through alerts based on metrics. Therefore, we'll move back to the beginning of the chain and explore some of the metrics we can use and try to convert them into meaningful alerts.

Let's open Prometheus and try to define an alert worthy of our scaling needs.

```
open "http://$CLUSTER_DNS/monitor"
```

Please use `admin` as both the **User Name** and the **Password** if you're asked to authenticate.

We'll start with an expression we already used in the previous chapters.

Please type the query that follows in the **Expression** field, click the **Execute** button, and switch to the **Graph** tab.

```
(sum(node_memory_MemTotal) BY (instance) - sum(node_memory_MemFree\
+ node_memory_Buffers + node_memory_Cached) BY (instance)) \
/ sum(node_memory_MemTotal) BY (instance)
```

As a reminder, the expression calculates the percentage of used memory for each instance (node). It does that by taking the total amount of memory and reducing it with free, buffered, and cached memory. Further on, the result is divided with total memory to get a percentage. Each segment of the expression is using `BY (instance)` to separate the results.

The output should be four graphs representing four nodes currently running in the cluster. Used memory should be somewhere between ten and forty percent for each node.

Don't get confused if you see more than four lines. We had more than four nodes and, during their lifespan, their metrics were also recorded in Prometheus.

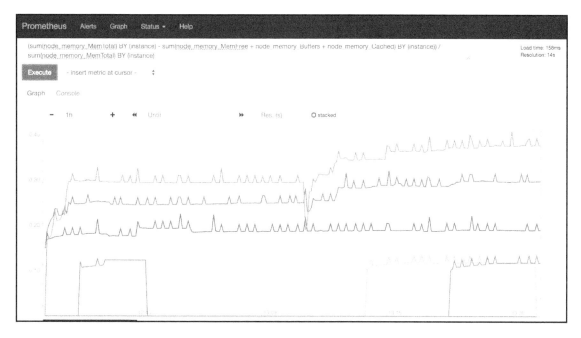

Figure 15-8: Prometheus graph with memory utilization

At this point you might be tempted to write an alert that would be fired whenever memory is, let's say, over 80%. That alert could result in a `POST` request to Jenkins which, in turn, would scale worker nodes.

What would such a spike in memory usage on one of the nodes tell us? If all nodes are using too much memory, it would not make sense to monitor them individually. On the other hand, if only one node has a spike, that would probably not indicate a problem that should be solved by scaling the number of nodes. The issue would, more likely, lie in incorrect memory reservations and limitations defined for one of our services. Or, maybe one of the services went wild with memory consumption. However, in that case, we probably did not even define its resources. If we did, Swarm would reschedule that service and, before that happens, we'd get a service-level alert. Such an alert might result in scaling of the service, or it might require some other type of actions. There might be other reasons for memory spike in one of the nodes but, in most of the cases, the resolution would have to rely on manual intervention. We'd need to (re)define service resources, fix a bug, or do one of many other actions that should be performed manually.

We, humans, should deal with unexpected anomalies and let the system correct itself when something predictable happens.

All in all, auto-scaling based on memory usage of a single node is, in most cases, not a good strategy. Instead, I believe that it would be better to base our auto-scaling strategy on memory usage of the entire cluster. After all, we already adopted the concept of treating the whole cluster as a single entity.

Let's try to write an expression that will give us the percentage of used memory across the whole cluster. We'll break it into two parts. First, we'll write a query that retrieves the number of used bytes and, later on, we'll get the total available memory of the whole cluster. If we divide those two, the result should be a percentage of the used memory of a cluster.

Please type the query that follows in the **Expression** field, and click the **Execute** button:

```
sum(node_memory_MemTotal) - sum(node_memory_MemFree +
node_memory_Buffers\
+ node_memory_Cached)
```

You should see that around 2 GB of memory is currently used in the cluster.

The expression we used is very similar to the one that did the calculation for each instance. The only significant difference is that we removed BY (instance) parts.

Next, we need to find out the total amount of memory of the cluster. That part should be easy since the previous expression already starts with the total.

Please type the query that follows in the **Expression** field, and click the **Execute** button:

```
sum(node_memory_MemTotal)
```

The output should show that we have 8 GB of total memory. You might see that the number was bigger in the past since we had a brief period with five or six nodes when we were experimenting with Jenkins' job aws-scale. You might still have it set to more than 8 GB. In that case, please wait for a few moments until metrics from the removed nodes expire.

If we combine those two expressions, the result is as follows:

```
(sum(node_memory_MemTotal) - sum(node_memory_MemFree +
node_memory_Buffers\
+ node_memory_Cached)) / sum(node_memory_MemTotal)
```

Please type the previous expression and click the **Execute** button. The result should be current memory usage of approximately 25%.

Figure 15-9: Prometheus graph with total memory utilization of the cluster

There's still one more problem we might need to solve. We should probably not treat manager and worker nodes equally so we might want to split metrics between the two. If we'd distinguish `node_exporter` services running on manager nodes from those deployed to workers, we could create different types of alerts for each server types.

Let's go back to the cluster and download an updated version of the `exporter` stack definition.

```
ssh -i $KEY_NAME.pem docker@$CLUSTER_IP

curl -o exporters.yml \
    https://raw.githubusercontent.com/vfarcic/docker-\
flow-monitor/master/stacks/exporters-aws.yml

cat exporters.yml
```

We entered the cluster, downloaded the `exporters-aws.yml` stack definition, and displayed its content. The output of the relevant parts of the `cat` command is as follows:

```
node-exporter-manager:
  ...
  deploy:
    labels:
      ...
      - com.df.alertName.2=node_mem_limit_total_above
      - com.df.alertIf.2=@node_mem_limit_total_above:0.8
      - com.df.alertLabels.2=receiver=system,scale=no,service=\
exporter_node-exporter-manager,type=node
      - com.df.alertFor.2=30s
      ...
    placement:
      constraints:
        - node.role == manager
  ...
node-exporter-worker:
  ...
  deploy:
 labels:
    ...
    - com.df.alertName.2=node_mem_limit_total_above
    - com.df.alertIf.2=@node_mem_limit_total_above:0.8
    - com.df.alertFor.2=30s
    - com.df.alertName.3=node_mem_limit_total_below
    - com.df.alertIf.3=@node_mem_limit_total_below:0.05
    - com.df.alertFor.3=30s
    ...
  placement:
    constraints:
      - node.role == worker
  ...
```

We split `node-exporter` service into two. We added two new label sets besides those we used before. They are `@node_mem_limit_total_above` and `@node_mem_limit_total_below` shortcuts that expand to alerts with the expression we wrote earlier. The first one will trigger an alert if the total memory of all the nodes where the exporter is running is above a certain threshold. Similarly, the other will be triggered if total memory is below the threshold. Those shortcuts are accompanied with labels `scale` and `type`. Default values of the `scale` label are `up` and `down` depending on the shortcut. The `type` label is always set to `node`. That way, we'll know whether to scale or de-scale and, through the `type` label, we'll know that the action should be performed on nodes. For more info, please consult **AlertIf Parameter Shortcuts** (`http://monitor.dockerflow.com/usage/#alertif-parameter-shortcuts`) section of the Docker Flow Monitor (`http://monitor.dockerflow.com/`) documentation.

You'll notice that the `node-exporter-manager` service does not have the `node_mem_limit_total_below` alert. The reason is simple. If memory usage is very low on manager nodes, there's still nothing we should do. We're not going to remove one of the managers since that would put cluster at risk. Furthermore, we changed the `node_mem_limit_total_above` default labels so that `scale` is set to `no`. That way, we can instruct Alertmanager not to send a request to Jenkins to scale the nodes but a Slack notification instead. All in all, when memory usage of manager nodes is too low, we will take no action. When it's too high, we'll investigate the reason behind that, instead of taking any automated actions.

The `node-exporter-worker` service will trigger automation in both cases. We'll configure Alertmanager to send requests to Jenkins to add or remove worker nodes if memory usage goes beyond defined thresholds. We put `node_mem_limit_total_below` limit to five percent. If this were a production cluster, that value would be too low. The more reasonable lower threshold would be thirty or forty percent. If total memory usage is below it, we have too many nodes in the cluster, and one (or more) of them should be removed. However, since our current cluster already has more capacity than we need, that would trigger an alert right away. Therefore, we decreased the limit to avoid spoiling the surprise.

Finally, both services have **placement constraints** that will make sure that they are running only on the correct node types.

We are about to deploy the exporters. Before we do that, please note that they will not trigger correct processes in Alertmanager. We are yet to configure it correctly. For now, we'll limit our scope only to alerts in Prometheus.

```
docker stack rm exporter

docker stack deploy -c exporters.yml \
    exporter

exit

open "http://$CLUSTER_DNS/monitor/alerts"
```

Since the new stack definition does not have one of the services contained in the old one and `docker stack deploy` does not delete services (only creates and updates them), we had to remove the whole stack. The alternative would be to remove only that service (`exporter_node-exporter`) but, since it's not critical whether we'll miss a second or two of metrics, removing the whole stack was an easier solution.

Further on, we deployed the stack, exited the cluster, and opened the Prometheus' alerts screen.

You'll notice that, this time, we have two sets of *nodeexporter* alerts. Let's start with those dedicated to managers.

Please expand the `exporter_nodeexportermanager_node_mem_limit_total_above` alert.

You'll see that it contains a similar expression as the one we wrote previously. It is as follows.

```
(sum(node_memory_MemTotal{job="exporter_node-exporter-manager"}) \
 - sum(node_memory_MemFree{job="exporter_node-exporter-manager"} \
 + node_memory_Buffers{job="exporter_node-exporter-manager"} \
 + node_memory_Cached{job="exporter_node-exporter-manager"})) \
 / sum(node_memory_MemTotal{job="exporter_node-exporter-manager"}) > 0.8
```

The difference is that we are limiting the alert only to metrics coming from the `exporter_node-exporter-manager` job. That way, we have a clear distinction between node types. The alert will be triggered only if total memory of manager nodes is above eighty percent.

Please click the link next to the `IF` statement.

You'll be presented with the graph screen with the alert query pre-populated. Please remove > 0.8 and click the **Execute** button. You'll see the graph with the memory usage of manager nodes. Whatever the values are, they should be way below eighty percent.

Please explore the `exporter_nodeexporterworker_node_mem_limit_total_above` and `exporter_nodeexporterworker_node_mem_limit_total_below`. They use the similar logic as the `exporter_nodeexportermanager_node_mem_limit_total_above`.

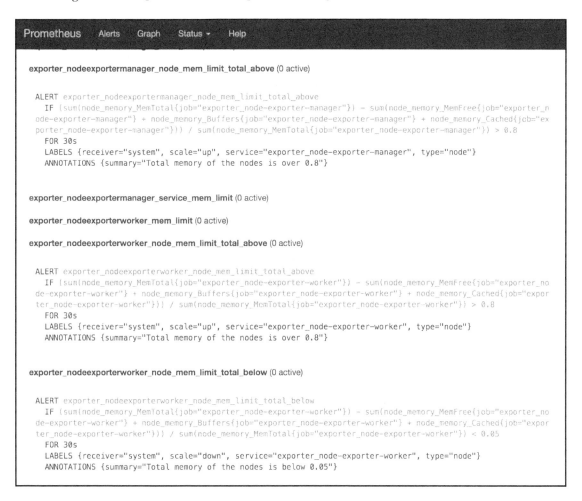

Figure 15-10: Prometheus alert based on total memory utilization of cluster managers

Now that we created the alerts, we should switch our focus to Alertmanager.

Since Docker secrets are immutable, we'll have to remove the `monitor` stack and the `alert_manager_config` secret before we start working on a new configuration.

```
ssh -i $KEY_NAME.pem docker@$CLUSTER_IP

docker stack rm monitor

docker secret rm alert_manager_config
```

Now we can create a new Alertmanager configuration and store it as a Docker secret.

```
source creds

echo "route:
  group_by: [service,scale,type]
  repeat_interval: 30m
  group_interval: 30m
  receiver: 'slack'
  routes:
  - match:
      type: 'node'
      scale: 'up'
    receiver: 'jenkins-node-up'
  - match:
      type: 'node'
      scale: 'down'
    receiver: 'jenkins-node-down'
  - match:
      service: 'go-demo_main'
      scale: 'up'
    receiver: 'jenkins-go-demo_main-up'
  - match:
      service: 'go-demo_main'
      scale: 'down'
    receiver: 'jenkins-go-demo_main-down'

receivers:
  - name: 'slack'
    slack_configs:
      - send_resolved: true
        title: '[{{ .Status | toUpper }}] {{ .GroupLabels.service\
}} service is in danger!'
        title_link: 'http://$CLUSTER_DNS/monitor/alerts'
        text: '{{ .CommonAnnotations.summary}}'
 api_url: 'https://hooks.slack.com/services/T308SC7HD\
/B59ER97SS/S0KvvyStVnIt3ZWpIaLnqLCu'
  - name: 'jenkins-go-demo_main-up'
```

```
      webhook_configs:
        - send_resolved: false
          url: 'http://$CLUSTER_DNS/jenkins/job/service-scale\
/buildWithParameters?token=DevOps22&service=go-demo_main&scale=1'
      - name: 'jenkins-go-demo_main-down'
        webhook_configs:
          - send_resolved: false
            url: 'http://$CLUSTER_DNS/jenkins/job/service-scale\
/buildWithParameters?token=DevOps22&service=go-demo_main&scale=-1'
      - name: 'jenkins-node-up'
        webhook_configs:
          - send_resolved: false
            url: 'http://$CLUSTER_DNS/jenkins/job/aws-scale\
/buildWithParameters?token=DevOps22&scale=1'
      - name: 'jenkins-node-down'
        webhook_configs:
          - send_resolved: false
            url: 'http://$CLUSTER_DNS/jenkins/job\
/aws-scale/buildWithParameters?token=DevOps22&scale=-1'
    " | docker secret create alert_manager_config -
```

Feel free to use the `15-self-adaptation-infra-alertmanager-config.sh` gist at `https://gist.github.com/vfarcic/efebfba9d42ba48eedabc118fcac7ed7` if you do not feel like typing the whole config.

Since the config needs environment variable `CLUSTER_DNS`, we sourced the `creds` file that already contains it.

We added two new routes. Alerts will be routed to the `jenkins-node-up` receiver if the `type` label is set to `node` and `scale` is `up`. Similarly, if the `scale` is set to `down`, alerts will be routed to `jenkins-node-down`. Both receivers are sending `POST` requests to build the `aws-scale` job. The only difference is the scale parameter that is either `1` or `-1` depending on the outcome we want to accomplish.

Jenkins builds will not be executed with the alert associated with managers. It has the `scale` label set to `no`, so none of the routes match it. Instead, we'll get a notification to Slack (default receiver). On the other hand, worker alerts will trigger Jenkins which, in turn, will scale or de-scale nodes of the cluster. Since `repeat_interval` and `group_interval` are both set to thirty minutes, new nodes would spawn every hour if memory usage does not drop.

Now we can deploy the `monitor` stack again. Alertmanager will, this time, use the new configuration and, if everything goes as planned, act as a bridge between Prometheus alerts and Jenkins.

```
DOMAIN=$CLUSTER_DNS docker stack \
    deploy -c monitor.yml monitor
```

Now that Alertmanager is using the new configuration, we can test the system. We'll start with a simple scenario and verify that increased memory usage of manager nodes results in a notification to Slack. Remember, we're not trying to scale managers automatically. That is reserved for worker nodes. Instead, we want to notify a human that there is an anomaly.

Since our current memory usage is way below 80%, we need to either increase the number of services we're running or change the alert threshold. We'll choose the latter since it is easier to accomplish. All we need to do is change the label of the `node-exporter-manager` service.

Before we proceed, let's confirm that all the services in the `monitor` stack are up and running.

```
docker stack ps \
    -f desired-state=running monitor
```

The output is as follows (IDs are removed for brevity):

```
1   NAME                            IMAGE                                          NODE              \
2                                   DESIRED STATE CURRENT STATE      ERROR PORTS
3   monitor_alert-manager.1   prom/alertmanager:latest                  ip-172-31-7-5\
4   6.us-east-2.compute.internal   Running        Running 2 minutes ago
5   monitor_monitor.1              vfarcic/docker-flow-monitor:latest        ip-172-31-7-5\
6   6.us-east-2.compute.internal   Running        Running 2 minutes ago
7   monitor_swarm-listener.1 vfarcic/docker-flow-swarm-listener:latest ip-172-31-33-\
8   127.us-east-2.compute.internal Running        Running 2 minutes ago
```

Now we can lower the upper memory threshold for the alert related to the `node-exporter-manager` and confirm that the alert associated with it works.

```
docker service update \
    --label-add "com.df.alertIf.2=@node_mem_limit_total_above:0.1" \
    exporter_node-exporter-manager
```

Since our memory usage is currently between 20% and 30%, setting up the alert to 10% will certainly result in fired event.

Let's go to Prometheus UI and confirm that the alert is firing.

```
exit

open "http://$CLUSTER_DNS/monitor/alerts"
```

The `exporter_nodeexportermanager_node_mem_limit_total_above` should be red. If it isn't, please wait a few moments and refresh the screen.

Once the alert is fired, we can confirm that a Slack notification was sent by Alertmanager. Please open *DevOps20* slack channel *#df-monitor-tests* and observe the note stating that *Total memory of the nodes is over 0.1.*

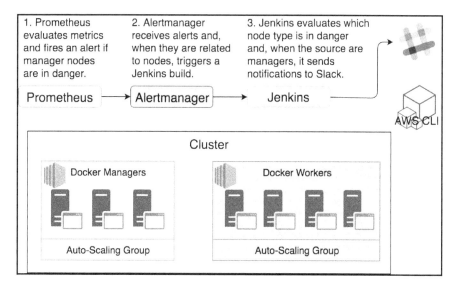

Figure 15-11: Prometheus initiated Slack notifications

Before we proceed, we should restore the `node-exporter-manager` alert definition to its previous threshold. Otherwise, another alert would fire an hour from now. We'll imagine that someone saw the alert and fixed the imaginary problem.

```
ssh -i $KEY_NAME.pem docker@$CLUSTER_IP

docker service update \
    --label-add "com.df.alertIf.2=@node_mem_limit_total_above:0.8" \
    exporter_node-exporter-manager
```

We entered the cluster and updated the service by adding (overwriting) the alert with 80% threshold.

Now we can test the real deal. We'll verify that automated scaling of worker nodes works as expected. We'll repeat a similar simulation by lowering the threshold. The only difference is that, this time, we'll update the node-exporter-worker service.

```
docker service update \
    --label-add "com.df.alertIf.2=@node_mem_limit_total_above:0.1" \
    exporter_node-exporter-worker
```

The alert is now set to fire when 10% of the total memory of worker nodes is reached. We can confirm that by visiting Prometheus one more time.

```
exit
```

```
open "http://$CLUSTER_DNS/monitor/alerts"
```

You'll notice that the exporter_nodeexporterworker_node_mem_limit_total_above alert is red. If it isn't, please wait a few moments and refresh the screen.

Since we configured Alertmanager to send build requests to Jenkins whenever an alert with the label type is set to node and scale is set to up, and those happen to be labels associated with this alert, the result should be a new build of the aws-scale job. Let's confirm that.

```
open "http://$CLUSTER_DNS/jenkins/blue/organizations/jenkins\
/aws-scale/activity"
```

You'll notice that the new Jenkins build was triggered. As a result, we should see a notification in Slack stating that worker nodes were scaled. More importantly, the number of worker nodes should increase by one.

```
ssh -i $KEY_NAME.pem docker@$CLUSTER_IP
```

```
docker node ls
```

We entered the cluster and listed all the nodes.

The output is as follows (IDs are removed for brevity):

```
1  HOSTNAME                                       STATUS AVAILABILITY MANAGER STATUS
2  ip-172-31-9-40.us-east-2.compute.internal      Ready  Active       Leader
3  ip-172-31-18-10.us-east-2.compute.internal     Ready  Active
4  ip-172-31-25-34.us-east-2.compute.internal     Ready  Active       Reachable
5  ip-172-31-35-24.us-east-2.compute.internal     Ready  Active       Reachable
6  ip-172-31-35-253.us-east-2.compute.internal    Ready  Active
```

You'll see that now we have two worker nodes in the cluster (there was one before). If, in your case, there are still no two worker nodes with the **Ready** status, please wait for a minute or two. We need to give enough time for AWS to detect the change in the auto-scaling group, to create a new VM, and to execute the `init` script that will join it to the cluster.

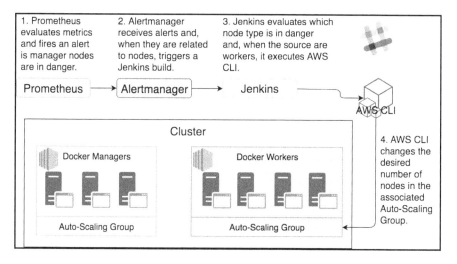

Figure 15-12: Prometheus initiated worker nodes scaling

Now that we confirmed that scaling up works, we should verify that the system is capable of scaling down as well. But, before we do that, we'll restore the label to the initial threshold, and thus avoid getting another node an hour later.

```
docker service update \
    --label-add "com.df.alertIf.2=@node_mem_limit_total_above:0.8" \
    exporter_node-exporter-worker
```

We'll follow the same testing pattern. But, since we are now testing the processes triggered when there's too much unused memory, we'll have to increase the threshold of the next alert.

```
docker service update \
    --label-add "com.df.alertIf.3=@node_mem_limit_total_below:0.9" \
    exporter_node-exporter-worker
```

The rest of validations should be the same as before.

```
exit
```

```
open "http://$CLUSTER_DNS/monitor/alerts"
```

We opened the Prometheus alerts screen. The `exporter_nodeexporterworker_node_mem_limit_total_below` alert should be red. You know what to do if it's not. Have patience and refresh the screen.

Jenkins build was executed, and we got a new notification in Slack. If you don't believe me, check it yourself. There's no need for instructions.

Finally, after a few minutes, one of the worker nodes should be removed from the cluster.

```
ssh -i $KEY_NAME.pem docker@$CLUSTER_IP
```

```
docker node ls
```

If you were patient enough, the output of the `node ls` command should be as follows:

```
 1   HOSTNAME                                          STATUS       AVAILABILITY  \
 2        MANAGER STATUS
 3   ip-172-31-25-180.us-east-2.compute.internal       Ready        Active
 4   ip-172-31-44-104.us-east-2.compute.internal       Down         Active
 5   ip-172-31-24-63.us-east-2.compute.internal        Ready        Active        \
 6        Leader
 7   ip-172-31-15-200.us-east-2.compute.internal       Ready        Active        \
 8        Reachable
 9   ip-172-31-32-99.us-east-2.compute.internal        Ready        Active        \
10        Reachable
```

One of the worker nodes was removed (or will be removed soon).

Before we move on, we'll restore the alert to its original formula.

```
docker service update \
    --label-add "com.df.alertIf.3=@node_mem_limit_total_below:0.05" \
    exporter_node-exporter-worker

exit
```

Among many other combinations and actions that we could perform, there is one area that might be very important. We might need to reschedule our services after scaling our cluster.

Rescheduling services after scaling nodes

We managed to build a system that scales (and de-scales) our worker nodes automatically. Even though we might need to extend alerts to other types of metrics, the system we created is already good as it is. Kind of... The problem is that new nodes are empty. They do not host any services until we deploy new ones if we updated some of those that are already running inside our cluster. That, in itself, is not a problem if we deploy new releases to production often.

Let's say that, on average, we deploy a new release every hour. That would mean that our newly added nodes will be empty only for a short while. Our deployment pipelines will re-balance the cluster. But, what happens if we do not deploy any new release until the next day? Having empty nodes for a while is not a big problem since our services have memory reservations based on actual memory usage. We observed metrics and decided how much each replica of a service should use. Having nodes with services that are using 80% or even 90% is not a problem. Still, we can do better. We can forcefully update some of our services and, thus, let Swarm reschedule. As a result, new nodes will be filled with replicas.

We could, for example, iterate over all the services in the cluster and update them by adding an environment variable. That would initiate rolling updates and result in better distribution of our services across the cluster. However, that might produce downtime. Some of our services (for example, `go-demo`) are scalable and stateless. They can be updated at any time without any downtime. Unfortunately, not all are created using distributed-systems principles. A good example is Jenkins and Prometheus. They cannot be scaled, so we cannot run multiple replicas. Update of a service with a single replica inevitably produces downtime, no matter whether we employ rolling updates or, for example, blue-green deployment. It does not matter whether that downtime is a millisecond or a full minute. Downtime is downtime. We might never be able to avoid downtime with services like those. Still, we should probably not produce it ourselves without a valid reason. Filling newly added nodes with services is not a reason good enough.

Therefore, we need to figure out a way to distinguish which services are safe to update, and from which we should stay away. The solution is probably obvious. We can add one more label to our services. For example, we can use a service label `com.df.reschedule`. If it's set to true, it would mean that the service can be rescheduled (updated) without any danger. Services with any other value (including not having that label) should be ignored.

We could use the command that follows to retrieve IDs of all the services with the `com.df.reschedule` label (do not execute it).

```
docker service ls -q \
    -f label=com.df.reschedule=true
```

The output would be the list of IDs (`-q`) of all the services with the label `com.df.reschedule` set to `true`.

Further on, we could iterate through that list of IDs and update services. Such an action would result in a redistribution of services across the cluster. We do not have to update anything significant. Anything should do. For example, we can add an environment variable called `RESCHEDULE_DATE`. Since its value needs to be different every time we update it (otherwise update would not trigger rescheduling) we can put current date and time as the value.

The command that would update a service can be as follows (do not execute it).

```
docker service update --env-add 'RESCHEDULE_DATE=${date}' ${service}
```

Finally, we should execute the process only if we are scaling up and skip it when scaling down.

All that, translated to a Jenkins Pipeline script, would produce the snippet that follows (do not paste it to Jenkins).

```
if (scale.toInteger() > 0) {
  sleep 300
  script {
    def servicesOut = sh(
      script: "docker service ls -q -f label=com.df.reschedule=true",
      returnStdout: true
    )
    def services = servicesOut.split('n')
    def date = new Date()
    for(int i = 0; i < services.size(); i++) {
      def service = services[0]
      sh "docker service update --env-add 'RESCHEDULE_DATE=${date}'
${service}"
```

```
      }
    }
  }
```

We start with a simple `if` statement that validates whether we want to scale up. Since it takes a bit of time until a new node is created, we're waiting for 5 minutes (`300` seconds). We could probably do a more intelligent type of verification with some kind of a loop that would verify whether the node joined the cluster. However, that might be an overkill (for now) so a simple `sleep` should do.

Further on, we are retrieving the list of all IDs of services that should be rescheduled. The result is split into an array and assigned to the variable `services`.

Finally, we are iterating over all IDs (`services`) and executing docker service update which will reschedule the services.

Let's incorporate the snippet into the `aws-scale` job we created earlier.

Please open the `aws-scale` configuration screen.

```
open "http://$CLUSTER_DNS/jenkins/job/aws-scale/configure"
```

Click the **Pipeline** tab and type the script that follows in the **Pipeline Script** field.

If you're not thrilled at the prospect of typing, feel free to copy and paste the script from the `15-self-adaptation-infra-jenkins-pipeline-02.groovy` gist at https://gist.github.com/vfarcic/dafb76fe3699e2241e1d6add228bf40e.

```
pipeline {
  agent {
    label "prod"
  }
  options {
    buildDiscarder(logRotator(numToKeepStr: '2'))
    disableConcurrentBuilds()
  }
  parameters {
    string(
      name: "scale",
      defaultValue: "1",
      description: "The number of worker nodes to add or remove"
    )
  }
  stages {
    stage("scale") {
```

```
      steps {
        git "https://github.com/vfarcic/docker-aws-cli.git"
        script {
          def asgName = sh(
            script: "source /run/secrets/aws && docker-compose\
 run --rm asg-name",
            returnStdout: true
          ).trim()
          if (asgName == "") {
            error "Could not find auto-scaling group"
          }
          def asgDesiredCapacity = sh(
            script: "source /run/secrets/aws && ASG_NAME=${asgName}\
 docker-compose run --rm asg-desired-capacity",
            returnStdout: true
          ).trim().toInteger()
          def asgNewCapacity = asgDesiredCapacity + scale.toInteger()
          if (asgNewCapacity < 1) {
            error "The number of worker nodes is already at the\
 minimum capacity of 1"
          } else if (asgNewCapacity > 3) {
            error "The number of worker nodes is already at the\
 maximum capacity of 3"
          } else {
            sh "source /run/secrets/aws && ASG_NAME=${asgName}\
 ASG_DESIRED_CAPACITY=${asgNewCapacity} docker-compose run\
 --rm asg-update-desired-capacity"
            if (scale.toInteger() > 0) {
              sleep 300
              script {
                def servicesOut = sh(
                  script: "docker service ls -q -f label=\
 com.df.reschedule=true",
                  returnStdout: true
                )
                def services = servicesOut.split('n')
                def date = new Date()
                for(int i = 0; i < services.size(); i++) {
                  def service = services[0]
                  sh "docker service update --env-add\
 'RESCHEDULE_DATE=${date}' ${service}"
                }
              }
            }
            echo "Changed the number of worker nodes from \
 ${asgDesiredCapacity} to ${asgNewCapacity}"
          }
        }
```

```
        }
      }
    }
  post {
    success {
      slackSend(
        color: "good",
        message: """Worker nodes were scaled.
 Please check Jenkins logs for the job ${env.JOB_NAME} \
#${env.BUILD_NUMBER} ${env.BUILD_URL}console"""
      )
    }
    failure {
      slackSend(
        color: "danger",
        message: """Worker nodes could not be scaled.
 Please check Jenkins logs for the job ${env.JOB_NAME} #${env.BUILD_NUMBER}
 ${env.BUILD_URL}console"""
      )
    }
  }
}
```

Do not forget to click the **Save** button.

We should add the com.df.reschedule label to at least one service before we give the aws-scale job a spin.

```
ssh -i $KEY_NAME.pem docker@$CLUSTER_IP

curl -o go-demo.yml \
    https://raw.githubusercontent.com/vfarcic\
/docker-flow-monitor/master/stacks/go-demo-aws.yml

cat go-demo.yml
```

We entered the cluster, downloaded the updated version of the go-demo stack, and displayed its content on the screen. The output of the cat command, limited to relevant parts, is as follows:

```
version: '3'

services:

  main:
    ...
    deploy:
```

```
...
labels:
  ...
  - com.df.reschedule=true
  ...
```

The only notable change, when compared with the previous version of the stack, is in the addition of the `com.df.reschedule` label.

Now we can re-deploy the stack and confirm that the updated Jenkins job works as expected.

```
docker stack deploy -c go-demo.yml \
    go-demo

exit

curl -XPOST -i \
    "http://$CLUSTER_DNS/jenkins/job/aws-scale\
/buildWithParameters?token=DevOps22&scale=1"
```

We deployed the stack, exited the cluster, and sent a `POST` request to build the `aws-scale` job with the `scale` parameter set to `1`.

If we go to the `aws-scale` activity screen, there should be a new build.

```
open "http://$CLUSTER_DNS/jenkins/blue/organizations/jenkins/aws-
scale/activity"
```

Let's go back to the cluster and confirm that the `go-demo` service was re-scheduled and, since the new node is empty (except for global services), at least one replica should end up there.

```
ssh -i $KEY_NAME.pem docker@$CLUSTER_IP

docker node ls
```

If you were quick, the output of the `docker node ls` command should reveal that the new node did not yet join the cluster. If that's the case, wait for a while until AWS creates and initializes the new node and repeat the command.

Once the new node is created, please copy its ID. We'll put it as a value of an environment variable.

```
NODE_ID=[...]
```

Please make sure that you replaced `[...]` with the actual ID of the new node.

If we continued with the fast pace and less than five minutes passed (`sleep 300`) since the new build started, the new node should be empty except for global services.

```
docker node ps \
    -f desired-state=running $NODE_ID
```

The output is as follows (IDs are removed for brevity):

```
NAME                              IMAGE                      NODE              \
                    DESIRED STATE CURRENT STATE         ERROR PORTS
exporter_cadvisor...              google/cadvisor:latest     ip-172-31-4-4.us-eas\
t-2.compute.internal Running        Running about a minute ago
exporter_node-exporter-worker... basi/node-exporter:v1.14.0 ip-172-31-4-4.us-eas\
t-2.compute.internal Running        Running about a minute ago
```

Once five minutes passed, the update was executed, and the `go-demo` service (the only one with the `com.df.reschedule` label) was rescheduled. Let's take another look at the processes running on the new node.

```
docker node ps
    -f desired-state=running $NODE_ID
```

The output is as follows (IDs are removed for brevity):

```
NAME                              IMAGE                      NODE              \
                    DESIRED STATE CURRENT STATE         ERROR PORTS
exporter_cadvisor...              google/cadvisor:latest     ip-172-31-4-4.us-eas\
t-2.compute.internal Running        Running about a minute ago
exporter_node-exporter-worker... basi/node-exporter:v1.14.0 ip-172-31-4-4.us-eas\
t-2.compute.internal Running        Running about a minute ago
go-demo_main.2                    vfarcic/go-demo:latest     ip-172-31-4-4.us-eas\
t-2.compute.internal Running        Running 3 minutes ago
```

As you can see, rescheduling worked, and one of the replicas of the `go-demo_main` service was deployed to the new node.

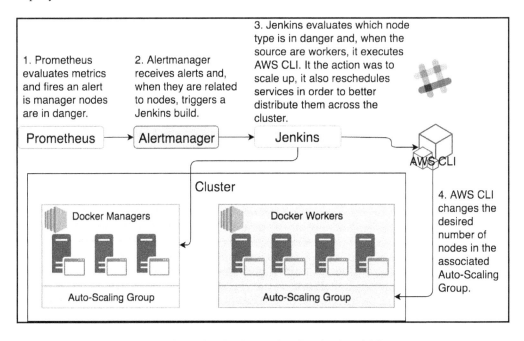

Figure 15-13: Prometheus initiated worker nodes scaling and service rescheduling

If you'd like to test that re-scheduling is not executed when de-scaling nodes, please exit the cluster and send a `POST` request to Jenkins with the scale parameter set to `-1`.

```
exit

curl -XPOST -i \
    "http://$CLUSTER_DNS/jenkins/job/aws-scale\
/buildWithParameters?token=DevOps22&scale=-1"
```

I'll leave to you the tedious steps of checking Jenkins logs and confirming that re-scheduling was not executed.

Even though our goal is within our grasp, we're not yet finished. There's still one more critical case left to explore.

Scaling nodes when replica state is pending

A replica of a service might be in the pending state. There might be quite a few reasons for that, and we won't go through all of them. Instead, we'll explore one of the most common causes behind having a replica pending deployment. A service might have memory reservation that cannot be fulfilled with the current cluster.

Let's say that a service has memory reservation set to 3 GB. All the replicas of that service are running but, at one moment, the system scales that service by increasing the number of replicas by one. What happens if none of the nodes have 3 GB of unreserved memory? Docker Swarm will set the status of the new replica to pending, hoping that 3 GB will be available in the future.

Such a situation might not be discovered with any of the existing alerts. The used memory of each of the nodes might be below the threshold (for example, 80%). The total used memory of the cluster might be below the threshold as well.

All in all, the system scaled the service, but the new replica cannot be deployed because there are not enough un-reserved resources, and none of the existing alerts noticed an anomaly. To make things even more complicated, if scaling was initiated as, for example, the result of slow response times, the same alert will fire again since the problem was not solved. Without the new replica, response times will continue being slow.

We can fix that problem by evaluating whether the number of containers that belong to a service matches the number of replicas. If, for example, we intend to have five replicas, we should have an alert that confirms that all five replicas are indeed running. Before we try to create such an alert, we should explore a query that will return the number of replicas of a given service.

Let's go back to Prometheus' UI.

```
open "http://$CLUSTER_DNS/monitor"
```

Since the number of replicas is the same as the number of running containers, the query can be as follows.

```
count(container_memory_usage_bytes{container_label_com_docker_swarm\
_service_name="go-demo_main"})
```

The query counts the number of metrics with, in the case, the label set to `go-demo_main`.

Please type the query into the **Expression** field, press the **Execute** button, and select the **Graph** tab. You should see that we are currently running three replicas of the service. If you are a fast reader, the result of the query might have revealed six replicas. When the system updated the `go-demo_main` service, it created three new containers and removed the old ones. Metrics from the old containers might be included in the count. If that's the case, wait for a few moments and repeat the query.

The expression we explored, translated to an alert, is as follows (do not try to execute it).

```
count(container_memory_usage_bytes{container_label_com_docker_\
swarm_service_name="go-demo_main"}) != 3
```

The alert would fire if the number of running containers (replicas) is different than the expected number (in this case 3). Since Swarm needs a bit of time to pull images and, in case of a failure, reschedule replicas, we'd have to combine such an `IF` logic with the `FOR` statement so that the alert does not produce false positives.

There's one more thing left to discuss. How do we get the desired number of replicas? We cannot hard-code a value to the alert since it would produce undesirable results when the service is scaled. It needs to be dynamic. The alert needs to change every time the desired number of replicas changes.

Fortunately, **Docker Flow Swarm Listener** (`http://swarmlistener.dockerflow.com/`) is, among other parameters, sending the number of replicas of a service to all its notification addresses. **Docker Flow Monitor** (`http://monitor.dockerflow.com/`), on the other hand, already has the shortcut `@replicas_running` that will expand into the alert we discussed and use the number of replicas from the listener. In other words, all we have to do is define `@replicas_running` as one more label of the service.

Please consult **AlertIf Parameter Shortcuts** (`http://monitor.dockerflow.com/usage/#alertif-parameter-shortcuts`) for more info about the `@replicas_running` shortcut.

I forgot to mention one more thing. Prometheus is already running that alert. It was defined in the last `go-demo` stack definition. So, let's take another look at the YAML file we used previously.

```
ssh -i $KEY_NAME.pem docker@$CLUSTER_IP

cat go-demo.yml
```

We went back into the cluster and listed the contents of the `go-demo.yml` file. The relevant parts are as follows:

```
services:

  main:
    ...
    deploy:
      ...
      labels:
        ...
        - com.df.alertName.4=replicas_running
        - com.df.alertIf.4=@replicas_running
        - com.df.alertFor.4=10m
      ...
```

There's no big mystery in those labels. They follow the same pattern as all other Prometheus-related labels we used throughout the book. The shortcut will expand into `count(container_memory_usage_bytes{container_label_com_docker_swarm_service_name="go-demo_main"}) != 3`. If we change the desired number of replicas, the listener will send a new request to the monitor, and the alert will change accordingly.

You'll notice that the `alertFor` label is set to `10m`. If a Docker image is big, it might take more than ten minutes to deploy a replica, and you might want to increase that time. On top of that, you should keep in mind that the more replicas we have, the longer it might take Swarm to deploy them all. However, since `go-demo` is very light, and we're running only a few replicas, ten minutes should be more than enough. If all the replicas are not running within ten minutes, the alert should fire.

Let's confirm that the alert is indeed registered in Prometheus.

```
exit

open "http://$CLUSTER_DNS/monitor/alerts"
```

Please observe the alert `godemo_main_replicas_running`. It should contain the definition we discussed.

We should test whether the system works so now we need to figure out how to force Docker Swarm to create a replica in the pending state. But, before we do that, we need to deal with the intervals we set in Alertmanager configuration.

Alertmanager is grouping alerts by labels `service`, `scale`, and `type`, and has parameters `repeat_interval` and `group_interval` both set to `30m`. That means that an alert will be propagated to one of the receivers only if more than an hour passed since the last one with the same labels. In other words, even though Prometheus is firing the alert, Alertmanager might be discarding it if less then an hour passed since the last time we scaled the nodes.

If you are impatient and do not want to wait for an hour, we can remove Alertmanager and put it back up again.

```
ssh -i $KEY_NAME.pem docker@$CLUSTER_IP

docker service scale \
    monitor_alert-manager=0

docker service scale \
    monitor_alert-manager=1
```

Scaling to zero and back up to one means that Alertmanager would start over and, as a result, we would not need to wait for an hour to test the new alert.

Now we can go back to the task at hand.

We can, for example, change memory reservation of the service to 1.5 GB. Since our nodes have 2 GB each, that should result in one of the replicas in the pending state. To be on the safe side, we can also increase the number of replicas to four.

```
docker service update \
 --reserve-memory 1500M \
 --replicas 4 \
 go-demo_main
```

We entered the cluster and updated the service.

Since Swarm is doing rolling updates, and it takes approximately twenty seconds for each replica, we should wait for a minute or two until all the replicas are updated.

Let's take a look at the stack processes.

```
docker stack ps \
    -f desired-state=running go-demo
```

The output is as follows (IDs are removed for brevity):

```
1   NAME            IMAGE               NODE                                        \
2    DESIRED STATE CURRENT STATE          ERROR PORTS
3   go-demo_main.1 vfarcic/go-demo:latest ip-172-31-47-61.us-east-2.compute.internal\
4    Running         Running 2 minutes ago
5   go-demo_db.1    mongo:latest         ip-172-31-47-61.us-east-2.compute.internal\
6    Running         Running 8 minutes ago
7   go-demo_main.2 vfarcic/go-demo:latest ip-172-31-36-187.us-east-2.compute.interna\
8   1 Running        Running 53 seconds ago
9   go-demo_main.3 vfarcic/go-demo:latest ip-172-31-36-187.us-east-2.compute.interna\
10  1 Running        Running 43 seconds ago
11  go-demo_main.4 vfarcic/go-demo:latest                                           \
12   Running         Pending 20 seconds ago
```

As you can see, Swarm could not deploy one of the replicas. None of the nodes has enough un-reserved memory so the state of one of them is Pending.

Let's see what happens with the alert.

```
exit

open "http://$CLUSTER_DNS/monitor/alerts"
```

Since the @replicas_running shortcut creates labels scale=up and type=node, there's no need to modify *Alertmanager* config nor the aws-scale Jenkins job.

Given that we set alertFor to 10m, the *godemo_main_replicas_running* alert should be red ten minutes after we executed the docker service update command.

For a short time, you might see "strange" numbers generated by the alert. For example, it might be in the pending state, saying that there are five containers instead four, while we're expecting to see three. Those "strange" results might be due to caching. The alert might be taking into account the old containers, those that were replaced with the recent update. Fear not. A short while later, the alert will stop counting the old containers and will report that there are three running, while it is expecting four. Ten minutes later it'll fire the alert.

Finally, let's confirm that Jenkins executed a new build.

```
open "http://$CLUSTER_DNS/jenkins/blue/organizations\
/jenkins/aws-scale/activity"
```

As you can see, a new build was executed, or, if less than five minutes passed, is about to finish. The auto-scaling group has been modified, and a new worker node joined the cluster.

```
ssh -i $KEY_NAME.pem docker@$CLUSTER_IP
```

```
docker node ls
```

The output of the `node ls` command is as follows (IDs are removed for brevity):

```
 1  HOSTNAME                                      STATUS       AVAILABILITY  \
 2      MANAGER STATUS
 3  ip-172-31-15-5.us-east-2.compute.internal     Ready        Active        \
 4      Reachable
 5  ip-172-31-26-189.us-east-2.compute.internal   Ready        Active        \
 6      Reachable
 7  ip-172-31-29-239.us-east-2.compute.internal   Ready        Active
 8  ip-172-31-36-140.us-east-2.compute.internal   Ready        Active
 9  ip-172-31-36-153.us-east-2.compute.internal   Ready        Active        \
10      Leader
```

A new worker node was created. There should be three manager and two worker nodes. If you don't see the new node, please wait for a while and re-run the `docker node ls` command.

Let's see what's going on with replicas of the `go-demo_main` service.

```
docker stack ps \
    -f desired-state=running go-demo
```

Swarm found of that, with the additional node, there is enough un-reserved memory and deployed the pending replica.

What now?

We have a self-sufficient system! It can self-heal and self-adapt. It can work without any humans around. We built Matrix! (http://www.imdb.com/title/tt0133093/) We'll... We're not quite there yet. You will have to observe metrics, look for patterns, create new alerts, and so on. You will have to be behind the system we built so far and continue perfecting it. What we have, for now, is a solid base that you will need to expand. You'll have to use the knowledge you got so far and adapt the examples to suit your own needs.

There are many other combinations and formulas you might want to define as alerts. You might want to perform some actions when CPU usage is too high or when a disk is almost full. I'll leave that to you with a word of caution. Don't go crazy. Don't create too many alerts. Don't saturate humans with notifications and try to avoid having the system collapse on itself with unreliable alerts. Observe metrics for a while. Try to find patterns. Ask yourself what should be the action when you notice some spike. Define and validate a hypothesis. Wait some more. Repeat the cycle a few more times.

You should extend your alerts only after you're confident in your observations and actions that should be performed.

Before we move on, please delete the stack we created.

```
exit

aws cloudformation delete-stack \
    --stack-name devops22
```

16
Blueprint of a Self-Sufficient System

We came a long way, and now we are at the end of the first stage of the journey. What will happen next is up to you. You'll have to expand on the knowledge I tried to transmit and improve the system we built. It is a base that needs to be extended to suit your needs. Each system is different, and no blueprint can be followed blindly.

Every good story needs an ending, and this one should not be an exception. I'll try to summarize the knowledge passed through the previous chapters. Still, I feel I should be brief. If you need a long summary of everything we explored so far, it would mean that I did not do my job well. I did not explain things well enough, or it was so dull that you skipped some parts hoping that they will be summarized at the end. Please let me know if I failed and I'll do my best to improve. For now, I'll assume that you got the gist behind the topics we discussed and dedicate this chapter to a concise summary of everything.

We split the tasks that a self-sufficient system should perform into those related to services and those oriented towards infrastructure. Even though some of the tools are used in both groups, the division between the two allowed us to keep a clean separation between infrastructure and services running on top of it.

Service tasks

Service tasks are related to flows that are in charge of making sure that services are running, that correct versions are deployed, that information is propagated to all dependencies, that they are reachable, that they behave as expected, and so on. In other words, everything related to services is under this umbrella.

We'll group service related tasks into self-healing, deployment, reconfiguration, request, and self-adaptation flows.

Self-healing flow

Docker Swarm (or any other scheduler) is taking care of self-healing. As long as there's enough hardware capacity, it will make sure that the desired number of replicas of each service is (almost) always up-and-running. If a replica goes down, it'll be rescheduled. If a whole node is destroyed or loses connection to other managers, all replicas that were running on it will be rescheduled. Self-healing comes out of the box. Still, there are quite a few other tasks we should define if we'd want our solution to be self-sufficient and (almost) fully autonomous.

Deployment flow

A commit to a repository is the last human action we hope to have. That might not always be the case. No matter how smart and autonomous our system is, there will always be a problem that cannot be solved automatically by the system. Still, we should aim for an entirely non-human system. Even though we won't manage to get there, it is a worthy goal that will keep us focused and prevent us from taking shortcuts.

What happens when we commit code? A code repository (for example, GitHub) executes a Webhook that sends a request to our continuous deployment tool of choice. We used Jenkins throughout the book but, just as any other tool we used, it can be replaced with a different solution.

The Webhook trigger initiates a new Jenkins job that runs our CD pipeline. It runs unit tests, builds a new image, runs functional tests, publishes the image to Docker Hub (or any other registry), and so on and so forth. At the end of the process, the Jenkins pipeline instructs Swarm to update the service associated with the commit. The update should, as a minimum, change the image associated with the service to the one we just built.

Once Docker Swarm receives the instruction to update the service, it executes rolling updates process that will replace one replica at the time (unless specified otherwise). With a process like that, and assuming that our services are designed to be cloud-friendly, new releases do not produce any downtime, and we can run them as often as we want.

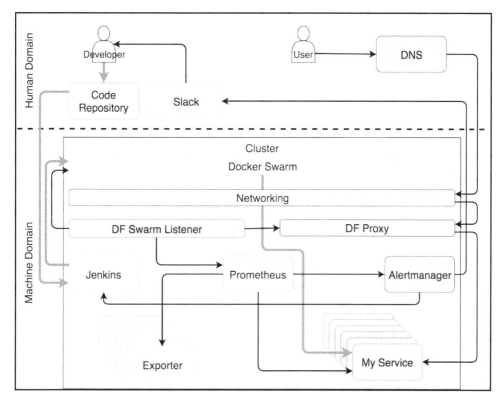

Figure 16-1: Continuous deployment process

Reconfiguration flow

Deploying a new release is only part of the process. In most cases, other services need to be reconfigured to include the information about the deployed service. Monitoring (for example, Prometheus: `https://prometheus.io/`) and proxy (for example, HAProxy: `http://www.haproxy.org/` or nginx: `https://www.nginx.com/`) are only two out of many examples of services that need to know about other services in the cluster. We'll call them infrastructure services since, from the functional point of view, their scope is not business related. They are usually in charge of making the cluster operational or, at least, visible.

If we're running a highly dynamic cluster, infrastructure services need to be dynamic as well. High level of dynamism cannot be accomplished by manually modifying configurations whenever a business service is deployed. We must have a process that monitors changes to services running inside a cluster and updates all those that require info about deployed or updated services.

There are quite a few ways to solve the problem of automatic updating of infrastructure services. Throughout this book, we used one of many possible processes. We assumed that info about a service would be stored as labels. That allowed us to focus on a service at hand and let the rest of the system discover that information.

We used **Docker Flow Swarm Listener** (**DFSL**) (`http://swarmlistener.dockerflow.com/`) to detect changes in services (new deployments, updates, and removals). Whenever a change is detected, relevant information is sent to specified addresses. In our case, those addresses are pointing to the proxy (Docker Flow Monitor (`http://monitor.dockerflow.com/`)) and Prometheus (Docker Flow Proxy (`http://proxy.dockerflow.com/`)). Once those services receive a request with information about a new (or updated, or removed) service, they change their configurations and reload the main process. With this flow of events, we can guarantee that all infrastructure services are always up-to-date without us having to worry about their configuration. Otherwise, we'd need to create a much more complex pipeline that would not only deploy a new release but also make sure that all other services are up-to-date.

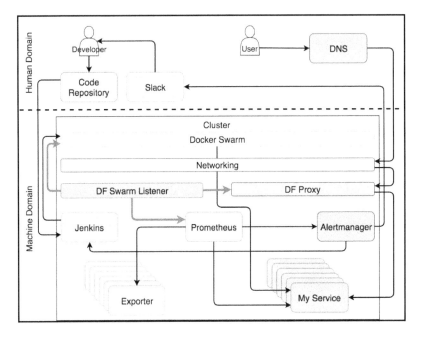

Figure 16-2: Reconfiguration flow

Request flow

When a user (or an external client) sends a request to one of our services, that request is first captured by the Ingress network. Every port published by a service results in that port being open in Ingress. Since the network's scope is global, a request can be sent to any of the nodes. When captured, Ingress will evaluate the request and forward it to one of the replicas of a service that published the same port. While doing so, Ingress network performs round-robin load balancing thus guaranteeing that all replicas receive (more or less) the same number of requests.

Overlay network (Ingress being a flavor of it), is not only in charge of forwarding requests to a service that publishes the same port as the request, but is also making sure that only healthy replicas are included in round-robin load balancing. HEALTHCHECK defined in Docker images is essential in guaranteeing zero-downtime deployments. When a new replica is deployed, it will not be included in load balancing algorithm until it reports that it is healthy.

Throughout the book, **Docker Flow Proxy** (**DFP**) (http://proxy.dockerflow.com/) was the only service that published any port. That allowed us to channel all traffic through ports 80 and 443. Since it is dynamic and works well with DFSL, we did not need to worry about HAProxy configuration beneath it. That means that all requests to our cluster are picked by Ingress network and forwarded to DFP which would evaluate request paths, domains, and other info coming from headers, and decide which service should receive a request. Once that decision is made, it would forward requests further. Assuming that both the proxy and the destination service are attached to the same network, those forwarded requests would be picked, one more time, by the Overlay network which would perform round-robin load balancing and forward requests to their final destination.

Even though the flow of a request might seem complex, it is very straight-forward from a perspective of a service owner. All that he (or she) needs to do is define a few service labels that would tell the proxy the desired path or a domain that distinguishes that service from others. User's, on the other hand, never experience downtime no matter how often we deploy new releases.

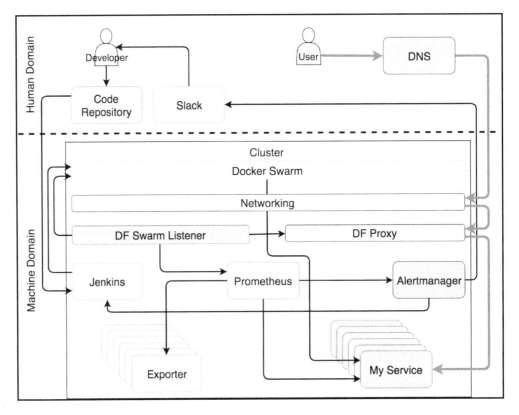

Figure 16-3: Request service flow

Self-adaptation flow

Once we manage to create flows that allow us to deploy new releases without downtime and, at the same time, reconfigure all dependent services, we can move forward and solve the problem of self-adaptation applied to services. The goal is to create a system that would scale (and de-scale) services depending on metrics. That way, our services can operate efficiently no matter the changes imposed from outside. For example, we could increase the number of replicas if response times of a predefined percentile are too high.

Prometheus (`https://prometheus.io/`) periodically scrapes metrics both from generic exporters as well as from our services. We accomplished the latter by instrumenting them. Exporters are useful for global metrics like those generated by containers (for example, cAdvisor (`https://github.com/google/cadvisor`)) or nodes (for example, Node exporter (`https://github.com/prometheus/node_exporter`)). Instrumentation, on the other hand, is useful when we want more detailed metrics specific to our service (for example, the response time of a specific function).

We configured Prometheus (through **Docker Flow Monitor** (**DFM**) `http://monitor.dockerflow.com/`) not only to scrape metrics from exporters and instrumented services but also to evaluate alerts that are fired to Alertmanager (`https://github.com/prometheus/alertmanager`). It, in turn, filters fired alerts and sends notifications to other parts of the system (internal or external).

When possible, alert notifications should be sent to one or more services that will "correct" the state of the cluster automatically. For example, alert notification that was fired because response times of a service are too long should result in scaling of that service. Such an action is relatively easy to script. It is a repeatable operation that can be easily executed by a machine and, therefore, is a waste of human time. We used Jenkins as a tool that allows us to perform tasks like scaling (up or down).

Alert notifications should be sent to humans only if they are a result of an unpredictable situation. Alerts based on conditions that never happened before are a good candidate for human intervention. We're good at solving unexpected issues; machines are good at repeatable tasks. Still, even in those never-seen-before cases, we (humans) should not only solve the problem, but also create a script that will repeat the same steps the next time the same issue occurs. The first time an alert resulted in a notification to a human, it should be converted into a notification to a machine that will employ the same steps we did previously. In other words, solve the problem yourself when it happens the first time, and let the machines repeat the solution if it happens again. Throughout the book, we used Slack as a notification engine to humans, and Jenkins as a machine receptor of those notifications.

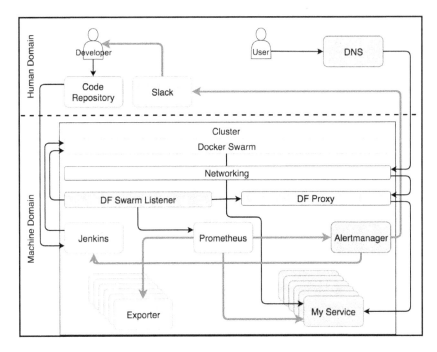

Figure 16-4: Self-adaptation services flow

Infrastructure tasks

Infrastructure tasks are related to flows that are in charge of making sure that hardware is operational and that nodes are forming the cluster. Just as service replicas, those nodes are dynamic. Their numbers are fluctuating as a result of ever-changing needs behind our services. Everything related to hardware or, more often, VMs and their ability to be members of a cluster is under this umbrella.

We'll group infrastructure related tasks into self-healing, request, and self-adaptation flows.

Self-healing flow

A system that automatically manages infrastructure is not much different from the system we built around services. Just as Docker Swarm (or any other scheduler) is in charge of making sure that services are (almost) always up-and-running and in the desired capacity, auto-scaling groups in AWS are making sure that desired number of nodes is (almost) always available. Most other hosting vendors and on-premise solutions have a similar feature under a different name.

Auto-scaling groups are only part of the self-healing solution applied to infrastructure. Recreating a failed node is not enough by itself. We need to have a process that will join that node to the existing cluster. Throughout the book, we used Docker For AWS (`https://docs.docker.com/docker-for-aws/`) that already has a solution to that problem. Each node runs a few system containers. One of them is periodically checking whether the node it is running on is the lead manager. If it is, information like join tokens and its IP are stored in a central location (at the time of this writing in DynamoDB). When a new node is created, one of the system containers retrieves that data and uses it to join the cluster.

If you are not using Docker For AWS or Azure, you might need to roll up your sleeves and write your own solution or, if you're lazy, search for it. There are plenty of open source snippets that can help you out.

No matter the solution you choose (or build yourself), the steps are almost always the same. Create auto-scaling groups (or whatever is available with your hosting provider) that will maintain the desired number of nodes. Store join tokens and IP of the lead manager in a fault tolerant location (an external database, service registry, network drive, and so on) and use it to join new nodes to the cluster.

Finally, stateful services are unavoidable. Even if all the services you developed are stateless, the state has to be stored somewhere. For some of the cases, we need to store the state on disk. Using local storage is not an option. Sooner or later a replica will be rescheduled and might end up on a different node. That can be due to a process failure, upgrade, or because a node is not operational anymore. No matter the cause behind rescheduling, the fact is that we must assume that it will not run on the same node forever. The only reasonable way to prevent data loss when the state is stored on disk is to use a network drive or distributed file system. Throughout the book, we used AWS Elastic File System (EFS) since it works in multiple availability zones. In some other cases, you might opt for EBS if IO speed is of the essence. If you choose some other vendor, the solution will be different, but the logic will be the same.

Create a network drive and attach it to a service as volume. Docker For AWS and Azure comes with CloudStor volume driver. If you choose a different solution for creating a cluster, you might have to look for a different driver. REXRay (`http://rexray.readthedocs.io/en/stable/`) is one of the solutions since it supports most of the commonly used hosting vendors and operating systems.

Before you jump into volumes attached to network drives, make sure you really need them. A common mistake is to assume that state generated by a database needs to be persisted. While in some cases that is true, in many others it is not. Modern databases can replicate data between different instances. In such cases, the persistence of that data might not be required (or even welcome). If multiple instances have the same data, failure of one of them does not mean that data is lost. That instance will be rescheduled and, when appropriately configured, it will retrieve data from one of the replicas that did not fail.

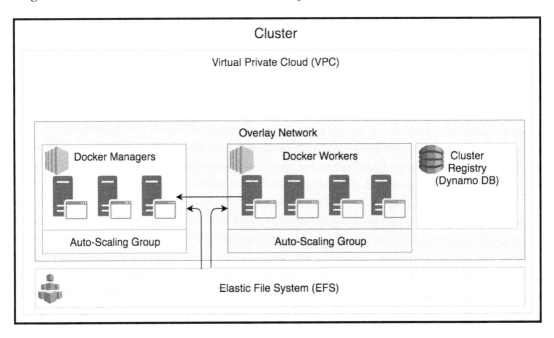

Figure 16-5: Self-healing infrastructure flow

Request flow

We already explored how to make sure that a request initiated by a user or a client outside the cluster reaches the destination service. However, there was one piece of the puzzle missing. We guaranteed that a request would find its way once it enters the cluster but we failed to provide enough assurance that it will reach the cluster. We cannot configure DNS with IP of one of the nodes since that server might fail at any moment. We have to add something in between the DNS and the cluster. That something should have a single goal. It should make sure that a request reaches any of the healthy nodes. It does not matter which one since Ingress network will take over and initiate the request flow we discussed. That element in between can be an external load balancer, elastic IP, or any other solution. As long as it is fault-tolerant and is capable of performing health checks to determine which node is operational, any solution should do. The only challenge is to make sure that the list of the nodes is always up-to-date. That means that any new node added to the cluster should be added to that list. That might be overkill, and you might want to reduce the scope to, for example, all current and future manager nodes.

Fortunately, Docker For AWS (or Azure) already has that feature baked into its template and system-level containers. Never the less, if you are using a different solution to create your cluster, it should be relatively easy to find a similar alternative or write your own solution.

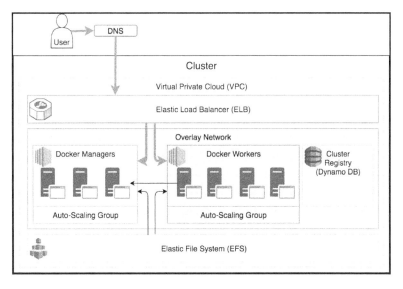

Figure 16-6: Request infra flow

Self-adaptation flow

Self-adaptation applied to infrastructure is conceptually the same as the one used for services. We need to collect metrics and store them somewhere (Prometheus) and we need to define alerts and have a system that evaluates them against metrics (Prometheus). When alerts reach a threshold and a specified time passed, they need to be filtered and, depending on the problem, transformed into notifications that will be sent to other services (Alertmanager). We used Jenkins as a receptor of those notifications. If the problem can be solved by the system, pre-defined actions would be executed. Since our examples use AWS, Jenkins would run tasks through AWS CLI. When, on the other hand, alerts result in a new problem that requires a creative solution, the final receptor of the notification is a human (in our case through Slack).

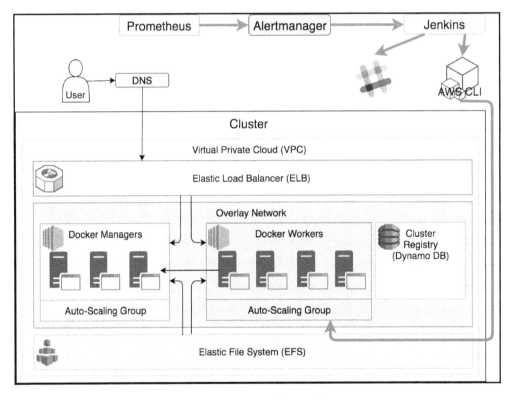

Figure 16-7: Self-adaptation infrastructure flow

Logic matters, tools might vary

Do not take the tools we used thus far for granted. Technology changes way too often. By the time you read this, at least one of them will be obsolete. There might be better alternatives. Technology changes with such speed that it is impossible to follow even if we'd dedicate all our time only on evaluation of "new toys."

Processes and logic are also not static nor everlasting. They should not be taken for granted nor followed forever. There's no such thing as best-practice-forever-and-ever. Still, changes in logic happen slower than in tools. It has much higher importance since it lasts longer.

I believe that the logic and processes described in this book will outlive the tools we used. Take that for what it's worth. Explore other tools. Seek for those that better fit your goals. As for me, I haven't even finished writing this book, and I can already see quite a few improvements over the tools we used. Some of them could be replaced with something better. Others might not have been the best choice from the start. But that does not matter as much as it might seem. Processes and logic are what truly matters, and I hope that those we explored will survive for a while longer.

Do not let this pessimistic attitude discourage you from implementing what you learned. Blame it on me and my never-ending quest for new and better ways to do something.

What now?

This is the end. Go and apply what you learned. Improve it. Contribute back to the community.

So long, and thanks for all the fish.

Other Books You May Enjoy

If you enjoyed this book, you may be interested in these other books by Packt:

Mastering Docker - Second Edition
Russ McKendrick, Scott Gallagher

ISBN: 978-1-78728-024-3

- Become fluent in the basic components and concepts of Docker
- Secure your containers and files with Docker's security features
- Extend Docker and solve architectural problems using first- and third-party orchestration tools, service discovery, and plugins
- Leverage the Linux container virtualization paradigm by creating highly scalable applications

Practical DevOps
Joakim Verona

ISBN: 978-1-78588-287-6

- Appreciate the merits of DevOps and continuous delivery and see how DevOps supports the agile process
- Understand how all the systems fit together to form a larger whole
- Set up and familiarize yourself with all the tools you need to be efficient with DevOps
- Design an application that is suitable for continuous deployment systems with Devops in mind
- Store and manage your code effectively using different options such as Git, Gerrit, and Gitlab
- Configure a job to build a sample CRUD application
- Test the code using automated regression testing with Jenkins Selenium
- Deploy your code using tools such as Puppet, Ansible, Palletops, Chef, and Vagrant
- Monitor the health of your code with Nagios, Munin, and Graphite
- Explore the workings of Trac—a tool used for issue tracking

Leave a review - let other readers know what you think

Please share your thoughts on this book with others by leaving a review on the site that you bought it from. If you purchased the book from Amazon, please leave us an honest review on this book's Amazon page. This is vital so that other potential readers can see and use your unbiased opinion to make purchasing decisions, we can understand what our customers think about our products, and our authors can see your feedback on the title that they have worked with Packt to create. It will only take a few minutes of your time, but is valuable to other potential customers, our authors, and Packt. Thank you!

Index

www.ingramcontent.com/pod-product-compliance
Lightning Source LLC
LaVergne TN
LVHW081514050326
832903LV00025B/1485